Guerrilla
Marketing
FOR
DUMMIES®

by Jonathan Margolis and Patrick Garrigan

Foreword by Jay Conrad Levinson
The Father of Guerrilla Marketing

Wiley Publishing, Inc.

Guerrilla Marketing For Dummies®

Published by
Wiley Publishing, Inc.
111 River St.
Hoboken, NJ 07030-5774
www.wiley.com

For general information on our other products and services, please contact our Customer Care
Department within the U.S. at 800-762-2974, outside the U.S. at 317-572-3993, or fax 317-572-4002.

For technical support, please visit www.wiley.com/techsupport.

Wiley also publishes its books in a variety of electronic formats. Some content that appears in print may
not be available in electronic books.

Library of Congress Control Number: 2008935261

ISBN: 978-0-470-28967-9

Manufactured in the United States of America

10 9 8 7 6 5 4 3 2

WILEY

About the Authors

Jonathan Margolis: Born and raised on Long Island, Jonathan Margolis knew early on that the world of marketing and promotions was where he belonged.

Jonathan began his marketing career in the theater industry, handling programs for both Broadway and Off-Broadway shows. Soon after, Jonathan heard the world of film calling and shifted his attention to "the big screen."

Jonathan's background in the film industry spans more than six years. During that time, he was responsible for implementing and overseeing all aspects of several motion-picture-industry trade shows that took place in the United States, Europe, and Asia.

After joining a marketing company that helped make big strides in the guerrilla space, Jonathan teamed up with a former business partner to launch the michael alan group, a company dedicated to a new era and form of nontraditional marketing. Over the years, the group has developed a steady client base consisting of major entertainment and lifestyle brands as well as numerous ad agencies and public relations firms. It has also received significant media coverage in both trade and consumer publications, as well as industry accolades and awards — including being named among the Top 100 Event Marketing Agencies in the country.

Jonathan has contributed articles to numerous trade publications and spoken before major trade shows and conferences around the country. On a pro-social level, he offers his time and experience to several nonprofit organizations to assist with their marketing initiatives and events.

He currently resides in New York City with his wife, Betsy, and son, Ethan.

Patrick Garrigan: Patrick comes to the field of guerrilla marketing from unlikely beginnings: the magical world of musical theater! After graduating from Syracuse University with a BFA in musical theater, Patrick began his career busily traveling across the country performing in theaters both modest and grand in shows such as *Disney's Beauty and the Beast, Titanic, Cats,* and *Bat Boy: The Musical,* among many others.

In 2005, Patrick shifted his focus slightly in an effort to harness his creative energies (and enjoy a steadier paycheck). The evolving arena of guerrilla marketing was a natural fit, and the nontraditional marketing firm the michael alan group, a perfect home. Since joining the group, Patrick has used his talents to conceptualize and coordinate many of the agency's more theatrical enterprises.

Currently, Patrick serves the michael alan group as a senior account executive, spearheading many of the agency's innovative initiatives. From parading dozens of fairies down Fifth Avenue to producing live celebrity performances, he has enjoyed successes both professionally and personally on behalf of the michael alan group's extensive roster of lifestyle and entertainment clients.

When not tinkering with wacky new concepts, Patrick keeps busy as a blogger, singer, and admirer of other people's dogs. He makes his home in New York City.

Dedication

Jonathan Margolis: To Ethan, my own little "guerrilla," and to Betsy, whose support means more to me than she'll ever realize. And a special thanks to Patrick, whose enthusiasm, dedication, and professionalism helped make writing this book a truly rewarding experience.

Patrick Garrigan: To my family — Dennis, Mary, Lisa, and Brian — and all their lovable eccentricities; and to my incredible friends whose support I desperately rely on and jokes I shamelessly steal. Last, to Mr. Margolis, whose mentorship, partnership, and friendship I am exceptionally grateful for.

Authors' Acknowledgments

We'd like to start by thanking our clients and partners who continue to entrust us with helping them design the most unique, entertaining, and educational programs for their products and brands. It's only through their trust and patronage that the concepts communicated in this book were able to be field-tested and guerrilla-approved.

Thanks to Mike Baker, our first contact with the good folks at Wiley Publishing. From the initial call, we knew we were in good hands, and we appreciate all his cooperation and support. Thanks also to Elizabeth Kuball, our editor on the project, for her impromptu conference calls, gentle guidance, and friendly "thank-you" e-mails after receiving each chapter — we truly appreciate and respect her expertise and professionalism shown throughout the entire process.

Thank you to Michael Joseloff, technical editor on the book, for your thoughts and feedback as the book was being written.

Special thanks to longtime friend and colleague Dennis Moore of dmstrategies. com for his contributions to the online chapters, and equal appreciation to Dennis Garrigan and The Garrigan Group for their assistance with the public relations aspects of this book.

To our colleagues at the michael alan group, including our staff across the country who drive vans, don costumes, and distribute premiums all for the sake of executing the perfect campaign. It's the collective experience of all these people whose knowledge we've been fortunate to draw upon and share.

Finally, thanks to you reading this right now — yes, you! Hey, thanks for picking up this book. Whether you're skimming it in the aisle of the bookstore because you liked the cover, or you're reading it in the comfort of your own home and plotting your marketing revolt, our hope is that much like guerrilla marketing, you'll find this book both entertaining and educational — which, in turn, will enable you to grow your business and achieve your marketing goals in ways you never thought possible.

Publisher's Acknowledgments

We're proud of this book; please send us your comments through our Dummies online registration form located at www.dummies.com/register/.

Some of the people who helped bring this book to market include the following:

Acquisitions, Editorial, and Media Development

Project Editor: Elizabeth Kuball

Acquisitions Editor: Mike Baker

Copy Editor: Elizabeth Kuball

Editorial Program Coordinator: Erin Calligan Mooney

Technical Editor: Michael Joseloff

Senior Editorial Manager: Jennifer Ehrlich

Editorial Supervisor and Reprint Editor: Carmen Krikorian

Editorial Assistants: Joe Niesen, Jennette ElNaggar, David Lutton

Cover Photos: © iStock.com/GlobalStock

Cartoons: Rich Tennant (www.the5thwave.com)

Composition Services

Project Coordinator: Erin Smith

Layout and Graphics: Reuben W. Davis, Nikki Gately, Christin Swinford, Christine Williams

Proofreaders: Caitie Kelly, Sossity R. Smith, Amanda Steiner

Indexer: Potomac Indexing, LLC

Publishing and Editorial for Consumer Dummies

> **Diane Graves Steele,** Vice President and Publisher, Consumer Dummies
>
> **Joyce Pepple,** Acquisitions Director, Consumer Dummies
>
> **Kristin Ferguson-Wagstaffe,** Product Development Director, Consumer Dummies
>
> **Kelly Regan,** Editorial Director, Travel

Publishing for Technology Dummies

> **Andy Cummings,** Vice President and Publisher, Dummies Technology/General User

Composition Services

> **Gerry Fahey,** Vice President of Production Services
>
> **Debbie Stailey,** Director of Composition Services

Contents at a Glance

Table of Contents

Foreword

*W*hen I wrote the original *Guerrilla Marketing* in 1983, it was for my students at the extension division of the University of California, Berkeley. They were people with big ideas but miniscule funds. They wanted the conventional goals of profits and balance and joy and fulfillment, but they had to resort to unconventional ways of attaining them. The book helped them accomplish their goals, sometimes growing into billion-dollar companies.

Marketing has changed a lot since I wrote that first book — and the 3 editions and 20 companion books that followed. You ought to know, right upfront, that guerrilla marketing is rapidly becoming mainstream marketing. So many people in so many nations have achieved so much success with guerrilla marketing while investing less money in the process, that traditional marketing has devolved to old-fashioned marketing.

There are still many principles of traditional marketing that continue to hold forth, but you can be sure that few of them have to do with the Internet, where half of all purchases will transpire this year, with more the next year and more the year after that. Basic human nature will also remain relatively the same, but methods of influencing that nature will differ dramatically from the last century.

From the outset, guerrilla marketing responded to a burning need for marketing savvy. It was created for people interested in growing their businesses rather than learning about marketing. Although enormous, well-funded companies have discovered guerrilla marketing, the soul and the spirit of the beast continues to be small business. The essence of guerrilla marketing is small business.

Guerrilla Marketing For Dummies starts by explaining exactly what guerrilla marketing is, and then the authors delve into all the elements needed to create a cohesive guerrilla-marketing campaign. Jonathan and Patrick make crystal clear the fact that marketing can be supercharged when it amazes, includes, and connects with a desired audience. They show that you can meet your goals in a whole host of ways — from street teams on limited budgets to highly publicized stunts and events.

Although Internet marketing was barely a gleam in a marketer's eye when I wrote my first book, we now know that what you do on the street can be augmented by what you do on the Internet. It's simpler than you may think, and the opportunities can be inexhaustible and inexpensive. The plain fact is that you need to be on the Web. It doesn't do the job for you, but it sure helps with the job.

Guerrilla Marketing For Dummies, though, does do a lot of the job for you off the Web as well, with its tips on getting the most from your marketing efforts by properly crafting a press release and pitching it to the right people. The authors even explain how to hire a professional publicist to help you gain the media attention that can speed you on the way to your goals.

An important part of guerrilla marketing is fusion marketing, where you connect up with allies who have the same kind of prospects and standards as you do. This book helps you determine who your fusion partners might be. And it points out the wisdom of working with a charity to help promote your offering. The authors conclude with a treasury of hints and advice in the Part of Tens chapters.

Readers are going to get a whole lot from *Guerrilla Marketing For Dummies* — information they can take to the bank, techniques and tactics to wage and win marketing battles regardless of the odds, clarity of a topic that to others seems complex (but is really simple and straightforward), and a major step forward in the lore of marketing. Of course, this book will make its prime contribution to you on your bottom line and the bottom lines of your clients.

Because it works so well, works for businesses of all sizes, works around the world, and is so darned simple, guerrilla marketing has become the gold standard for inexpensive marketing. Best of all, you now hold the keys to the vault in your hands with this book.

Jay Conrad Levinson
The Father of Guerrilla Marketing
DeBary, Florida

Introduction

*G*ood guerrilla marketing only takes a moment:

7 a.m.	You wake up and, as you open your morning newspaper, you find a special insert shaped like a dog bone. What you thought might be an ad for pet food is actually a promo piece for a new reality series appropriately titled *Man's Best Friend.*
8 a.m.	As you walk to the subway, you notice dozens of posters along the scaffolding by your building. As it turns out, your favorite band's in town this month — good to know.
8:45 a.m.	As you exit the subway, a friendly, attractive, outgoing young woman hands you a sample-size box of cereal and tells you to have a nice day.
1:30 p.m.	During a lunch meeting at a local restaurant, you make a quick stop to the restroom. As you wash your hands, the ad on the wall actually *talks* to you, gushing about how good looking you are — and oh, you should really try this new cologne, Attraction.
1:45 p.m.	At the end of lunch, when the waiter brings you the check, he also leaves behind three individually wrapped mints with the brand name written right there along the side, causing you to wonder, "Who exactly paid whom here? Did the restaurant owner specifically buy this brand, or did the brand approach the owner with some sort of in-kind sampling opportunity? Hmm. . . ."
6:15 p.m.	After work, you stop by a bar with some friends, and a liquor company is there giving out all sorts of cool stuff — T-shirts, hats, and your personal favorite: free drinks.

Perhaps without even realizing it, you encountered six points of contact with guerrilla marketing tactics. Surprised? You shouldn't be. As brands fight like a middle child in the pursuit of your attention, guerrilla tactics have made this pursuit personal through direct, unique modes of contact. In this book, we introduce you to this ever-developing method of reaching consumers where they live, work, and play.

About This Book

We've long been toying with the idea of writing a book on guerrilla marketing. For one, it's a relatively new, exciting, and ever-changing industry filled with fearless agencies, fun projects, and boundless opportunities. Plus, what agency *wouldn't* want a chance to say they "wrote the book" on the industry they work in?

So when the publisher of those ubiquitous *For Dummies* books asked if we'd be interested in writing *Guerrilla Marketing For Dummies,* of course we said, "When do we start?" As we immersed ourselves in the project, we realized that we were producing something more than an ego-booster. It was less about bragging rights and more about providing a great resource for anyone interested in connecting with consumers in an innovative, targeted, and cost-effective way.

With that goal in mind, we've compiled tools, tricks, idea starters, and even a few trade secrets for everyone from entrepreneurs to small and midsize organizations. This book arms you with cutting-edge solutions to achieve maximum marketing results with minimal resources. We show you how — using equal parts hard work and imagination — you can cut through the constant marketing clamor to grab your target audience's attention and best position your product or service.

Give yourself credit for your innate marketing savvy, and take the tips and pointers we provide and run with them. Although it would be easy for us to simply say, "Call Joe Blow Agency and they'll hook you up," this fix-all approach won't be the most helpful to you in the long run. Why? Because you can produce many of the marketing initiatives we outline in this book, on your own, without the expense of an outside agency. And even if you *do* decide to hire a marketing agency, you'll want to identify, approach, and qualify the firm yourself to ensure that they offer and can provide exactly what you're looking for. Don't worry — although we don't give you names of agencies to call, we do tell you how to find them, as well as give you questions to ask agencies you're considering working with.

Finally, we know you probably have a long list of books to read and sudoku puzzles to solve. So you don't have to read this book cover to cover. Don't worry, we won't take it personally if you skip around. In fact, this book is modular, which means that you can dive in and read only the sections you need — you don't need to have read everything that's come before to understand what you're reading now. We cross-reference other sections or chapters, so that you can find more information on a particular topic if you need it.

Conventions Used in This Book

We don't use many conventions in this book, but there are a few you should be aware of:

- ✔ **Italics:** Anytime we introduce a new term that you may want to know, we *italicize* it and define it shortly thereafter (often in parentheses).

- ✔ **Bold:** We use **bold** for the key words and phrases in bulleted lists (like this one), as well as for the action parts of numbered lists.

- ✔ **Monofont:** We put Web addresses and e-mail addresses in `monofont` to help separate them from the surrounding text.

When this book was printed, some Web addresses may have needed to break across two lines of text. If that happened, rest assured that we haven't put in any extra characters (such as hyphens) to indicate the break. So, when using one of these Web addresses, just type in exactly what you see in this book, pretending as though the line break doesn't exist.

What You're Not to Read

You don't have to read this book cover to cover. And you can also skip *sidebars,* text in gray boxes. The sidebars contain things like case studies that we think you'll find inspirational, but you can skip them without worrying that you're missing something critical.

You can also skip anything marked by a Technical Stuff icon. (For more on icons, check out the "Icons Used in This Book" section, later.)

Foolish Assumptions

Right out of the gate, the fact that you picked up our book means that you're likely to be a curious, creative person eager to embrace — or at least take a chance on — concepts that may at first glance seem a little out there. We take for granted that you're willing to say, "Okay, that sounds a little silly," but you'll give it a try anyway. And for that we already like you!

We believe that you have at least some exposure to the traditional forms of media such as TV, radio, and print and the ratio of cost to return. But even if we overstep that assumption a bit, we quickly review these outlets in relevant chapters to ensure that we're all speaking the same language.

Last, we see you as a person who has perhaps experienced someone else's guerrilla marketing effort and whispered to yourself, "I can do that . . . maybe even better!" By the way, we agree with you, and we look forward to seeing how you can adopt these principles and make them your own so you, too, can contribute to the guerrilla field and ultimately benefit your business.

How This Book Is Organized

Each of the seven parts of this book deals with a different phase of guerrilla marketing. Like moving into a new home, we want you to settle in and get comfortable. To help acclimate you to this environment, we get you familiar with the language and the lay of the land. From there, we work chronologically, helping you design your plan from the ground up, execute your initiatives, and monitor the success of the program. Here are the details of what we cover in each part.

Part I: It's a Jungle out There — Be a Guerrilla

Unable to resist a good homophone, we start by setting the basic parameters as to what guerrilla (not gorilla) marketing is. Then we address the elements needed to create a cohesive guerrilla marketing campaign, whether it's seeking insight from friends and colleagues via an internal brainstorming session, or calling in the help of a guerrilla marketing firm to help with design and/or execution.

Part II: Marketing at Street Level

In Part II we cover some of the more common and fun initiatives that guerrilla marketing has to offer. This part focuses on the fact that marketing can be most effective when it amazes, includes, and connects with a desired audience. From street teams on shoestring budgets to highly publicized stunts and events, we supply you with all the specifics necessary to do them — and do them well.

Part III: Opportunities All around You: Nontraditional Media

In keeping with the theme of this book, the methods of advertising are as innovative as the practices used to promote them. These days you may see advertising on the outside of a building, inside a restroom, even on the forehead of the individual *using* that restroom! We've got you covered inside and out.

Part IV: Driving It Home: From the Street to Your Site

Equally as important to what you do on the street is what you do on the Internet. The opportunities are endless — and potentially inexpensive. If you want to reach people where they live, work, and play — which is the goal of guerrilla marketing — you need to be on the Web.

Part V: If a Tree Falls in the Woods . . . The Power of the Press

In this part, we help you get the most out of your marketing efforts by properly informing the people who can best help spread the word on your product or brand — the press. We tell you how to draft a press release and put your best foot forward when it comes to pitching yourself to those who matter. Last, we fill you in on hiring a professional publicist to help you garner as much media attention as humanly possible.

Part VI: You Scratch My Back . . .

Identifying and approaching noncompetitive yet complimentary products or brands can prove very worthwhile when you're designing a marketing plan. In this part, we help you figure out which brands may be good matches, show you how to approach them, and identify the opportunities available after you've forged a relationship. We also discuss the benefits of working with a charity when promoting your product or brand.

Part VII: The Part of Tens

The final part provides you with all kinds of helpful hints and advice. Chapter 21 picks ten commons types of brands and services and matches each with a multifaceted guerrilla campaign, using many of the practices we define throughout the book. Chapter 22 gives you ten reasons why we love guerrilla marketing, and why we think you will, too. And Chapter 23 gives you ten ways you can go guerrilla on *any* budget.

Icons Used in This Book

What kind of *For Dummies* book would this be without the symbols that sit in the margin, alerting you to valuable information and sage advice? An icon-free one, that's what kind. Lucky for you, we include icons throughout this book for your reference. Here's what they mean:

From past campaigns, we've picked up an few little touches that have helped to take an average marketing effort over the top — moving it from good to exceptional. To help you get the most out of your initiative, we offer some friendly pointers.

During the course of planning leading up to your guerrilla marketing campaign, you have to handle a multitude of details. The Remember icon reminds you of the essentials so that you can deal with them beforehand — and so that they don't throw a wrench in your plans on-site.

Some municipalities don't take kindly to guerrilla marketing. Your campaign may be met with a variety of reactions — from disapproving shakes of the head to jail time. Anything marked with the Warning icon lets you know that you need to take a second look at what you're doing and consider whether you should first call a lawyer, contact city hall, or scrap the idea entirely.

We understand that you probably have finite budgetary options and that, when executing guerrilla efforts, you may need to stick to the basics. When you see the More Money icon, we tell you about times when you may want to spring for an item that may, at first glance, seem like a luxury — either to lighten your load or to put a more professional sheen on your campaign.

Whenever our inner geeks come out and we get technical, we mark the paragraph with this icon. This is the kind of stuff you don't *need* to know but that'll impress the hell out of your friends when you talk marketing.

Where to Go from Here

We want you to feel completely unrestrained, so start wherever you like. If you're curious about a particular aspect of guerrilla marketing, use the index or table of contents and check it out!

If you're new to the idea of using guerrilla marketing to promote your product or brand, start with Chapter 1. If you want to get a couple people on the street this weekend to promote an upcoming event, turn to Chapter 6. If you've got pre-promotion covered but could use some advice on producing the event itself, Chapter 8 is what you're looking for. Finally, say the food's been ordered, and the RSVP list is packed, but now you just need the press to attend — Chapter 16 is for you.

Use this book from start to finish or cherry-pick the contents that suit you best. As long as you have a sense of the options available to you when devising a plan, and you have a grasp on the essentials needed to execute that plan in a timely, efficient, cost-effective way, you're good to go!

Part I

It's a Jungle out There — Be a Guerrilla

The 5th Wave   By Rich Tennant

"Bad news – Buddy flipped the van, spilling eight crates of samples into rush-hour traffic. Good news – the van flipped logo-side up."

In this part . . .

Upon explaining to our families (who've never fully grasped exactly what it is that we do) that we were penning a book on guerrilla marketing, we received an onslaught of inarguably bad jokes: "I like gorillas and everything, but is it really necessary to market to them?" Or sarcastically, "Yeah, I've been trying to get a lot more gorillas into my store — I might need that."

They can have their jokes at our expense, but we have the last laugh when we start asking some questions of our own. Do you want to make the most out of your marketing dollars? Do you want to reach your consumers in a way that's unlike anything they've ever seen before? Would you like to receive some free press for your business? When the response to these questions is inevitably yes on all counts, we coyly reply, "Then buy the book."

Lucky for you, you have bought the book! In this part, we put you in the driver's seat, with some careful guidance, and set you on a course toward achieving your goals by thinking nontraditionally. We get started by clearing up any guerrilla/gorilla confusions and let you know exactly what guerrilla marketing is. From there, we look at the possibilities available with guerrilla methods and begin the tactical selection process. After you've made some choices, we address some of the best ways to make your campaigns a success by dreaming up concepts, fully fleshing out your ideas, and finding the people who can help your marketing plan be the best it can be.

Chapter 1

Entering the Jungle: An Introduction to Guerrilla Marketing

*W*elcome aboard! It's time to begin your preparations to enter the guerrilla jungle. Machete? Check. Muted linen attire with pockets that serve no real purpose? Check. Strategic nontraditional marketing plan? Um . . . check? No cause for alarm, you've got the machete and the duds — we'll help with the rest.

You've heard about it, you've read about it — but do you know what guerrilla marketing is? Not sure? Not to worry. *Guerrilla marketing* is a type of marketing that reaches consumers in an engaging and — this is key — *unexpected* way. Beyond the intoxicating buzzwords — *out of the box, viral,* and *grassroots* — guerrilla is about using your own creativity and the tools at your disposal to make a genuine connection with your customers (the ones you already have and the ones you hope to attract).

The best thing about going guerrilla is that, as you take stock of your *current* marketing assets, you're likely to find that you already have many tools to craft a campaign that will put you in direct contact with your customers in a truly unparalleled way.

We're getting ahead of ourselves, but it's to be expected. We guerrilla marketers are an excitable bunch, and as we tackle the elements that go into becoming a successful guerrilla marketer in the sections and chapters to follow, we think you'll agree there's a lot to be excited about! But before you can swing in the guerrilla jungle, it's important to have a little background about exactly what you're entering into.

Before you devote precious time, energy, or resources to going guerrilla, you need to know what goes into successful marketing in general. From there, we address how you can tilt, twist, or flat-out ignore these critical constructs when you apply them with guerrilla sensibilities.

Last, we take to the marketing buffet and explore a few of the more common outlets to which guerrilla marketing can easily be applied, and usher you on your way to becoming a marketing whiz kid yourself. Sound good? We think so. Now if only we could figure out what to do with all those jungle accoutrements.

Marketing 101

Marketing, advertising, public relations — what do all those terms even mean? Between you and us, there are probably people who work in these fields who have little or no idea what they mean, so if you're a little hazy on the details, it's not surprising. Although we could break these terms down in stodgy textbook definitions, we think noted humorist and marketing pro S. H. Simmons put it in a more relatable context by viewing these related fields through the prism of wooing a foxy lady:

> If a young man tells his date she's intelligent, looks lovely, and is a great conversationalist, he's saying the right things to the right person and that's marketing. If the young man tells his date how handsome, smart, and successful he is, that's advertising. If someone else tells the young woman how handsome, smart, and successful her date is, that's public relations.

Like concocting an exotic dish, successful marketing plans may involve a pinch of advertising and a dash of public relations (or more depending on the desired result). But marketing itself tells your consumers that they are intelligent, nice to talk to, and pretty, so to speak. In other words, the goal of *marketing* is to communicate brand messaging to targeted consumers by appealing directly to their wants and needs, with the intention of motivating them to buy into (literally or figuratively) a product or belief.

When flipping through the business sections of your local newspaper en route to the movie reviews and sports scores, you may catch snippets of headlines in your periphery touting, "OmniCola launches $5M cross-platform marketing campaign," and you think to yourself, "Why are they spending $5 million on a marketing campaign? If I had $5 million to spend, I'd quit my job, buy a solid-gold hovercraft, and write the screenplay for that buddy flick I just know I have in me." Or maybe that's just us.

However you would spend $5 million dollars, the question of why companies participate in marketing is a very good one. The simplest answer is that companies participate in marketing efforts *to make money.* That may be an oversimplification of the question, but it gets to the heart of the matter. Mom-and-pop storefronts and multinational corporations all participate in marketing because doing so allows them the opportunity to reach out to their target consumers, appeal to their consumers' sensibilities, and shape the consumers' perception of their products or services.

For example, maybe despite the fact that you haven't been able to build big muscles since your days of intramural shuffleboard in the ninth grade, you've committed yourself to creating the perfect workout attire. After spending seemingly countless hours studying athletes, fiddling with fabrics, and scanning through French fashion magazines, you've designed a recreational revolution: Cupid & Psyche, the finest fitness attire ever produced by man. What now?

To a certain extent, you've run into the old "If a tree falls in a forest and no one is around to hear it, does it make a sound" riddle. If you've created the most incredible spandex and cotton workout garment ever to hug human curves, and no one knows about it, does it really exist? Well, of course it does, but it probably isn't getting the respect it deserves. This is where marketing comes in. Marketing gives the product *life* in the form of public perception and positive consumer contact.

Marketing can be used to make people love your product as much as you do. As CEO of Cupid & Psyche, one tactic you may employ could be to offer free attire to sports figures and other athletic supporters or influencers whose mere donning of your attire creates the perception that your threads are the only thing to wear if you're serious about being in excellent shape. From there, you may launch a series of sexy, targeted ads featuring chiseled, toned couples dressed in the threads, with simple tags such as, "You Are a Legend."

Why take the time to do any of this? Because marketing helps you create the perception that your product or service is essential to consumers. Beyond getting consumers to buy, you're setting a tone that you're not just offering a great product, you're offering *the* great product — which will, with any luck, perpetuate the success of your business.

Honestly, everyone likes to be liked. A flirty glance while you're out shopping for groceries can totally make your day. As applied to marketing, brands look to find ways to get that flirty look from potential consumers. They do so by attempting to make themselves as appealing as possible while they're out in the "marketplace."

You don't need to major in marketing or advertising in order to design or execute a marketing campaign. Although it certainly may help to have a background in the field so that you can drop impressive-sounding terms (most of which can be made up at your discretion and dropped with confidence at appropriate moments) in meetings, the thing you do need is to know your brand. But even beyond that, you need the creativity, ambition, and audacity to create new methods to present your company in a way that makes it clear that you're in a class all your own.

The one thing we can't stress enough is when it comes to creating a marketing plan: Don't stress. Creating a strategy is about looking to the cornerstones of your business to help guide the trajectory of your marketing plans. To get started, you need to break down your business to barebones. Ask yourself the following questions:

- ✔ **Who am I trying to reach?** Who are your likely customers? To best position yourself, first identify those who most directly could benefit from your product and then expand from there.

- ✔ **What am I trying to tell or sell them?** What do you want? Do you want them to buy something, visit a Web site, talk to their friends? Clarify what you want to communicate so you can package your message accordingly.

- ✔ **Where is the best place to reach them?** Where are these elusive folks you're looking to reach? Sporting events? Quilting bees? Again, look specifically to where the most easily attainable consumers are and grow your reach from there.

- ✔ **When is the best time to reach them?** Say your product is a sleeping aid. The morning commute is probably not the best time to try to reach your consumers. When you try to communicate with your audience, when are they most likely to listen?

- ✔ **Why would they be interested in my product, brand, or service?** What are you bringing to the table that's unlike anything else? The answer to this question will help you craft a message that is persuasive and effective.

- ✔ **How can I make what I do stand apart from everyone else who does it?** Consider what's being done by the competition and try to figure out how you can make your efforts outshine those who may be after the same customers.

Going back to brand basics

Picture yourself at an archery range. You have your quiver of arrows and a longbow. If you're particularly theatrical, maybe you even brought along your Robin Hood costume, but that's not a prerequisite. Clumsily, you head to the shooting line and place an arrow on your bow and a bag on your head. You spin around three times, and let your arrow fly. Releasing a campaign without specificity has about the same odds of hitting your target and could prove just as dangerous for your brand.

Considering the basics of what your product and service is and who you're trying to reach enables you to size up the direction of your marketing plan, take aim at your target, and launch a targeted, effective strategy. Having this sort of focus puts you and your brand in the position to make smart choices that position you to achieve your goals through careful planning of objectives.

Environmental groups and concerned persons the world over have worked diligently to promote a culture where we waste as little as possible. Having an objective understanding of your brand enables this same sort of frugality for your own natural resources. Possessing a firm grasp of your company, what you're offering, and who you're offering it to puts you in a position to cut waste by enabling you to avoid spending time and resources on people who may have no use for your product.

If you're selling baby strollers, you do yourself a great disservice by launching a marketing campaign late nights in city hot spots — your target went to bed four hours ago in the hopes they could get a few hours of sleep in before they had to wake up in the middle of the night to feed a crying baby. Careful consideration of brand basics enables you to cherry-pick ways to reach your target directly, while carefully side-stepping those who have no need for your offering.

Going Guerrilla

Before you step into the ring with guerrilla marketing, you're likely to be full of uncertainties. "Would I be better off going the traditional route and simply placing my ad in the local newspaper?" We can't say for sure. What we *can* do is arm you with the information necessary to be an educated marketer.

In this section, we give you the basic introduction to what going guerrilla actually entails. We begin the getting-to-know-you process by exploring exactly what this unique slant on marketing is.

What is guerrilla marketing?

Guerrilla marketing is a shape-shifting form of marketing that takes a brand's messaging and presents it to the desired consumers in a way that is personally engaging and wholly unexpected.

The term *guerrilla* conjures imagery of bearded revolutionaries and makeshift armies. Though perhaps lacking the modern sex appeal of a Che Guevara, non-traditional tactics have not strayed too far from the military roots that are so often correlated with what it means to be guerrilla. Guerrilla tactics, in terms of their militaristic roots, were created by armies who didn't have the resources to reach their political and military goals through traditional methods. As a result, they had to look at the resources available and get creative with how they chose to approach and engage. Or, if you prefer, "You got lemons? Make lemonade."(For more on how the old tactics of the guerrilla are new again, turn to Chapter 2.)

As used in warfare, guerrilla strategies involve picking opportunities where the opponent will not expect to engage them in order to make their best assault and then blend back into the background. In many ways, these are the essential principles of guerrilla marketing. The tactics follow a similar basic plan of attack:

1. **Identify your target (audience).**

2. **Strategize where they are and how you can make the most effective impression.**

3. **Hit them in a way that is completely unexpected and impactful.**

To be successful in guerrilla marketing, you have to be innovating constantly. You can't expect to make an impact on consumers if every time you approach your audience you're decked out in a fully-branded tuxedo, performing an elaborate tap dance. The first time you do this, you may be met with applause and raves — but if you don't change up your act, over time you may quickly find that the performance that once used to slay them in the aisles now has them sarcastically rolling their eyes.

Guerrilla marketing tactics are invigorating because they empower all businesses to be able to use what they have to work with to appeal to their consumers in a way that is unique to their brand. Unless you work at the marketing department of a major company, you probably don't have tens of thousands or millions of dollars to spend on your efforts. But that doesn't mean that you shouldn't do anything. It just means that you need to get inventive with how you apply the resources you have. Much like the definition of marketing discussed in the previous section, you want to find ways to shape consumers' views and opinions of your product, but do it in a way that has direct and motivational impact on your consumers.

Whereas, traditional marketing uses tried-and-true methods to reach consumers, guerrilla marketing turns the approach of reaching consumers upside down in order to cause consumers to look at a product differently. Even though guerrilla marketing can use traditional methods (such as print, TV, and radio) to get the word out, what sets it apart is that it breaks traditional expectations by applying these tools in a different way. Guerrilla marketing gives the consumer something tangible and experiential, something more intimate and meaningful than just another ad.

For example, a guerrilla marketer may buy a billboard on the side of a building to promote her brand, but she would never be satisfied to stop there. To the guerrilla marketer, this is not a $5,000-per-month ad space — no way! This billboard is a blank canvas. She must decide how she'll take this canvas and produce something that's unmissable.

Maybe the board becomes a multimedia display that dazzles consumers. Maybe the board is outfitted with motion-detecting capabilities so it spews coupons when consumers approach it. Or maybe it's as simple as printing a small Web address in the center that's dwarfed by the space thereby drawing consumers in to wonder, "Why would they buy this space just to print that tiny URL?"

By its very nature, guerrilla marketing affects consumers in a more intimate way than more traditional marketing or advertising. Guerrilla marketing has also been refereed to as "relationship marketing" or "love marketing," because of the desired intimacy of the connection. Although we can't guarantee a love match, over time we've discovered that in a society overwrought with robo-calls and automated everything, reaching out to consumers as individuals is consistently well received; it engages and empowers your target to work not only as potential customers for your brand, but as advocates to spread the love for you. And that's the *real* power of guerrilla marketing.

Who does it?

Who does this stuff anyway? Is it rag-tag garage bands looking to drum up some more attendees at their rock concerts? Is it major companies looking to get some publicity? The answer to the question "Who's doing guerrilla marketing?" is, "Everyone." As advertising rates for traditional media soar into the stratosphere, brands big and small are looking for innovative ways to reach their audience.

What may have initially begun as a grassroots push to help get the word out about a particular cause or product has grown across the marketing industry as an accepted, effective way to market to consumers. Brands are coming to recognize the fact that speaking directly to consumers in ways that are uniquely personal enables them to have a firm connection to the product or service and instills a certain degree of brand loyalty if these connections are consistently positive.

Although we could provide you with countless headlines touting how a variety of industries are shaking up their marketing approach to speak more directly to their consumers, we're not really telling you anything you don't already know. Consider your week for instance. On your walk to work, you may have seen a smiling brand ambassador distributing a coupon or sample complete with a peppy tagline. Perhaps during lunch you went to your favorite Web site, and entered an enter-to-win contest to win a pampering spa treatment. Then when you arrive home, you turn on the boob-tube only to see that, in the town square today, 500 people were made up with body paint and posed to create a living sculpture garden to promote the kickoff of a local arts festival.

Everyone from the food industry to consumer electronics is turning to guerrilla marketing initiatives to help get the word out on their product or brand. Even charitable groups and nonprofit organizations are jumping onboard, because they've seen how cost-effective it is to produce something that's dynamic in order to help raise awareness and drum up support from people who are most likely to be influenced by their message.

Why do they do it?

Traditional methods work. We're not going to deny that for a second. Why else would they be called *traditional?* If they didn't work, they'd be called "flash in the pan methods" or "fads," but the truth is, to get your message out to a large community, the instantaneous reach of TV, radio, and print is impressive. However, consumers demand more customization and the high operating costs for these media can cause headaches for advertisers.

Take TV commercials for instance. We're sure without really thinking you can easily rattle off three of your all-time favorite TV commercials. That speaks directly to the impact of such advertising efforts. The problem for brands and media buyers looking to stretch their budgets as far as possible is that, well, the cost of airing a TV commercials can still be pretty expensive.

What you see on-air is only the half of it. To produce that commercial, the agency had to hire actors, directors, writers, caterers, studios space. and likely a best boy grip or two (whatever they do). That's just to get it produced. Then from there they have to pay the networks crazy amounts of money to air the ad. Seeing dollar signs? So are the agencies. You add DVR machines to the mix, and suddenly agencies are wondering if consumers are even seeing these commercials!

Then there's print media. As much as we love the act of reading the paper while sipping on our morning coffee, most people these days are opting to get their news, sports scores, and gossip from the Internet. The wider breadth of information and the fact that most of it is free make for a relatively easy choice for consumers.

These obstacles require innovation, and that's why brands are embracing guerrilla tactics — because there's a *need* for it. Marketing budgets vary from year to year, so instead of spending it all in one large ad buy, brands are able to stretch those dollars further in nontraditional mini-bursts that are lower on cost but high on consumer connection. These programs are gaining steam for the following reasons:

- ✔ **They're unique.** The whole point of guerrilla is to do something that's never been done before to make the greatest connection to consumers.

- ✔ **They're targeted.** Instead of spending money where it doesn't need to be spent, you're hitting your target consumers directly where they reside.

- ✔ **They're cost-effective.** The money you spend is directed specifically at creating a desired effect for a specific consumer in a specific way at a specific time, so the money is spent on the people it will have the greatest impact on.

- ✔ **They're buzz-worthy and often press-worthy.** You do something truly unique, and you're bound to attract attention. It may be just among your target, but if you're lucky you could also be picking up some press exposure as well!

Can it work for me and my brand?

In a word, yes. Producing a guerrilla marketing campaign requires you to design something that's exciting and that connects your consumers. So chances are, you can find a way to use it to fit the needs of your brand, product, service, or site.

Our advice: Don't come out guns blazing. Feel free to test it out. Many times we get calls from people saying that, although they may not have a marketing budget per se, they're willing to give it a try and see if it works. And if it works, they'll do a lot more. Now that last part may have just been a ploy to "encourage" us to come in low on our initial estimate. Regardless, testing the waters is always a smart proposition before jumping into the deep end. (To dip your toes further in the water, check out Chapter 4.)

Not every company may see the same return on the investment of a guerrilla campaign, but that doesn't mean you should throw out the whole guerrilla marketing thing. Instead, it may mean that you need to take a second look at your methods and refine from within. This may require redefining your target demographic and campaign specifics and then attacking it from a different angle.

Taking the Road Less Traveled

Perhaps you've been told that you march to the beat of a different drum — or maybe you've always wanted to be told that. If so, we welcome you into the non-traditional fold with open arms. Guerrilla marketing encompasses a variety of broad methods to connect with consumers, and all of them are best executed when done so with fearless creativity and wild (yet targeted) ideas.

In this section, we explore a few of the more common methods that guerrilla marketers use to touch consumers in unexpected ways. We fill you in on street-level initiatives, the creation of new forms of innovative media, the power of the Internet, how to get the press exposure for your deeds, and the various partners who can help make your efforts a success.

Hitting the streets

That old advice "You're never going to make any friends, if you don't put yourself out there" is particularly true when it comes to reaching target audiences. The goal of street-level efforts is not only to put your brand out there, but also to make yourself the most engaging and fun person at any party. You do this by giving consumers the chance to see, smell, touch, and even taste your product (assuming it's edible).

There are a wide array of methods to make these unique one-on-one connections — your basic street-team distribution and sampling campaign (Chapter 6), the spectacular publicity stunt (Chapter 7), and events (Chapter 8) to help give your target the opportunity to experience your product in an uncluttered and personal way.

Developing new outlets

You don't like street teams? Billboards too boring for you? Come up with your own outlet! The best marketing idea is the one that you haven't created yet. Across the board, the most exciting thing about guerrilla marketing is that it's constantly evolving with new platforms created by inventive entrepreneurs.

The *guerrilla sensibility* is the idea that everything you encounter could be a platform to reach a specific group of customers. It's kind of fun to think that you could be the person who invents a whole new form of marketing.

Ushering in experimental the theatrical, dot-com way

We first felt the taste of guerrilla marketing in the theater industry. Why? For starters, often, theater professionals are big on passion, but not so big on funds. Plus, New York theatrical groups are constantly seeking to reach a highly targeted demographic — usually tourists roaming the streets of Midtown, and sometimes even more specific than that (depending on the show and its demographic appeal, among other factors). These circumstances provided rich guerrilla training grounds.

We realized what we were doing in the theater industry could also be applied to more commercial brands, which just so happened to occur at the same time as the explosion of the dot-com era — a group of tenacious entrepreneurs that were fiercely fighting for your eyeballs. So instead of being like the next guy, these young highly motivated MBA graduates were charged with trying to find ways to cut through the clutter.

This maverick style gave the guerrilla community the chance to put our skills (and their dollars) to the test. We could propose the unimaginable, design the incredible, and, with any luck, achieve the impossible. Being creative was crucial to survival, because the market was simply saturated and the competition was fierce.

We sampled, we stunted, we toured, and we gave out more free points, offers, and T-shirts than you could ever imagine. So although most of those dot-com companies have since shut down (none due to our efforts, of course), they offered us some of the most fearless case studies of taking experiential marketing to the streets, some of which we show you throughout this book. We were able to use guerrilla tactics to market theater, as well as the big ideas of the dot-com era — and we're confident you'll find applications for your brand, too!

How is your target entertained? Where do they congregate? What do they talk about? Surveying these sort of things and looking for available opportunities could cause a brand-new marketing platform to make itself known to you, which you can then sell and use the profits to retire to a tropical island somewhere. (For more on developing new outlets, check out Chapter 11.)

Harnessing technology

People love that information superhighway. Back in the early days of the Internet, one of the most commonly uttered phrases was, "It's just so addictive. One site just leads right to another." These days it's only gotten more so. Tech-savvy guerrilla marketers have fully embraced the Internet and technology on the whole as the latest battleground in the struggle to reach consumers.

Embracing current trends and new technologies in the digital age work to further connect with consumers where they most commonly play — online. This can be as simple as creating a dynamic Web site or as involved as creating a thrilling custom game to further attract your consumers.

Beyond the Internet, another method of plugging into your base is to look to technological developments to entertain and inform. (To plug into your target, check out Chapter 13.) What's available right now that you can use to reach your consumers? Maybe you want to use talking posters in restrooms, reflexive multimedia displays that are sensitive to consumers' movements, or customizable green-screen video booths that place participants in the action of their favorite movies or video games. Looking to the things that thrill and entertain is yet another way to tempt the consumer "buy" button.

Publicizing your efforts

A distribution team or spectacle may touch hundreds or even thousands of potential customers in that instant, but leverage the power of the press and you can reach hundreds of thousands or even millions! So much of creating an effective guerrilla campaign is about connecting with consumers to shape impressions, but another facet of guerrilla marketing is applying the techniques to help raise awareness for your brand.

Finding partners

Hey, we're all people — people . . . who need people. What makes *you* the luckiest person in the world is the knowledge that you don't have to (and shouldn't) engage in a guerrilla campaign alone. Depending on which avenue you choose to apply your marketing efforts, you're likely to find that you'll need the assistance of co-workers, the industry, or perhaps even the help of a guerrilla marketing, advertising, or media buying agency. Here are a few of the calls you may want to consider making.

Colleagues and friends

You probably have numerous talented, skilled co-workers, friends, or family members — people whose skills may be just the thing to tap when you're looking to produce a guerrilla campaign. Whether it's wrangling your sister Lisa to distribute materials, calling up your good buddy Lou to host an event, or sending an e-mail to brother-in-law Dan who writes for the local paper to write some ad copy, these immediate resources should be your first line of attack for a guerrilla effort. As you consider methods to monopolize your inner circle's skills, you may find that you have all the necessary tools available to you at the family reunion or social gathering place!

Charity

Doing a good turn just makes you feel good. Doing a good turn that may serve to benefit your brand feels even *better*. If you decide to produce an event, you may consider getting a charity involved. Give them a call! More often than not adding a charitable component to your campaign or plan will not only serve the good of the cause, but also help raise awareness of your product or brand by placing it in a very positive light.

Industry

Depending on your field and industry, resources may be available to you by virtue of your participation in the trade. Maybe there's an industry magazine, trade show, Web site, e-newsletter, or association related to your product or service. Some of them may be free; others may cost a few bucks. Nevertheless, it may be exactly what you need to keep you on the cutting edge of your game and pick up some important contacts along the way.

Agency

You're no amateur. You want to make sure that everything that you create to market your brand jives with the image you'd like to have in the industry and among your consumers. As you examine your resources, you may decide you can't do it all — so why not get the help you need.

Whether it's hiring an agency to design your entire marketing plan or just using one to execute your next event, sometimes calling in people who have experience in the field can set your mind at ease by ensuring that everything goes off flawlessly. Such agencies are likely to have the experience, manpower, or resources to help achieve your goals in the most efficient and cost-effective way.

Chapter 2

Scoping Out Your Options

*A*s a consumer yourself, you have one very powerful weapon: choice. Every day, global walls fall down, communication increases, and consumer perspectives shift from "What can I get?" to "What *can't* I get?" When you have the world at your fingertips, you can afford to be choosy. It feels good to be powerful, doesn't it?

All this competition creates a challenge for all businesses — from international corporate titans to corner stores — to make sure that they stand out in this rapidly changing landscape. As businesses scratch and claw to carve out their nook in the public's minds, the methods that they use to communicate just how great their product is, as a result, must change as well. For most businesses, the key to swaying that coveted consumer choice in their favor is thinking differently, thinking guerrilla.

In this chapter, we tackle guerrilla head on. We begin by defining how guerrilla is different from some of the marketing tools you may be approached with every day. Then we discuss the origins of guerrilla tactics and why guerrilla is necessary today.

From there, we move on to the measure of reaching your consumers, known as *impressions,* and what you can expect to pay to have your message dancing in each of your consumer's heads. Finally, because the field quickly is so quickly evolving, you'll be wondering, "Where is all this crazy, guerrilla thinking going — and will it all last?" We like where your head's at, and we answer that question as well.

How Is Guerrilla Different?

Do you like following rules and being told how to do things? Neither do we, and that's why guerrilla marketing is perfect for free-wheeling thinkers like us. All marketing is interested in reaching consumers. The difference comes in how you accomplish that goal. *Traditional marketing* uses more traditional media — today, that includes print, radio, and TV. *Guerrilla marketing* consists of more street-level, out-of-home, event marketing. The focus with guerrilla isn't the "what," it's the "how": *How* are you approaching the consumer? Guerrilla is about reaching your audience in a way that's exciting, unexpected, and memorable. It's this attitude and approach that sets guerrilla apart from other forms of marketing.

One of the key ways in which guerrilla marketing is different is that it doesn't work within an established set of parameters like more traditional marketing does. The fearless guerrilla marketer knows that the opportunities don't lie exclusively within the more conventional media platforms. Instead, guerrilla marketing is focused on reaching consumers by creating an experience exclusive to your target audience.

However, just as clothes change from being out of fashion to chic vintage, reimagining ways to use traditional media can, itself, become nontraditional. In the dog-eat-dog business of who can be the most clever, agencies and brands stay competitive by coming up with ways to use traditional media in nontraditional ways.

The guerrilla spirit is your chance to fully embrace all those times that you thought it might be interesting if you tried X to generate interest. Guerrilla marketing allows you to take these impulses — these "crazy" ideas — and not only capitalize on your own creativity, but reach your audience in an unparalleled way. And that's an awfully nice by-product of embracing your own imagination!

Throughout the course of this book, we outline essential terms of guerrilla marketing, but the fact of the matter is that these definitions are time-sensitive — what it means to be guerrilla changes with every street team, stunt, event, or previously unexplored concept that is executed to promote a product or service. It's this upstart spirit that's the truly thrilling part of creating and using guerrilla tactics. There is a sense that, whether you have $100 or $100 million, the playing field is relatively level, because the effectiveness of your message is only limited by your ability to present it in a way unlike anything people have ever seen before.

Standardizing the unstandardizable

Guerrilla deviates from more traditional efforts primarily in that there's no universal measurement tool and no defined rate card that guerrilla marketers all work from. This lack of structure can be frustrating if you're the type who needs to be able to see defined facts and figures, but we find that it ultimately allows for greater business-specific customization. If you want to reach people in a way that's unique, who wants to stage a campaign that's already been done a million times before?

In the past, people have tried to more categorically define methods and the return that users might see. In fact, a little while back there was a movement to come up with a universal tool to measure event marketing campaigns in particular.

What's with "the man" trying to pin guerrilla down? Well, the appeal lies in the simple fact that approaching the public differently works, and the smart ladies and gents on Madison Avenue have taken notice. With this allure comes a need to define it in terms that can easily be packaged and sold to their clients.

Even the leading advertising trade publication *Ad Age* agrees: "agencies [are] struggling to define and measure a growing number of non-traditional media forms that are steadily gaining share in the media mix." The problem, however, lies in the fact that defining and classifying new media platforms that are constantly evolving is difficult.

As time goes by and more ad agencies continue to incorporate guerrilla initiatives into their campaigns, we may start seeing "official" definitions of words like guerrilla, grassroots, and stealth. Perhaps there'll be a governing organization that will standardize guerrilla tactics and campaigns, and create precise tools for the measurement of their success — but frankly, we hope not.

Much like people, we feel it's the quirks and eccentricities that make guerrilla marketing so arresting. Most guerrilla marketers' personal flair for change and oddity will prove likely to prevent us from ever establishing a formal set of rules and guidelines. And that's the way guerrillas like it.

Guerrilla marketing requires people to be a product of their own environments and circumstances. In order to be effective, guerrilla marketers must defy convention to get attention, because that's what makes for good marketing. If you think about it, wasn't it the standardization of the advertising and marketing world that brought about guerrilla tactics in the first place? If we're all the same and standardized, then how do we expect to stand out?

Why Is Guerrilla Necessary?

When people first hear about guerrilla marketing, a common response is, "Is that *really* necessary?" Some argue that you may be able to achieve the same effectiveness of guerrilla marketing with your standard ad in the community newspaper. In some instances, that assertion may be correct. The problem with a standard ad is that it's just that: standard.

Guerrilla marketing picks up where basic, more traditional methods of reaching consumers may fall short. Here are a few of the main benefits that guerrilla marketing offers businesses:

- ✔ **It's targeted.** Guerrilla marketing zeroes in on the specific consumers where they live, work, and play, at times where they'll be most receptive to your message. In contrast to a large billboard that may or may not reach your consumers, guerrilla takes your message directly to your audience. By placing your brand in front of your ideal group at targeted times and locations (with the precision of cherry-picking the market, the location, and even the street corner), you can create a message that's both nimble and effective.

- ✔ **It's cost-effective.** Guerrilla marketing allows you to create custom initiatives that can make the best use of your resources. Suppose tomorrow you win the lottery and, after purchasing the obligatory solid gold bust of yourself, you decide you want to blow the rest of your fortunes on purchasing nonstop TV ads for your company. Your message will definitely get out there. However, most people (and most major brands for that matter) don't have the resources to get that kind of continuous saturation. Instead of running up this silly expense, guerrilla marketing evaluates the available resources — financial, proprietary, or creative — and uses them to maximize the quality of your message while keeping costs down.

- ✔ **It's press-worthy.** Guerrilla marketing is about creating unique experiences that pique media interest, so you get mass exposure on a local budget. So you can't afford the big TV ad buy — big deal. Why not create a campaign so incredible, so outstanding that the press would be fools not to cover it? This kind of backdoor approach to getting mass exposure allows you the chance to keep your campaign specific, while getting media coverage, courtesy of the press, for whatever brand-related boffo you were able to cook up.

In addition to these pluses, technological developments have only made a stronger case for the need for new methods to reach consumers. People are busy these days — there's work, yoga class, and a never-ending list of social engagements. Because of these overactive schedules, people are highly selective about how they choose to spend their downtime. These days, consumers are looking to get to the meat of the matter. People skip the commercials with TiVo, get their print news from a variety of outlets, and subscribe to satellite radio to avoid the commercials. With these threats to the survival of traditional forms of media, all sorts of brands both tiny and titanic, are looking for alternatives for reaching the consumer in a targeted, cost-effective way. More and more, business owners are looking to guerrilla tools to help achieve this goal.

Everything old is new again

There's an old saying that "there's nothing new under the sun." To a certain extent, that could be said of guerrilla marketing. Many of the basic concepts of guerrilla began before the forms of mass media that we enjoy today were even invented.

Especially, around the turn of the 20th century, crafty businessmen had an exceptional grasp on the idea that if they wanted to turn a good profit, they needed to get their message out there to the people who might patronize them. For example, boxing promoters were exceptional with their use of posters to help promote their fights. Large, brightly colored posters featuring bare-chested brutes enticed consumers to come down and enjoy the blood sport. These old-time boxing posters have morphed into what we now consider wild postings (see Chapter 9).

Another striking example are the "newsies" of the 1900s. Set to specific street corners to peddle their papers, armed with headlines or talking points, they acted as the publication's street-level spokespersons. These chatty paper hawks have given way to the modern street team, outfitted in branded attire to promote a selected product (see Chapter 6).

With the invention of television, these street-level initiatives gave way to advertising on the airwaves. Over time, TV shifted from being a cutting-edge rich man's toy to a staple form of media.

Now, as the Internet continues to boom, marketers are challenged to create unique experiences on the Web. The Internet is the latest marketing battleground, and it provides fertile ground for creative opportunities for more smart businessmen and women to present their message to consumers where they work and play (see Chapter 12).

As time passes, the core techniques of guerrilla marketing essentially remain the same; the thing that changes is the palate of options available to present them.

Stocking Your Arsenal

How much do you love a good, fully stocked, Vegas-style salad bar? The possibilities are endless! A little bit of romaine lettuce, some cucumbers, maybe some of those hairy anchovies for the daring among us, a sprinkling of bacon bits and croutons, a dab of this, a sprinkle of that, and — *voilà!* — you've designed a masterpiece.

When crafting a marketing plan, imagine yourself the King of Vegas and belly up to the bar to hand-select your components. By mixing both traditional and guerrilla, you can help shape a brand image that will leave you with a full plate of business.

Delicious analogy aside, it's pretty clear that when good marketing practices are employed, there should be very little differentiation between traditional and guerrilla campaigns. Good marketing is good marketing — whether it consists of traditional methods, nontraditional media and guerrilla methods, or some combination of the two.

As we've oft been told, you shouldn't put all your eggs in one basket. This is a good thing to keep in mind when picking your presence. After taking an introspective look at your company and who you want to market to, it's time to explore the big questions:

- ✔ What kind of budget do I have?
- ✔ Where will my target consumers be most likely to view my message and have it stick?
- ✔ What types of media would most appeal to me and represent my brand well?
- ✔ What type of interaction (if any) do I want to have with consumers when communicating my message?

By considering these points, you should have a better sense of the kinds of media and tactics that will best meet your needs. After you have a better sense of what will benefit your brand, you can make choices about the avenues that will drive your message home. (For more on picking the best campaigns for your brand, check out Chapter 21 for inspiration.)

Don't ever feel like you have to box yourself into one format or another. It's possible and — more often than not — extremely useful and beneficial to engage in guerrilla tactics even while using the more traditional, mainstream media.

Think how impressive it would be for your target audience to see your sizzling ad in the *Town Crier,* only to step outside and have the message reemphasized by smiling street teams distributing branded materials right outside their doorstep. Frequency and variation of methods is what helps to rustle up interest for your brand.

Making an Impression and Knowing Its Cost

Imagine how simple life would be if all you had to do was offer a product or service and magically business would come to you. Although it happens occasionally, the reality is that most businesses must work hard not only to produce something of quality, but also to make sure that people know about it. Unfortunately, getting the word out usually isn't free.

In this section, we fill you in on what an impression is — you may have heard that term bandied about — and how much it'll cost you.

What is an impression?

Luckily for all of us, marketing and advertising impressions have nothing to do with Cousin Earl doing a rather bogus impersonation from his comedy catalogue. When it comes to marketing, an *impression* is the number of times an ad is rendered for viewing — one impression is equivalent to one opportunity to see an ad.

Impressions are calculated based on a number of factors. Some of them include the foot traffic that a particular location gets, the amount of time that consumers spend in front of the ad, and other environmental considerations. The number of estimated impressions is usually presented by the vendor of the advertising and is very, *very* loosely regulated by the going rate in the marketplace.

Not all forms of media and marketing are able to guarantee you a specific impression measure. Especially for campaigns that have never been executed before, the best you can expect as far as number of impressions is a basic estimate based on the foot traffic for that location during the time of your initiative and/or the number of people you're expected to reach via your distribution elements (if you have any) and the amount of possible press.

How much do I have to pay for it?

The cost of an impression is given in terms of cost per mill (CPM), which is the cost per thousand impressions. CPM is what allows media vendors to provide their clients with a measure of what they can expect for their investment.

Many forms of media, especially the buzzing industry of online advertising, utilize CPM impression pricing to calculate their ad rates. Using this format, let's say you own Sweet Tooth Candy Shop, and you decide you want to advertise on *Twisted Sugar,* the one-stop-shop for the latest in online candy industry gossip. Furthermore, let's say that you have $5,000 that you want to devote to a year's worth of advertising on the site.

You find *Twisted Sugar*'s ad page (on a Web site, this is usually a link that says "Advertise" or something along those lines), and you see the following:

$100–$500	$500–$1,000	$1,000 and up
$10 CPM	$5 CPM	$1 CPM

The amount of money you decide to spend dictates your CPM rate. So what does this mean? Well, because you have $5,000 to spend, you're able to secure the steal of a rate, $1/CPM. Now that you've secured a CPM rate, how much will you be paying for each impression? To find out, simply divide the CPM rate by 1,000 (because CPM stand for cost per thousand).

$1 ÷ 1,000 = $0.001 per impression

Not too shabby, eh? So now that the rate and cost per impression is decided, you need to work out the number of CPM units or media-specific measures (such as the number of months the ad will run, the number of times the ad will appear, and so on) they want to buy. You can do this by dividing the total amount you're looking to spend by your CPM rate:

$5,000 ÷ $1 = 5,000 CPM units (or ad runs or media measures)

You may think this is all well and good, but you want to see how many impressions you can expect with this $5,000 ad buy. You can find out by taking the number of CPM units and multiplying it by 1,000 (because CPM stands for a thousand).

5,000 CPM units × 1,000 = 5,000,000 impressions

Given that the nature of the candy business is such a specialized, niche market, 5 million impressions during the life of the $5,000 ad buy is a pretty good way to spend some money.

For the purposes of illustration, the CPM rate for Sweet Tooth was quite low. But many factors could impact this CPM rate:

- ✔ **Popularity and traffic of the outlet:** If you select a major outlet, such as an international publication or one with a certain notoriety, you can expect that the CPM rate is going to be much higher because the number of people the outlet reaches will be significantly higher than your local newsletter.

- ✔ **The quality of the interaction:** This rate speaks to the involvement the consumer enjoys with your ad. Are you front and center? Do you have some sort of game or contest component? The inclusion or absence of these elements will dictate how much or how little you're ultimately paying per impression.

- ✔ **How targeted is the medium?** Who picks up this outlet? Is it 16 year old teeny boppers, or independent movie theatre owners? Understanding who sees this media will help shape what outlets you select and how you choose to use them.

- ✔ **The amount of time the consumer is exposed to the message:** How long will consumers see this ad? Is it a 30-second radio spot or is it a small corner of the local ladies journal? To fully arm yourself, look to the costs for different media where there is a captive audience (such movie-theater advertising) versus platforms that are fleeting (such as the side of a moving bus). Not only will it enable you to make an educated choice, it may help you negotiate the best rate possible.

Depending on the media you lean toward, you'll want to make sure that it fits within your budget. To get yourself started, here are some sample CPM rates:

- ✔ **Outdoor:** $1 to $5 CPM
- ✔ **Cable TV:** $5 to $8 CPM
- ✔ **Radio:** $8 CPM
- ✔ **Online:** $5 to $30 CPM
- ✔ **Network/local TV:** $20 CPM
- ✔ **Magazine:** $10 to $30 CPM
- ✔ **Newspaper:** $30 to $35 CPM
- ✔ **Direct mail:** $250 CPM

Much of the CPM pricing is created based on more traditional forms of media such as TV, radio, and print. What does this mean for guerrilla marketing? The challenge lies with the user. How can you tailor guerrilla efforts to make the greatest use of these more traditional methods and measures? What can you do that's new and exciting and makes the best use of this defined number of impressions? You may want to create a campaign or contest that utilizes the perceived number of people who will see this ad. For example,

> 10,000 people will see this ad. 5,000 will click on the link. 1,000 will win a new car.

How will you put the numbers in your favor? How can you use the information gained from CPM measures to craft your message? Using this information successfully is the hallmark of the guerrilla marketer.

Where's it all going and will it all last?

The world of guerrilla marketing generates all sorts of new and interesting ways of creating visibility and awareness for a product or brand. As you scan these pages, you may be asking yourself, "Where's it all going, and is this trend in advertising going to last?"

The beauty of guerrilla marketing is definitely in the eye of the beholder. Whether these forms of alternative marketing will continue to proliferate and flourish depends on who you ask.

The skeptics are still skeptics. The sometimes immeasurable nature of the beast dissuades a lot of people from taking full advantage of the potential — the totally justifiable argument being, "How can I justify spending $20,000 on a regional campaign, if I can't guarantee a single sale." Twenty grand is a lot of cash — we can understand a hesitance to part with it.

At the other end of this spectrum, however, are the businesses that enjoy great successes by implementing tactics that haven't been used over and over again. Taking advantage of unique practices allows these guerrilla marketers to enjoy an exclusive corner in the marketplace.

The bottom line is this: Brands will use what works, and when what they're doing doesn't work, they'll find something else that does. Consumers will let brands know, and in turn, brands will let agencies know if they've failed in their mission by both paying parties taking their business elsewhere. It's marketing Darwinism, and it will help ensure the development of innovative marketing solutions indefinitely. It's primal and it's cold, but this idea of natural selection allows for a rolling, changing industry that's electrifying to watch and, even better, participate in (no matter your level of involvement).

Chapter 3

Guerrillas Plan, Too: Developing Your Marketing Plan

Guerrilla marketing can be wild and crazy — but at least when it comes to going guerrilla, wild and crazy still involves having a plan. In this chapter, we explore some of the steps and techniques necessary to concoct a fruitful guerrilla campaign. We start by helping you articulate your goals, pin down what you want to do, and shape how you're going to do it with minimal troubles. From there, we define your target audience and strategize how to reach them. Next, we address Murphy's Law and help you anticipate those little snafus that can pop up during the course of your campaign. Last, we turn our attention to those sometimes unpleasant spreadsheets, and help you create a budget that acknowledges the expenses you can plan for in the early stages of your campaign.

Having a plan doesn't mean you're dull — it means you're doing everything possible to make sure your guerrilla campaign succeeds.

Setting Goals, Objectives, and Strategies

Guerrilla marketing makes thrifty use of available resources to reach your consumers with spot-on accuracy. Quite a lofty goal when you think about it. One way to take the scare out of this somewhat overwhelming ambition is to develop a plan.

The fact that originality is what shapes and defines the guerrilla marketing industry provides certain challenges. Truly unique implementations don't come with existing "how-to" guidelines. That means you have to very carefully strategize (in other words, come up with a plan) before putting your plan into action.

As you're brainstorming ideas for your guerrilla campaign, start by asking yourself, "Why am I doing this?" Odds are, you don't have a million-dollar marketing budget, so clarifying what you want to achieve will help you stretch what you *do* have to its fullest. Are you trying to drive traffic to your dazzling new Web site? Build industry buzz? Or simply get people walking through your front door?

After figuring out why you're executing a guerrilla campaign and what you hope to accomplish with it, you can start thinking like a general and strategize about how you'll achieve these objectives.

In the following sections, we walk you through defining your guerrilla goals, as well ways to reach those goals.

Defining your goals and objectives

The alarm clock goes off and you think to yourself, "Ugh, do I really have to go to work today?" In a spiky, "I don't have to do anything I don't want to do" sort of way, the answer to this question is: No, you don't. However, you have the goals of taking that dream vacation, buying a house, finding a gorgeous date, and the profound desire to not hear your parents tell you to go get a job. So in the name of pursuing these noble goals, you decide putting in a hard day's work is a pretty effective way to put yourself one step closer toward achieving these objectives. Because you've defined your intent so clearly, the case for heading into work pretty much makes itself. Sleeping in will just have to wait until Saturday.

Executing guerrilla programs requires this same sort of clarity. Plainly laying out what you hope to achieve will help you decide what you want to do and how you'll go about doing it.

No one knows the goals of your guerrilla campaign better than you do. Maybe your goal is to break out of your normal methods with something different, or maybe it's to one-up your annoyingly flashy competition with something exciting and unique. Whatever your personal motivation, in the following sections we fill you in on some of the more popular reasons that brands and services consider and/or execute guerrilla campaigns to reach consumers.

Raising awareness of your brand

Why does anyone market to consumers? Well, that's probably a much larger question to be answered by very serious-looking people and grad students writing their MBA theses. But the bottom line is that you market to consumers because you want to sell your product or service. People can't buy what you're selling if they don't know about it.

Whether you're opening a new hair salon, or promoting the next big Hollywood blockbuster, the reason that you place that ad, wrap that vehicle, sample that product, sponsor that event is so people know who you are and will think of you and not that other guy the next time you can fill a need of theirs.

The degree of connection you'll have with your potential customers varies depending on what kind of campaign you settle on. Maybe the link between you and the consumer is just for a split second. But that split-second apprehension of your logo or message could prove very beneficial to you the next time shoppers are deciding where to go to get their haircut, or which movie will provide that evening's entertainment.

Driving traffic: In store, online, or both

Maybe your motto is ABC: Always be closing. You're a master salesperson. You may not care whether you're number one in your field. What matters to you is that you see people walking through your doors — either literally or on your Web site. From there, you know you can close the deal.

A *call to action* is a request on the part of the company for consumers to actually *do* something — for example, redeem a coupon for a potential prize or simply seek additional information from a storefront or Web site. To help craft your call, consider incentives such as special offers, rewards (in exchange for participation), in-store discounts, or coupons.

This sort of consumer participation, beyond basic awareness, involves asking the consumer to take a few moments to engage your brand. Be realistic with what you're asking. Consider the responsibility-to-reward ratio. What is the responsibility of the consumer in relation to what you're willing to reward them? If you're not rewarding them highly, you can't make them responsible for much.

For example, if you're asking consumers to participate in a challenging city-wide scavenger hunt culminating at your store, you'd better provide consumers with *something* in step with the time and effort they'll exert on your behalf. Ask yourself, "Would *I* be excited about doing *x* for this reward?" If so, you're on the right track. If not, come up with a bigger reward, or a less-demanding call to action.

Building buzz

Buzz is not only getting consumer to see and know your brand, but to talk about it as well. To generate buzz, you need to put on a compelling campaign — something that causes a stir, that sticks in people's minds, and that has them talking around the water cooler Monday morning.

These days, college students and easily distractible employees waste countless hours on video-sharing Web sites, which are rampant with cases of viral videos that are so hysterical, racy, or thought-provoking that Web junkies just can't keep it to themselves. The videos end up getting shared on social networking sites, being e-mailed to friends, and, perhaps the most effective, being talked about and personally recommended by people who've seen them. This chatter — or buzz — is the same kind of thing that can help to increase visibility and interest in your brand or service.

Garnering press

Yet another great thing about executing a guerrilla campaign is that if your initiative is particularly noteworthy, you can get the press to help spread the word for you! As a businessperson, you know that no matter the format, good ink can be difficult to come by — and it's a blessing when it happens. When you're in the planning stages of your guerrilla campaign, consider how much of a focus garnering press will be in your activities.

With a little luck and hard work, your guerrilla endeavor will be so thrilling that the press would be fools not to cover it (see Chapter 8). That said, some initiatives lend themselves more toward getting press attention than others do. A basic open house may get mentioned by your small-town newspaper or free weekly flier, whereas a huge blowout event, with celebrities and mascots and people parachuting in, may make it to the front page or onto the TV news.

We're not saying that one type of event is better than another — but if your goal is getting lots of press attention, you need to do something press-worthy. (For more on press, see Chapter 16.)

Keeping costs down

The goal of staying within budgetary restrictions may seem obvious, but sometimes it's the most obvious goals that elude us. Guerrilla thinking is freeing and invigorating because you can put on that creativity cap and go nuts with inventive, evocative concepts. But when you're entertaining all these imaginative ideas, it's not uncommon for realism to take a backseat.

It's great that you're giving your inner visionary a voice, but you should never try to execute a campaign — guerrilla or otherwise — that's beyond your means. You know that your company only succeeds by staying aware of what you're spending and what you're earning. The same goes for executing a guerrilla operation. From the very beginning, you need to make the most prudent use of your resources by careful planning. Laying out your budget, assessing the costs, and watching both as you spend may not be particularly sexy, but it will ensure that whatever you do, you're able to successfully stay within your budget.

Evaluating your assets and using what you've got

Back in elementary school, we had to take assessment tests to help evaluate our strengths and interests. We were asked whether we felt we were better at English or math, gym or art class, lunch or recess, peas or carrots. Then, based on the answers we provided, we were matched with general occupations that would mesh — such as a policeman, actor, doctor, lawyer, firefighter, or veterinarian. We were encouraged to develop and hone these skills so that we might one day achieve our dreams.

Planning for a guerrilla initiative may not be a lifelong dream of yours, but evaluating your strengths and existing assets will help make your desire for a successful campaign a reality. Assessing what you already having going for you will help you strategically use your strengths to help achieve your goals.

Here are a few quick questions that will help you take into account your existing assets and strengths:

- ✔ **What do you have at your disposal?** Take an internal inventory of what's available to you. What resources do you have (or can you easily get) that can help you achieve any or all of your goals and objectives? Do you have access to talent? Large quantities of samples that you can distribute at little or no cost? A place where you can hold an event or produce a stunt with minimal resources?

- ✔ **What can you leverage about the product or brand being promoted?** Public opinion and existing partnerships can be particularly helpful when you're angling to get the most out of a guerrilla campaign. What sort of brand collateral do you have? Are you a band with a die-hard fan base? Is your product made entirely of recycled goods? What inherent qualities can you leverage to get the most out of your campaign?

- ✔ **Is there something unique about your product or brand that you can work into your strategy to get the most out of your campaign?** Maybe your company is the only one in the world that makes left-handed cellos. If so, then you should make sure that the cello community and music lovers at large know that you're the only game in town when it comes to southpaws pursuing baritone stringed instruments.

If you provide an unparalleled product or service, creating or reinforcing the perception that you're the standard bearer when it comes to your industry should be an important consideration in your strategy.

Describing Your Target Audience

You probably behave differently in front of your parents than you do in front of your girlfriends or your buds at the bar. You conduct yourself differently around your boss than you do around your family — well, as least we hope you do . . . we'd hate to see you walking around the office in your skivvies.

The bottom line: You make choices about the things you say and do based on who you're communicating with and how you want to be perceived. Knowing your audience helps determine the tone, location, and content of your communication.

The same thing is true when you're trying to sell your product or service. You need to define your *target audience* (the clearly defined set of consumers who you're trying to reach through your marketing campaign — the same people you're trying to sell your product or service to) so that you can know what kind of message to communicate and how to best get that message across.

Here are some questions you can ask yourself to define your target audience:

- ✔ **Are they male or female?** Who is most likely to use your product or service? If you're looking to sell high-end makeup with real flecks of gold for that undeniable shimmer, putting on a guerrilla campaign that targets football-tailgating manly men is not the best use of your resources.

Some products aren't quite as cut and dried as this scenario, though. Your product or service may not be entirely geared toward men or entirely geared toward women. Maybe, based on your research and past sales, you think that 45 percent of your target audience is male and the other 55 percent is female.

✔ **How old are they?** Although it's fashionable to say that companies are for all people, as a guerrilla marketer, you need to be just a bit more specific.

Although your customer base may extend from 18 to 72 years of age, who is the *primary* user of your product or service? (Typically, for marketing entertainment brands, the age range is usually within the 18-to-49 bracket.)

If after careful consideration, you still can't define the specific age range of your target audience, create a specific age range that you would *like* to reach with your specific campaigns. You may have a 50-year span in the ages of people who use your product, but when it comes to this specific campaign who do you want to reach?

✔ **Where do they live?** Reaching your target audience can be as simple as knowing where they are. Are your consumers harried city dwellers, suburban soccer moms, or rural ranchers? Knowing where your audience lives will help determine where and when you should try to reach them.

✔ **Where do they work?** If you own Sartorial Sam's Fine Suits and you know that the majority of your customers are Wall Street execs, you can tailor (pardon the pun) your initiatives to appeal to this target where they work — right down on Wall Street itself.

✔ **What size household are you targeting?** Families? Newlyweds? Single people who live alone? Brand-new parents? If your product is geared toward new parents, it probably doesn't make a lot of sense to stage a guerrilla event at 9 p.m. near all the downtown bars. And if your target is singles, you probably don't want to hold an event at the local playground. The size of the household determines, to a large degree, the lifestyle of the people who live in it. If you know something about the household, you know something about where to reach your consumers.

✔ **What's their household income?** People with more money to spend participate in different activities and have different spending habits then those who don't have as much money and have to watch their wallets carefully.

If you have a general idea of your target audience's annual household income, that information can influence where you choose to reach them and how you present your message. If you're a luxury brand targeting people with cash to burn, presenting your product as chic and in vogue may be the direction to head. If your target has a lower household income, you may want to position your product as one of these essential "must-have" items, something that'll save them money in the long run.

Also, consider income when you're figuring out where to stage an event. If your target is families, and you know you want to reach families with a lower annual income, you may be better off placing your street teams near the local (free) playground than at an indoor play facility that charges admission.

✔ **Are they educated and, if so, to what degree?** A person's educational background may have an effect on his life experiences, his tastes, and the activities he participates in.

Much of what you're doing here is making sweeping generalizations about a population — and generalizations ensure that you're getting the most bang for your buck. For example, if your target audience is made up of wealthy people with advanced college degrees, you may be more likely to hit a greater number of them at a local museum or symphony than you would at the hometown football game. Does that mean that wealthy college-educated people don't attend sporting events? No. And does that mean that people without college degrees don't rock out to Beethoven. Nope. It just means that you're more *likely* to hit a greater percentage of your target audience if you go with the generalization.

✔ **What do they watch, read, and listen to?** Does your target audience spend all their downtime online, looking for funny videos to send to their friends? Does your audience read the tabloids, romance novels, or books on motorcycle repair? Are their MP3 players stacked with Britney Spears or Radiohead?

Because guerrilla marketing's goal is to be constantly ahead of the curve, you have to be plugged into how consumers are entertained. The best guerrilla marketing campaigns have been the ones where consumers were simultaneously educated and entertained. It's pretty near impossible to entertain your consumers if you're out of touch with what amuses them.

✔ **What might appeal to them?** This is where you get to the nitty-gritty of what you can do to attract your target. What will appeal to them on a visceral level? Is it humor? Sex appeal? A mental puzzle? The promise of millions? What will get them to stop and take notice?

Suppose you're targeting people who attend comic-book conventions. You may want to appeal to the inner superhero of these comic enthusiasts and create branded superhero costumes, complete with cape, cowl, and brand-related gizmos, and give them the opportunity take their picture in front of a branded backdrop.

✔ **What might turn them off?** Tastes and sensibilities vary from region to region and mindset to mindset. Especially when you're trying something a tad edgier, you want to make sure that won't offend your target's sensibilities. Coming up with something clever and different can be exciting, but if that "clever" and "different" concept turns off your target, it may have the exact opposite result. We're not saying that you need to edit yourself within an inch of your life, but take into account who will be seeing your creation and at least acknowledge any potential backlash. From there, you can decide if that risk is one you're willing to take or if you need to revise your plans to make them a little tamer.

Figuring Out When and Where You Want to Strike

After identifying your target audience and what you want to communicate to them, it's time to put on that general's helmet and get to strategizing. Each guerrilla campaign is unique, but here are a few of the big issues to consider when you're selecting where and when you approach your target consumers:

✔ **Morning, noon, or night?** What time of day do you think your target consumers will be the most receptive to your message? Is it in the morning, so they can log into a site when they arrive at their computer? Are you sampling a mini-hamburger that rushed employees can enjoy on their lunch break? Or is your product something like taking a cruise where the target will have to take the information and discuss it with his spouse or partner?

A good reality check: If you were a consumer, and you didn't know anything about this product or campaign, what time of day would *you* be the most receptive?

✔ **Weekday or weekend?** Do you want to reach them during the work week when they're sharp and analytical about your proposition? Or do you want to catch them on the weekend, when they may be a little more relaxed and open-minded? Maybe you want to contrast the analytical work week with something silly and frivolous? Specifically choosing when to approach your target demographic may also influence how you go about speaking to them.

✔ **What time of year?** If you're trying to get people to purchase your new line of toasty long johns, sending staffers dressed in them in the middle of August isn't a good idea. Aside from the risk of staffer heat stroke, not many people are in the market to stay warm in the heat of the summer. Instead you may want to look to early fall when people start to sense a nip in the air and are in the market for cozy attire.

Another element to be conscious of are holidays and other seasonal markers that are associated with a time of year. For example, does your product ward off the effects of seasonal allergies? Is your product something that lends itself to being given as a holiday gift? Or maybe your full-service online storefront enables shoppers to avoid Black Friday entirely? If so, keep these issues in mind when you're timing your big marketing push.

These are just a few of the major considerations to take into account when deciding your timing and locations. Depending on your goals, target audience, and campaign, you may find you have more or less issues that you need to account for. Our hope, however, is that these items will help you make strategic choices when it comes to the where and when of your campaign.

Addressing and Overcoming Obstacles

There's an old saying that nothing good comes easy. That's definitely true of executing guerrilla campaigns. The key to making things a little easier on yourself is anticipating larger issues in the planning stages. On the day of your guerrilla campaign, you'll have enough little fires to put out (see the following section), so if you can tackle the broader problems ahead of time, you'll be able to handle the smaller stuff on-site.

Some of what we call big-picture problems include the following:

- ✔ **Problems with the brand:** Is there something inherent about your brand that lends itself to not always working, showing results, possibly being seen as offensive? Are there specific internal problems or past public-relations issues that need to be acknowledged so that you can help avoid a bad outcome?

- ✔ **Problems with the media:** Does it feel like the press just has a "problem" with the product or service and as a result you have a difficult time getting coverage? If so, what can you do to win them over?

  Or, does your campaign itself rely solely on press presence and participation to succeed? What if some breaking news overshadows your program? How will you counter this press diversion?

  One way to avoid this outcome is to document the event yourself so that you'll be able to send a photo or video to the press after the fact and still possibly get that coverage, if you run into this problem.

- ✔ **Problems with securing permission:** Do you have all the permits and permission needed to stage your dog-and-pony show? Think how awful it would be if you spent weeks and months pulling together all your fancy production materials, complete with lighting and fog effects, only to find your entire event brought to a screeching halt by a hard-nosed enforcement officer who is shutting down the entire operation due to your lack of a street activity permit.

If you're executing a big event or stunt, contact the proper authorities and see what they require in the way of permits. On the other hand, if you're executing a truly guerrilla street-level initiative, you may want to keep your plans to yourself — just execute your program and make on-site modifications to your campaign if problems arise. (For more on getting permits, check out Chapter 7.)

✔ **Problems with consumers:** Similar to the issues with the brand itself, is there something about the product or service that consumers would be initially wary or cautious about? Do you have a problem with a certain sect of your target demographic this seems resistant to your brand? If so, is there a way to acknowledge, avoid, and/or incorporate this opposition into your marketing plan in order to possibly avoid any confusion or conflict?

Preparing for the Unforeseen

Tackling the big obstacles will allow you to avoid problems that could prove fatal to your plans (see the preceding section), but on the day of your campaign, little unforeseen problems will crop up. In fact, we're just sick enough to believe that it's these little incalculable on-site hiccups — and the problem-solving they require — that makes doing this sort of work exciting!

From our past experiences, here are a few of the more foreseeable unforeseeables, and our solutions to the problem:

✔ **Locations:** In your careful calculations leading up to your guerrilla extravaganza, you've detailed exactly where you want to be, where you want to be set up, and how it's all going to go off. Then you get there the day of the campaign and discover that the gas company is doing emergency repairs on that block, or the picketing local union has blown up an enormous inflatable rat at the location next to yours.

The immediate on-site fix to this is to see if you can wait it out. If the gas company is just finishing up or the picketers are only permitted during certain hours, you may be able to simply delay your campaign 20 or 30 minutes and you'll be back on track. If that isn't the case, then it's time to go to Plan B: Alter your campaign by going to a (pre-scouted) backup location or opting for scaled-down plans. Having contingency plan(s) will help you avoid any confusion on-site if you suddenly need to relocate or otherwise alter your original plan.

Always have backup locations and backup plans in place, and make sure everyone knows what they are. If you get stuck in an elevator without cell service, and your team shows up to find the gas company on-site, you want to be sure they all know what Plan B is, so they can go forward with it without instruction from you.

✔ **Weather:** You craft the perfect event, everyone arrives on time and you're in good shape. Suddenly, the heavens open and you find all your plans are all wet. No one — agency or otherwise — can guarantee great weather.

If it's rain that's putting a damper on your campaign, a quick fix is to have pop-up tenting and clear rain ponchos for your staff to wear. If it's strong wind, have an alternate plan such as moving to an indoor venue or rescheduling for another date.

The time of year will dictate a lot of the contingency planning. If you're putting on a campaign in Seattle in December, Seattle's rainiest month, plan on rain being a factor. If you're putting on a beach event in Los Angeles in June, plan on it being overcast — "June gloom" is legendary in Southern California.

If you're new to the area or don't find the Weather Channel high entertainment, do your research to find out what the weather is typically like in your area at that time of year. (Check out www.weather.com for all the statistics you need, including average monthly temperatures and precipitation.) Also, keep your eye on the weather the week leading up to your campaign, so you and your team are ready for nearly anything.

✔ **Protests:** If you're doing something involving animals, you may be picketed by an animal rights group. We've even seen such drastic cases as people protesting events in Times Square because they thought it was commercializing the space!

Keep your ear to the ground, and have your people do the same. If you catch wind of a protest brewing, see what you can do to appease the protestors or at the very least have a clear answer to the issue that they have with your activities. Finally, if you're working with the city to produce your campaign, use the backing of the city to marginalize these problems as much as possible. The big idea for this one is to make sure that no matter what, the protest doesn't upstage your efforts.

✔ **Copyrighted material:** You've got all your printed materials produced, complete with logos and images, and your event playlist all cued up only to find that you don't have permission to use any of these copyrighted materials.

Get honest with yourself. Do you really *need* this copyrighted material? Is using it worth having to pay fees or winding up in court? Chances are, the answer is no.

You can prevent this from ever being a problem by securing the necessary permissions in advance.

✔ **Questionable legality:** Guerrilla marketers sometimes toe the line and sometimes they blatantly cross it. We're not the judgmental types, so we're not going to condemn those who break the law, but we do advise the more cautious, conservative approach in order to avoid this problem entirely. If you decide to throw caution to the wind, do so knowing that you may face serious repercussions — beyond just the shutting down of your campaign.

Additionally, consider the people who are carrying out your campaign on your behalf. If a member of your street team (see Chapter 6) is caught doing something illegal, that person is the one who'll get the ticket, fine, or jail time — not you. Your employees need to be aware of the potential repercussions, and you need to be able to live with yourself the next day. Don't ask your employees to do anything that you wouldn't do yourself.

✔ **No-shows:** You may have hired great staff — they're chipper, peppy, and ready to go. Peppy as they might be, the night before your campaign, they may stay out just a little too late and, coincidentally, their alarm clock "just didn't go off." Okay, maybe we're being cynical and it really didn't go off — either way, you're suddenly in a tight spot.

Always try to have an ace in your pocket. If you have a team of five, one person may be a no-show. Take this into account and have a friend or alternate on standby. (Pay them a modest honorarium, of course — whether you need to use them or not.)

If you're working with a staffing agency, have a contact number that you can reach someone from the office in the event of a problem. There's a good chance they'll either have alternates standing by, or be able to utilize their database to replace someone a lot quicker than you might be able to on your own.

✔ **Problems with vendors and partners:** This one's tough. You find yourself planning an event and have little choice but to rely on select vendors or partners to help pull it off. Sometimes despite your efforts putting the success of your event in the hands of others doesn't always come out with the happy ending you hoped for.

Make a pest of yourself — in the most endearing way possible, of course. Going over the game plan (and Plan B) several times may annoy your vendors and partners, but we'd rather be annoying than have our partners unclear about what's expected of them. Additionally, make sure that you have cellphone numbers (and maybe even home numbers) of your vendors to get progress reports if someone's running late. This way, you also have someone to call if something gets off track.

Also, don't think that just because they've arrived onsite you can excuse yourself. No one knows your plan like you know your plan. Stick around to supervise. It's easy to self correct as things are being prepared, but once things are done, a lot of times they're done. Hanging around ensures that they're done right.

Crunching the Numbers

Way back in the beginning of your planning process, you set out the admirable goal of staying within budget. After considering all the elements necessary to execute a guerrilla campaign, you need to make some choices and figure out what you can afford.

Here's a laundry list of a few of the items that you may need to include

- ✔ **Staff,** including event managers, distribution teams, labor crew, and talent.
- ✔ **Permits and permissions,** including city permits (for sound, street activity, parking, and so on) and permission to use copyrighted material.
- ✔ **Production elements,** such as audiovisual touches and signage.
- ✔ **Premiums, printed pieces, and distribution apparatus.** Be sure you know what you're giving to consumers and how they'll receive it.
- ✔ **Transportation expenses,** including production vehicles and out-of-town travel.
- ✔ **Venue fees.**
- ✔ **Attire and/or costuming.**
- ✔ **Public relations or publicist costs (see Chapter 17).**
- ✔ **Pre-promotional marketing efforts, such as billboard, restroom, radio, or other more traditional media buys.** (See Chapters 9 and 10 for more traditional forms of media buys.)
- ✔ **Work that is subcontracted,** such as catering or other specialized services.
- ✔ **Miscellaneous or contingency funding.**

Not all of these elements will be needed for every campaign. For example, a street-team campaign is not likely to incorporate talent fees and the out-of-town travel that goes along with a large-scale spectacle.

After identifying the elements that you'll need, you need to create a budget. Table 3-1 shows a sample street-team budget. (**Remember:** These figures are just estimates, and they won't work for every campaign.) You can create the same kind of budget for any type of marketing campaign.

Table 3-1	Street-Team Budget for Eight Staffers, Two Days, and Four Hours Per Day			
Item	*Quantity*	*Hours*	*Cost Per*	*Client Total*
Event manager	1	8	$35	$280
Distribution staff	8	8	$35	$2,240
Labor crew	2	8	$35	$560
Van/gas/ parking tolls	1	1	$350	$350
Attire	8	1	$40	$320
Printed pieces	10,000	1	$0.10	$1,000
Premiums	10,000	1	$0.50	$5,000
Miscellaneous				$500
			Total	**$10,250**

Chapter 4

Thinking Like a Guerrilla

*A*rt is hard. Guerrilla marketing requires a certain artistry in its inception and, ultimately, its execution. After all, could just anyone come up with the idea of dressing up 200 people as frankfurters to promote a hot-dog brand during baseball's opening day? Or having real, live NASCAR cars race down Main Street to celebrate the new season? Or harnessing people to the sides of a skyscraper to paint a brand's logo across a white canvas hung out for just the occasion? No! These feats require an artist's sensibility — someone who is focused, pragmatic, and creative.

No matter what business you're in, brainstorming for guerrilla tactics requires you to take all those moderately psychedelic thoughts that pop into your head before you fall asleep, inside jokes you've had around the office, and general craziness and see how you can refurbish them to work specifically for your brand. Many people find that going guerrilla is one of the most freeing and informative times of their lives — a time that allows them the opportunity to not only come up with some stellar nontraditional ideas, but also get a greater understanding of their brand itself by exploring it from a variety of angles.

In this chapter, we step into the ring and get a little *loco*. We walk through the tactics that help you explore every crevice of your brand to mine every creative nugget that can be used to benefit your business. To kick it off, we set up basic brainstorming parameters to get possibilities percolating. When we've set the tone for your groupthink, we move on to some thought starters by looking to what's been done before for inspiration. When you find yourself in the midst of a conceptual monsoon, we take the time to let the potential ideas settle, make a choice, and take steps toward enacting your polished marketing initiative.

Staying Open-Minded, Creative, and Involved

Throughout the course of your business life, you have to deal with a lot of things that, frankly, just stink. Angry clients, missed deadlines, and "the account that won't go away." We have good news: This section is nothing like that — it's fun! Doing some guerrilla brainstorming is your chance to take all the things that excite you about your brand and play around to see what kind of marketing ideas you can produce by maximizing what's good about what you do and what resources you have at hand. (Oh, and often, food is involved in brainstorming, and that's always a bonus.)

Brainstorming for the guerrilla is about looking at your brand both cumulatively and modularly. It's about looking at it through a wide lens and riffing off what you can use, and then breaking down all the pieces to make sure that you've exhausted every possibility. Then after you've done so, you ask yourself the question, "What can I do or say that will enable me to stand out from everyone else?"

To do that, we show you how to create the environment to help get everyone in the mood — well, not *that* kind of mood (we don't want to create some major office controversy), but the kind of mood that puts everyone in the role of creative consultant, free to say relatively anything that'll help create a guerrilla campaign that has everyone slapping their foreheads and declaring, "That's it!" And when that does happen it's pretty electric.

Sound good? We thought so.

Creating the environment

When you want to relax, maybe you go to a spa where luxuriating in assorted muds, exfoliating with raspberry and avocado facials, and drifting off to the melodies of New Age harp music provide the perfect environment to escape the daily grind. Retreats such as these have mastered an element that is essential to brainstorming sessions as well as relaxation: environmental context.

Resorts have environmental context down to a science. Each room is painted in soothing pastels, water is available everywhere to refresh and reinvigorate you, calmly cheerful staff usher you to your acupuncture treatments and massages, scents may even be circulated through purified air, all set with the aim of one emotional response: relaxation.

When you're getting ready to hold your brainstorming session, you need to create an environment that's set on your *own* desired response: creativity.

Before you go dumping your aftershave in the A/C vents, consider what will help to produce an environment conducive to creativity. The answer will vary from one group of people to the next, so you need to talk to your team and see what *they* would like to have as a part of the process. Sometimes it's ordering in some Chinese, playing some tunes, and stocking the cocktails of choice. Maybe it's cupcakes and coffee. Or maybe they just want a clean, quiet room and some blank white boards.

What could be fun for a tight-knit, friendly team could be out of line or at the very least awkward for an unfamiliar or reserved group, so test the waters before diving into something that not everyone will be comfortable with.

Push the envelope, a bit. After gauging the group and getting a sense of what people will be comfortable with, throw in a wild card. Maybe it's providing everyone with large artist's sketch pads, adding music, or a brief live performance by someone. Yeah, it may get a few eye rolls initially, but it may also be an environmental element that sparks a creative revolution!

In some people's view, a meeting is a meeting is a meeting. To grease the wheels, and encourage participation in future efforts, reward attendees with a small token of your appreciation. A gift card to the local coffee shop or some other small incentive says that you appreciate their attendance and participation.

Laying out the tools

Imagine you're trying to come up with ideas to market to bakers a new delicious butter that makes people skinnier, but all your team has ever worked on is marketing olive oil. Ever diligent, your team is eager to hustle coming up with ideas for your oil-based ingredients, but they just don't know this specific realm. What can you do to get your team mobilize for this fat-burning foodstuff?

Give them the tools to work for you:

✔ **Background:** What product are you looking to promote? What's unique about it? Does the brand or product have any existing marketing efforts? A tagline? What exists about this product that can be used to generate ideas?

✔ **Sample:** Provide product samples and give people a chance to try it. Give your team the opportunity to experience your product. If it's food, a sample. If it's a product or equipment, a demonstration or a tour. If it's entertainment, a sneak peak at the feature. This may take a little bit of time, but you can only know something so much by seeing a picture or hearing about it. Giving your team a first-hand look at the product will generate far more leads than you ever thought imaginable.

✔ **Internet access:** Look to the product's Web site for additional information. Web sites have grown from basic landing pages to mini-periodicals about products. The site will give your team answers and the ability to see how it's currently being presented.

✔ **Access to experts:** If you're looking to market to bakers, bring a couple of toqued kneaders into your thinktank to help come up with ideas and provide their thoughts. Invite some of your target audience into your circle and see how their feedback may flavor your ideas.

Having a couple members of your target audience on hand may be a good idea to help keep the dialogue firing, but try not to go overboard. If you feel the need to involve a larger cross-section of your target, you may want to hold a separate *focus group* (a meeting of invited target consumers, where you pose a series of predetermined questions and open conversation for the purposes of getting a greater sense of what appeals to them).

Setting out the parameters

The preparations have been made, and now it's time to give life to your team's creativity! At this point, you're probably champing at the bit to get going — but alas, there's just one more thing, we promise. Before you set your imaginative minds to task, lay out *considerations* (basic parameters that guide and inform a brainstorming session):

✔ **Goals and objectives:** Everyone's wondering why you called them here today. Tell them. What are the goals and objectives of the brainstorming session? What do you hope to achieve from this gathering? Ideas for a one-off stunt or the beginnings of a year-long plan?

✔ **Your target demographic:** We love shoes and don't really care for cats. That information may be helpful if you're looking to market to us and wholly irrelevant if you're not. Lay out to your team, as specifically as possible, who you're looking to reach with this campaign. Who is your target? Are they 13-year-old girls who love pop music, or 70+ men who enjoy fly-fishing? This precision honestly will generate more specific, actionable ideas and better inform what you choose to do.

- ✔ **Timing:** You don't want to let the timing hinder your ideas, but it can be helpful in coming up with a framework for your concepts. Are you looking for a couple of big ideas to be done throughout the upcoming year? The next three months? In the summertime or the dead of winter?

- ✔ **Locations:** Don't let location limit you, but how does where you're looking to execute your campaign color the tone? If you're hoping to produce something deep in the heart of Texas, are chaps and ten-gallon hats in your future? If you're launching a campaign in Malibu, do you need to be looking to surf shops to ride a tidal wave of ideas?

- ✔ **Key attributes of the brand:** If something has worked in the past, throw it into the idea potpourri. If there are things that are synonymous with the brand — such as campaign slogans, mascots, jingles, or other icons — consider how or if they should be worked into your concepts.

Appointing a scribe

The considerations have been laid out for all to view and consider, and you're mere seconds from opening the flood gates. But before you do, you need to delegate a stenographer or scribe to document what's sure to be a flood of great ideas.

Working the right side of the brain taps into the creative mind and many people find it helpful to be able to see the ideas in front of them to better visualize what's been thrown out there. If you have got some visual learners among you, have your delegated scribe write these ideas on a chalkboard, dry-erase board, or tear-off pad on an easel. (This can also serve as a written record of what was said, so you don't forget any potentially helpful suggestions.)

For one wickedly irreverent comedy client, we held a wilder brainstorming session, and writing it down just wasn't an option. The ideas flowed too quickly, and we just couldn't find someone we could rope into taking to the whiteboard. In this case, we simply dropped a voice recorder in the center of the table and went off to the races. This approach created a far more casual roundtable feel, while providing a record that could be referred to later. The effect was an hour of hilarious ideas that were presented to a pleased client.

Starting the brainstorming

The stage has been set, considerations have been laid forth, and your method of recording has been set. Let 'em loose! As the ideas come forth, either as a trickle or a flood, keep the following pointers in mind so that you can make the most of your time.

Don't judge

"I think that's an awful idea."

When you're brainstorming, this sentence — or any variation on it — should never be uttered. Furthermore, anyone guilty of this utterance should be slathered in honey and dropped in the nearest wildlife refuge to fend for himself. Okay, so that *may* be a little extreme, but the point is, negativity of this sort has no place in your brainstorming session. It's only through the creation of what psychologists call a "safe space" that you can produce a group dynamic that will yield the positive results you desire.

What may start as the stupidest thing you've ever heard could grow to become the brilliant campaign that nobody saw coming. People may come up with crazy notions they had on their way to work or in the shower that morning, and, although the ideas may not be fleshed out quite yet, it's more productive to entertain a thought than to shoot it down immediately because of superficial flaws.

Allow for piggybacking

When you're brainstorming, an effective tool to keep the process moving forward and evolving into what could be the idea you're looking for is *piggybacking* (taking someone else's thought or idea and adding your own unique addition to the concept). You can use this technique when you find yourselves stumped, or you can use it to build upon a previously submitted idea. A decent idea can inspire someone else to tweak or improve upon it, and from there it gets passed around until resulting in the best idea of the night.

Don't be afraid to be literal

Brainstorming your ideas should be fun, so why make the work any harder than it needs to be. Say your company's tagline is, "We Take You Higher," and your boss says to you, I want to *really* take our customers higher. Take him at his word: Produce a branded hot-air balloon and offer free rides and photos with every purchase. You can't take your customers much higher than 1,000 feet!

Take them out of the conference room!

Each year, all the major television networks take to the conference rooms of the big ad agencies as they present their case as to why the firm should buy advertising spots on their networks. This time, known somewhat infamously as "Upfront Season," commonly involves the presentation of hundreds of predictable PowerPoint pitches.

One network charged its ad sales department with simple direction: Take them out of the conference room. Their team responded literally by not just taking their guests out of the room, but out of the building, making their presentation on a fully branded bus that looped around the block as the pitch was made. Getting the buyers out of the office and showcasing the network in a very different way allowed the network the opportunity to make an unparalleled impact. The campaign was also recognized with an industry award.

Campaigns are frequently most press-worthy and connect with consumers when the association is easy to make, if not blatantly obvious. Consumers are bombarded with thousands of messages a day, so if you can make your association immediately recognizable, they're most likely to notice and retain the information.

See how you can take what seems to be the painfully obvious choice for your brand and make it work in a way that's both clever and effective. Check out the nearby sidebar, "Take them out of the conference room," for an example of getting literal.

Exploring the Explored and Refining the Existing

There's an old tune called, "There's Nothing New Under the Sun," which makes the case that, essentially, we've seen it all before. Although we would make the cheerier argument that the best is yet to come, there are patterns from past campaigns and efforts that can be helpful tools in bringing forth ideas for your own campaigns.

Have you ever seen a marketing initiative taking place and thought, "Now, why didn't *I* think of that?" Or maybe you've noticed something special that you felt you could tie into your brand (like a bike shop branding the spoke hubs of a fleet of bicycles to spread their message). This is your time to throw ideas like this into the pot. Maybe one or more of the ideas will float off to the wayside, but one of them could also make its way to the top. Don't rule out anything!

In the following sections, we show you how you can borrow from campaigns of the past and make it work for your brand.

Why hasn't anyone thought of *this* before?

The inverse of looking to the past and thinking, "Why didn't *I* think of that?" is thinking "Why hasn't anyone thought of *this* before?" Our answer: Because you're just that good. Who knows? There may be a variety of reasons that the items you stir up haven't been executed in the past:

✔ **It's so obvious that no one ever thought of it.** You're in a rush to get out the door, you're already late, and, of course, you can't find your keys! Frantically, you ransack your home only to discover the keys have been in your pocket the entire time — or, worse, in the door itself! Similarly, the most perfect concepts may have been overlooked simply because they're so obvious that no one ever thought they would be effective.

To avoid this fate, leave no stone unturned. By fully exploring *all* the possibilities — obvious and abstract — you may find an idea that will have someone else wondering why *he* didn't think of it first.

✔ **Maybe someone else thought of it but just never thought it could happen.** Naysayers have no place in guerrilla marketing. You simply have to view everything as a possibility until you're 110 percent sure that it can't or won't work. And really, who likes a naysayer anyway?

Don't fall into the trap of saying no before your idea even gets off the ground.

Especially in the brainstorming phase, consider *everything* a possibility! Time travel? No problem. Maybe you *can't* alter the time-space continuum, but you can create branded environments that can take people to the future or the past. At this point, the world is your oyster, so give it all a whirl — you'll figure out how to actually *do* it later.

✔ **Someone tried pulling it off but, for some reason or another, couldn't make it happen.** As you know, the business world is constantly changing. Seemingly endless financial resources can dry up overnight, Chief creative officers can pack it in to write their memoirs in a cabin somewhere. Your great idea may be *so* great that someone else shared your excitement but it just wasn't in the cards for some reason. You can use these circumstantial losses to your benefit when you come up with something super and make it happen!

✔ **Someone, somewhere did it, but you just never heard of it.** The world is a big, beautiful place full of countless creative people. Just because you've never heard of your idea being executed before, doesn't mean it hasn't been. On the plus side, if *you* haven't heard of it, chances are good that no one else in your area has heard of it either. So take advantage of (at the very least, the regional) notoriety for your brand.

Embracing campaigns that have worked in the past

Lots of marketing methods have proven effective and have been used over and over again — and there's nothing wrong with that. In fact, having a strong grip on what has proven successful is key in creating innovative, new ideas. The challenge is to pare the killer ideas that have worked in the past down to their essence and see what made them stand out. After you've pinned down the core themes that made these ideas resonate, you can use them to bring about your own creative ideas.

When breaking down why a particular campaign worked in the past, try to summarize its success in one overarching core sentence — for example: "This campaign worked because consumers were able receive a valuable coupon and redeem it on a local level, and because the brand was able to easily track its success."

Let go of the desire to tie your ideas directly to your brand. What activities, events, entertainment, or other experiential engagements made an impression on you? Did you go to a concert that had a "wow moment" that helped the artist connect with the audience? What was unique about this moment? What tools were applied to make this impact? Use these visceral connections from seemingly unrelated experiences to generate ideas that can be later implemented and tailored to make *your* guerrilla campaign compelling.

Whether it's something you read about, saw, or did yourself, there's nothing wrong with using that reference, knowledge, or experience to help build your latest campaign. We're not suggesting copying or plagiarizing, but if building a giant structure in a highly trafficked area seems to grab the attention of your target media, maybe it's worth considering something similar (yet different enough from what's been done in the past) for your latest stunt. Or if consumers seem responsive to receiving materials and information at select venues and events, maybe adding those locations to your distribution schedule would be a wise move.

The edgiest way to use past marketing efforts to your benefit is to take the elements that have become accepted as traditional and thumb your nose at them. Many of the techniques used today by marketers are easily recognizable to most consumers, so when a brand goes against the grain to mock or turn these accepted practices on their ear, they tend to attract quite a bit of attention. Is there something within your industry (a silly trade practice, a notable icon) that you can parody or present in a completely different way that will attract the attention of your target audience? (For an example of shaking up the commonplace see the sidebar "We'll cover your ass," in this chapter.)

We'll cover your ass

Sometimes if you want people to take notice, you've got to shake things up a bit. in an attempt to land a coveted account with Chrysler, notable ad-agency exec and now TV host Donny Deutsch decided to challenge conventional wisdom when he stepped into a role with his father's advertising business. Although other agencies were spinning their wheels pursuing the traditional methods to land the account, this fellow decided to try something with a little more panache. So naturally, he headed to the junkyard and picked out the rustiest Chrysler bumper he could find, packaged it neatly, and shipped it off to his potential clients. When the automakers opened the box, they found the bumper affixed with a sticker that read, "We'll Cover Your Ass." The move was brassy to be sure, but ultimately his boldness paid off when he landed the account.

Tweaking what works to fit your brand

As you look to what's been successful in the past, you may find campaigns — or, at the very least, common denominators — that you think would have been perfect for your brand, if only you'd thought of them first. Okay, so maybe you *didn't* think of them first, but maybe you can take what has been fruitful in the past and add your own finer touches to it to produce something impressive and (seemingly) original.

Likely, your head is spinning with campaigns that you've loved in the past and you're excited to put your brand's imprint on them. You may be wondering, though, whether if you remount a campaign, detractors will point, laugh, and call you a poseur — a feeling you haven't had since you opted for that Flock of Seagulls haircut in the '80s. To avoid the wrath of these people, follow these tips for taking the program and making it your own:

- ✔ **Change where it's been done.** One of the guerrilla marketing programs we like to do — basically because it's fun and press-worthy — is custom sand sculptures. In some markets, however, custom sand sculptures can seem passé. So we propose a change of venue. Say you own a company that sells luxurious yachts. Seeing a custom sand sculpture on the beach is a pretty predictable choice for your brand. So, be *un*predictable! Have sand delivered to your storefront or other venue where your boats will be on display, and craft the work of art live on-site. The creation and presentation of the finished product *in a unique setting* could prove just as intriguing as the work itself.

✔ **Change who's participating.** People love a fish-out-of-water story — it's one of our favorite narratives. Whether it's a construction worker required to blow out women's hair or a Wall Street power player who suddenly is forced to bail hay down on the farm, we love the hijinks that are guaranteed to be the result of someone experiencing something for the first time.

If a previously executed idea was clearly a success, take another look at it and see what might happen if you swap out the original participants or invitees with a group that will make your initiative stand out. Maybe that's snagging local celebrities, the high school choir, or your local senior center — it all depends on what will create the most dynamic contrast with what's being executed.

✔ **Improve on how big it's been or how long it lasted.** Louder, faster, funnier, bigger, better, longer. . . . You like an event that that had 500 attendees? Well, throw an event that has 5,000 attendees! Impressed that those dancers set the record for dancing nonstop for 24 hours? To top that, assemble your own dance crew to cut a rug for 72 straight hours all while raising money for charity! Guerrilla marketing involves a certain degree of one-upmanship. Sometimes, the idea isn't to deny the power of a campaign — it's to blow it out so that prior attempts pale in comparison. Also, even though no one likes a braggart, it's nice to be able to claim those bragging rights.

Imitation may be the highest form of flattery, but make sure you aren't flattering your competition. Taking an idea and running with it could be the perfect strategy for making your program a hit, but be careful when choosing what to improve upon. Reinventing something that's been done before only works if you make it better. And this is especially true if you're borrowing the gem of a concept recently executed by a direct competitor.

Letting It Rip, Letting It Stew, and Figuring It Out

This is the stage in your creative process where you maximize your paternal and maternal instincts. That's right, these ideas are your babies and they shouldn't be forced through their paces — they should be nurtured, coddled, and left to blossom. Although the imagery may cause you to cringe, it's true that the ideas you've produced are precious and should be given the time to gestate.

After you've unleashed your forces, come up with some great new concepts, and explored successful efforts of the past, step away from this for a little bit. Give your ideas a chance to settle. The creative process can be exhausting, so give yourself and your cohorts an opportunity to catch your collective breath.

After you and your team have had the opportunity to stew on the ideas, come back and review the top ideas, weigh their pros and cons, make a choice, and set charting a plan for your success. When you've regrouped, here are a few questions to ask yourselves in order to select the best program:

- ✔ Which concept will best appeal to your target? Are you trying to reach consumers or press? Which concept best positions you to effectively reach them?
- ✔ Which concept is the most innovative and original?
- ✔ Which concept best represents the brand?

After you've reviewed the ideas and considered these few guideposts, one idea is likely to stand out from the rest. From there, you need to further refine the chosen concept adding nuances and elements that will make it as powerful as possible, and draft the necessary plans to make this collaboratively created concept a reality.

If at the conclusion of the brainstorming and selection process, you still don't have that one concept that pops, give it a rest for a day or two and repeat the process with a fresh perspective. Lather, rinse, and repeat.

Putting plan to paper

You've researched, brainstormed and decided what you want to do. Now it's time to mobilize your plan. In this phase, be sure to tell everyone on your team your strategy and give them the necessary tools to help you make your plan a reality.

If you're a business that's launching a larger program with many moving pieces, you'll want to prepare what we refer to as a *project brief* (a document that lays out all the details of your program for all to see). Regardless of the concept you choose, your project brief should include the following:

✔ Date(s) and timing of your campaign

✔ Location(s)

✔ All staff involved and needed

✔ Production elements

✔ Venue details (if applicable)

✔ Status of each element (pending, approved, secured, and so on)

✔ Press opportunities or considerations (if applicable)

✔ Required permits or permissions (if applicable)

Everyone involved in the campaign should have a chance to review the document before it's finalized, so they all have the opportunity to throw in their 2 cents. (Think how frustrated you'd be if you were working in the PR department and were suddenly charged with selling an initiative to the press that you knew didn't have a chance of getting picked up.) Plus, seeking input from everyone involved will enable you to further clarify the plan and shape it into something that'll achieve your goals (after all, if the PR folks know that the press won't cover what you're planning, you want to know that sooner rather than later). Getting feedback from everyone also gives you the chance to work out the kinks and clear up any problems before they become insurmountable obstacles that topple your plans. (For more on the parties that should be involved, turn to "Assembling your team," later in this chapter.)

Creating a budget

You run a successful business not by giving away the store, but by carefully monitoring what you're spending versus what you're bringing in. Especially if you have a limited marketing budget, it can be painful to part with every single dollar. To ensure that you get the most out of the money you're spending, you need to create — and stick to — a budget.

In this book, we lay out various expenses that are commonly associated with specific types of guerrilla marketing campaigns, but regardless of the kind of campaign you choose to do, taking the time to craft a budget is important. Table 4-1 gives you an example of a basic budget.

Table 4-1		A Basic Budget		
Item	**Quantity**	**Budgeted**	**Actual**	**Notes**
Staff	6	$250	$200	2 event staff, 4 street staffers
Attired	6	$120	$120	
Materials	500	$250	$225	Saved on shipping costs.
Venue	1	$5,000	$5,000	
Signage	4	$1,600	$1,200	Sourced cheaper signage alternative.
Miscellaneous	1	$2,000	$1,225	
Recap Report	1	$50	$50	
	Totals	**$9,270**	**$8,020**	
	Amount Saved	**$1,250**		

Especially if this is your first guerrilla marketing campaign, you may go over budget in some areas. To help offset these extra costs, give yourself some wiggle room by including a "Miscellaneous" category to help cover unforeseen costs.

Breaking up your budget into budgeted costs and actual costs will help you keep tabs on where you were able to save money and where you spent more than you anticipated. Laying out your budgets in this way will help you on your next campaign.

Assembling your team

You've collaborated on ideas, you've begun budgeting — now it's time to hand-pick your team members. Depending on the nature of your campaign, this may just involve convincing Rob from Accounts Payable that he needs to dress up as a giant piece of broccoli for four hours. Or it may mean that you need to tap a PR specialist or other marketing professional to give your campaign the finish you're looking for.

Later in this book, we fill you in on the necessary team members who will be involved in each kind of initiative. But in the following sections, we offer a quick overview of the people you should consider.

Putting together street teams

When you're assembling a street team, make sure you have the following people on your team before setting them loose on the streets:

- A group of friendly, attractive, outgoing individuals who can efficiently represent you and your brand on the street

- A manager who can be the street-level liaison between the teams and yourself — someone who's standing by day and night, so you can get your beauty rest

See Chapter 6 for more on street teams.

Planning an event

Whether you're having people over for snacks and a training video or holding a VIP launch party (see Chapter 8), there are a few people you'll want to have in your corner:

- Audiovisual people to handle lights and sound

- A caterer to handle food, beverage, rentals, and basic décor

- Some sort of entertainment — a band, a DJ, or maybe even a fortune teller to entertain your guests during the event

- Staff to assist with everything from greeting guests to stuffing goody bags to cleaning up after the night is over

To find the crew to make your event a success, look first to the venue. Many venues have in-house or preferred vendors who can work for you. If that isn't the case, check with online production resources such as BizBash (www.biz bash.com) for options and potential vendors.

Creating distribution materials or premiums

Never underestimate the power of the *giveaway* — some sort of premium that consumers can take away from your efforts (see Chapter 20). To help create materials that are professional and appealing, you'll want to enlist the services of the following staff and vendors:

- **Someone to handle layout and design:** Often, this can be as simple as hiring a graphic designer to use her artistic talents in concert with your guidance to present your logo in an exciting way. If you don't have access to these resources, you may try calling upon the vendor that's producing the distribution pieces to see if they can assist with this.

- **Vendor for the production of distribution elements:** Your local printer may be able to help you print up postcards. Or you may have to call in a company specializing in branded promotional items to assist with customized tote bags.

✔ **Delivery apparatus:** Whether you're hiring a fulfillment house (whose services range from receiving to packaging and delivery) to distribute on your behalf, or you're looking to use street teams, you want to build in some way to get what you create into the hands of the people you intend to persuade.

Going online

As we discuss in Chapters 12 and 13, the Internet is highly fertile ground to plant the seeds for your brand into your consumers minds. To help you do this most effectively, you want to enlist the following Internet innovators:

✔ **A Web designer:** Your business's site is far too important to rely on elementary Web-design skills. Make sure you tap a designer who gets you and your brand — and can present both in the most positive light.

✔ **A Webmaster:** You want to make sure someone is overseeing your site and your Web initiatives.

Someone should also be responsible for watching the bottom line and tracking which online marketing efforts worked and which ones didn't. That way, next time you'll have en even better idea where to spend your hard-earned money.

Preparing to pull the trigger

You've nursed your beautiful guerrilla campaign from creative inception through budgetary struggles and surrounded yourself with a team of people who are just as committed as you are to making the campaign a success. You've embraced the process entirely and, as a result, you have a fully formed, goal-oriented program. Before you launch your campaign, make sure you do the following:

✔ **Double-check the details.** You may have taken in the big picture, but sometimes in the hustle and frantic nature of bringing campaigns to life, some of the details get overlooked or just plain ignored. So before you strike out on the campaign, double-check the specifics — even the simplest stuff, such as date, time, location, weather, and so on — and make sure everyone on your team knows these specifics as well.

✔ **Review the printed materials.** Prior to launching any of your materials into production, demand a proof of everything so that you can make sure the details are all correct. Make sure to review all dates, times, brand information, Web sites, and other specifics — and make sure you pass this info around the office for others to do the same. If these elements are takeaways, you want to make sure that your target audience is taking away the right information.

✔ **Check in with your staff.** For better or for worse, you're only one person. Inevitably, you're going to have to rely on the talents and abilities of others to help see your initiatives realized. Even so, never take for granted that everyone knows what they're supposed to be doing. When appropriate, hold training sessions. The day before your campaign, have your staff call in to confirm they'll be there. Make sure everyone knows the specifics of your campaign.

✔ **Make sure you're ready to pay your venue and vendors.** If you're executing your big idea off your property or utilizing vendors whose participation is crucial to the success of your campaign, see if anyone requires payment on-site and have checks ready. Knowing this ahead of time will help you avoid problems that could derail an otherwise perfect program. Also, make sure you've got a little extra cash on hand for those last-minute things like emergency items and tips.

✔ **Document everything.** When people have a baby, they document every moment — they take pictures and video of every moment. Sure, this is a marketing campaign and not a human being, but that's no reason why you shouldn't record all the details of its entry into the world. Have your digital camera, video camera, and pen and paper standing by to record every beautiful moment. You may also consider hiring a professional photographer to cover your event (see Chapter 8). Not only will this documentation provide you with a record of your effort, but it'll help you later analyze the successes and shortcomings of your campaign.

Chapter 5

Bringing in the Big Guns: Guerrilla Marketing Firms

In This Chapter

▶ Knowing when to hire a marketing agency

▶ Finding the right agency for you

▶ Considering cost

▶ Knowing when to say goodbye

*Y*ou've taken the time to sit at the table with the most brilliant, creative minds you could collect or bribe with pizza, and you've crafted a strategic marketing mix of exciting events, nontraditional media, cleverly outfitted street teams — you've even opted to name a star after your company for good measure. Yes, pride begins to swell in your chest — until one of those brilliant minds chimes in, "How are we ever going to do all this?"

Don't let this inquisitor rain on your parade. As we outline in this book, many, if not all, of the programs you've created you can do yourself. But in some cases, you may decide it's time to seek out some assistance and call in the big guns. Here, we look to address how to utilize the resources of guerrilla marketing firms to help you aim for the stars — literally or figuratively — and make your plan a reality.

We start by addressing when it's time to reach out for help, weighing some of the common considerations that drive companies to seek out the capabilities of a nontraditional agency. From there, we suggest where to look for help and, ultimately, help you decide who to hire. After you've selected your special marketing forces, we take a look at what this collaboration will cost you. Finally, we talk about parting company — letting you know when it's time to wrap up your relationship and move on.

Knowing When It's Time

You've got big plans. You want them to be realized through flawless, execution. After a company inventory, you decide that the best way to achieve that peerless execution is simply to have someone else do it. Good for you. Reading all those self-help books, you learned that a good manager is one who knows when to delegate, dump, or do it — and you've opted to delegate so you can do it.

We know bringing in someone you don't know, to do something you've never done before, can be a big deal, and a bit overwhelming. Your head may be aflutter with all sorts of questions. Am I ready to make this commitment? Is this the best use of my resources? Is there someone out there I can trust? We completely empathize.

Deciding you want to use guerrilla tactics, in and of itself, can be a trailblazing decision for some companies. Naturally, you want to make sure it's the right choice for you and your brand. With that in mind, we look to a few of the more typical reasons that businesses look to guerrilla marketing firms.

When you don't have the money for big media

You're in the process of mapping out your marketing game plan, and you've suddenly realized that you've developed some strange sort of tunnel vision where everything you see, you envision in terms of how you can advertise your product or service. It's gotten to the point where it's started to take over your life.

In your car, on the way to work, you see your product splayed on a huge digital billboard and swear that if you could just hear your company's peppy jingle perkily chirping on your car radio, that business would skyrocket. The obsession doesn't end there. Unable to sleep, you find yourself watching those late-night infomercials and conclude that if you only had a catchy toll-free number with teams of attractive operators "standing by" to take your customers' call, you wouldn't have to worry about little Timmy and Danielle's college tuition ever again.

After seeing these strange mirages, you decide it's time to get down to business and make some calls about these big media outlets. But it doesn't take long for you to discover that if you spend your money on these outlets, the only college the little ones will be able to attend will be clown college. Now you have a new problem: Where to go from here?

One possibility is to look to a guerrilla marketing firm to see what existing resources they have available. One of the main reasons people turn to nontraditional media is that it can usually be executed for less money than most forms of traditional media. Plus, many guerrilla agencies already offer an existing framework of services that you can use to get your product out there, for a price tag that fits more closely within your budget.

For example, an agency could execute a simple street campaign (maybe even with attractive staffers singing that jingle you had dancing around in your head) for under $1,000. Or you could have the agency produce a simple, fun microsite (see Chapter 13) to create a unique online presence. This relevant form of media can — depending on how fancy you get — be professionally designed for as little as $2,500.

When stacked up against more traditional methods, which can begin around $10,000 and quickly shuttle up to several hundreds of thousands (depending on the outlet), more and more businesses are using guerrilla agencies to help provide them with options that provide a big bang for much less buck.

When traditional methods won't cut it

Expectations are important when you're spending those precious marketing dollars. Maybe it's just us, but if we pay someone a lot of money to run a brilliant TV spot featuring dancing, price-cutting scissors and catchy tunes, and the commercial doesn't yield an increase in sales or even leads, we think it's time to scrap that commercial and think about another way. One alternative method may be hiring a guerrilla firm to grab your target audience.

Another way in which traditional outlets may not be the direction you're looking to go is when print, radio, billboards, or other mass media just can't do what you want. This problem is an exceptionally good one to have! Why? Because if you've conceptualized a campaign that is so knock-your-socks-off good that these outlets aren't capable of executing it, chances are, you've created something truly unexpected — or, at the very least, something truly guerrilla and buzz-worthy. In these situations, many brands find it helpful to hire a nontraditional agency that can assist in shaping the effort and making sure that it comes off the way they've envisioned it.

When you have to move fast

When you wake up and head into work, you probably have a mental picture of how your work day will play out: e-mails, proposals, follow-up calls, an extended lunch hour, four trips to the bathroom, and so on. Later, as you head home and reflect on your day's achievements, you may be surprised to find that the day you planned out and the one you actually experienced bore little resemblance (with the exception of the extended lunch hour — you made sure you got that!). Business moves fast. What was yesterday's top priority suddenly finds itself in the trash today, and that silly side project quickly takes center stage.

With these shifting priorities, many companies find that, when they finally do nail down their campaign, they need to kick the campaign into full gear immediately. Given the tight window, they may not have the time and in-house support needed to pull off the campaign. This is where guerrilla firms can step in and lend a hand.

Most reputable firms have the experience, contacts, materials, and man-power already in place to help you realize your concept and your schedule. Time is money, so while we're wholeheartedly confident that if you had the time you'd be able to figure it all out, when in a crunch, opting to seek the services of those already in the know may end up saving you both time and money.

Deciding Who to Hire

In showbiz they have a saying that the real work of a movie is done in the casting process. You put people who best tell your story in the right roles, and you've got yourself a hit. This isn't just good advice from a cigar-chomping Hollywood producer — it's a good rule of thumb when selecting the agency that'll be telling your story to consumers.

Although the hiring is completely subjective, you need to make sure the agency you select has the right resources and a secure grasp of your needs. In this section, we shed some light on who's out there, what they do, and what you can expect in return for your money.

Identifying the agencies and options

Whether it's the money, the ideas, the time line, or some other decider, you've determined that enlisting a guerrilla agency to handle your campaign is in your best interests. Now the question becomes, "Where do I look?"

If you don't have the time to get out there and research agencies yourself, freelancers and consultants can begin this search for you. These consultants can either help you identify which agency is right for you and hire them for the job, or they may even be able to handle the work themselves. Usually, consultants are reserved for larger companies. You can find them by doing a simple online search for "guerrilla marketing" or search for the specific genre of guerrilla marketing you're interested in, such as "street sampling," "mall tours," or "online marketing." Also, reach out to existing trade resources.

Agencies themselves come in all shapes and sizes. Some are as small as five people; others are as big as a network of 500, plus national or international employees. Some are independently owned; others are owned by larger firms.

The key to finding the agency that's right for you is knowing what you need. Following are some common requirements, along with information on who you should be looking for to help you fill that need:

- **Buying and placing media:** If all you need is someone to help you buy and place media, you may not need to hire anyone at all. Instead, you can work directly with vendors. This approach offers a more direct line of communication, and it has the added benefit of cutting down on your overall costs.

- **Handling the press and taking care of public relations (PR):** If you already have all your ducks in a row to execute your event, and you just need a hand with your press and PR, you may not want to call on a guerrilla marketing firm. Instead, you can hire a freelance publicist or PR firm to help you out. (For more on hiring PR, see Chapter 17.)

- **Hiring a street team:** If you decide that you want to use a street team, you may want to call on a staffing agency to assist you. Although the agency may not have the resources or the background to help you shape a broader marketing plan, it should have a database of staff available. Often, a staffing agency can help match staff to fit your criteria, as well as supply headshots and short bios if you want to see who they're putting out there on your behalf. For example, if you want your street team to look like they just walked off a runway in Milan, staffing agencies will work with you to help you find the look you're seeking.

Although staffing agencies will help match you with people who have experience in promotional work, if you're looking for true models, you may want to think about working with modeling agencies. Just note that the more specialized the request and duties, the higher the final invoice.

- **Executing a full-on guerrilla marketing plan:** If you've decided to go for the meat-and-potatoes of guerrilla marketing — which frequently involves some variation of street teams, publicity stunts, wrapped vehicles, and so on (all of which we elaborate on in Part II) — the time has come to call upon those who specialize in grassroots guerrilla marketing. They can help you come up with a strategy and execute it.

There's good news on this front. There aren't as much guerrilla agencies as there are traditional ad agencies and media buying outlets, which means you can spend less time qualifying the candidates and more time working toward a successful campaign.

Although many agencies offer the world, some agencies will clearly specialize more in one area than another. For example, one agency might specialize in national touring vehicles or stunts, while another might excel in online programs and partnerships. Be sure to ask what the agency you're considering specializes in.

It's a big world out there. Don't feel that you need to use an agency located down the block, simply because they're down the block. If you're buying local media, you may want to stay local — but when it comes to having a group design and implement national ideas and campaigns, it's okay to look beyond the town square for the right agency.

Just because you're hiring a firm halfway across the country doesn't mean you won't receive personal attention. The digital age enables clients and agencies to enjoy as much or as little contact as the client needs.

When lining up potential agencies, don't judge an office based on its size. The versatile nature of guerrilla can cause looks to be deceiving. Smaller groups have worked for much bigger companies, and bigger agencies sometimes take on much smaller clients.

Also, just because the agency doesn't know about your business doesn't mean you should rule them out. In your everyday, you have many discussions about issues that you don't have a PhD in, but that doesn't make your contribution to the conversation any less valid. Sometimes bringing in agencies with other focuses can breathe new life into existing efforts — they'll approach your brand in a way that you may not have considered before.

Qualifying the candidates

You're getting closer to picking that agency that'll be the standard bearer for your organization. How do you make the final selection? Just like buying a car, it's time to kick the tires, and get all the juicy inside details from someone who's already been in the position in which you now find yourself. There are several common ways to do this:

- ✔ Scope out the agency's Web site and dig up any trade info you can find.
- ✔ Issue a request for proposal, and see how they respond to your needs.
- ✔ Ask for references from companies that have worked with them in the past.

So grab your driving gloves and let's get to qualifying!

Reviewing the agencies' Web sites

As we discuss in Chapter 2, most guerrilla marketing firms don't have a standing rate card. So agency Web sites serve as excellent calling cards to help give you a sense of the company's focuses and capabilities.

More often than not, an agency's Web site will contain case studies of past work, otherwise known as the agency's *portfolio.* The site should provide a cross section of the agency's methods of operation. Things to look out for include details of past campaigns, the sort of clients the agency has (or has had) relationships with, detailed case studies, and client responses.

As you look over the site, consider your response. Does this agency share the kind of vision that you have for your company? If the answer is yes, send an e-mail or pick up the phone to request more information.

Issuing a request for proposal

After getting the basic information, you need to take the agency out on the road, so to speak, and see how it "handles." You can start by issuing a *request for proposal* (RFP), a document prepared in order to elicit bids from potential vendors for a product or service.

We don't advise issuing an RFP for a simple street distribution campaign, to get some help with some signage, or for some other smaller campaign. If you're prepared to spend the time and money on a campaign with a budget of upwards of $50,000, however, issuing a formal RFP can help you vet a handful of select agencies that you think meet your criteria.

An RFP takes some time to prepare — and the agencies will need some time to prepare their responses. Here are some things to include in your RFP:

- **Specific information on the services you're looking for, in as much detail as possible.**

- **What information you'd like to receive about the agency bidding on the business:** For example, you may be interested in the history of the agency, the number of employees, and who will be assigned to the project if they're awarded the business.

- **Any criteria for vendor eligibility or disqualification:** This might include working with competing brands, having enough staff to meet your needs, and having experience with campaigns like yours.

- **Relevant dates:** This includes the deadline for application, the deadline for submission of supplemental information, dates for any associated interviews or open meetings, the date when the decision will be made, and you're desired timeframe for the project.

Some companies even implement a qualifying process to begin the qualifying process. In the past, we've received a request for qualification (RFQ), a survey in which agencies are first asked to answer a series of questions and supply several case studies in order to qualify for receiving the RFP itself.

Here's a sample RFP — you can customize this to meet your own needs:

Client: A well known music cable network called Tunes.

Project: Create an on-site presence for the network at a popular music festival called MusicFest.

Background: Tunes is a network that allows its audience to find content, technology, trends, and music at their inception. As the exclusive multi-media sponsor for MusicFest since 2006, Tunes provides MusicFest with special MusicFest themed content on all platforms (on-air, online, mobile, and video on demand). We will have full access to MusicFest assets and want to fully integrate them into our on-site activities including:

- Themed structure
- Trained brand ambassadors
- Distribution materials
- E-mail acquisition component
- Branded giveaways

Tunes also produces and airs MusicFest promotional spots to promote ticket sales (pre-sale and on-sale). Tunes will also provide MusicFest with one microsite on www.tunes.com with original and entertaining content.

Assignment: Develop and execute the Tunes on-site sponsorship at the MusicFest. The Tunes area should be an experience that communicates to festival attendees what the Tunes brand is and also offers an opportunity to interact with our brand through all senses. Your experiential marketing expertise should be used to make our brand come alive in a way that is unique and exclusive to the Tunes network.

Objective:

- Heighten exposure to the MusicFest audience for the Tunes brand
- Promote tune-in for Tune's programming
- Leverage network content and talent relevant to key demo

Target Profile:

- Majority of MusicFest attendees: Adults: Ages 15 to 22
- Tunes target demo: Adults: Ages 16 to 34
- 50 percent male, 50 percent female

Concept:

- Concept ideation for a unique and high-impact on-site presence
- Manage all promotional components (premiums, vehicle wrap, data collection, and so on)
- Create and manage timelines
- Work with Tunes personnel to manage project status and secure relevant materials, provide design/copy direction with Tunes Creative Services and/or any outside agencies on collateral designs/production
- Develop and maintain budget to include all related costs
- Provide Tunes with weekly updates from the road with pictures, as well as a recap report at the conclusion of the event showing success measurement

Additional Thought-Starters:

- Integrate emerging technologies — Tunes is multiplatform (online, on-air, mobile).
- Should be experiential, interactive, and create a spectacle.
- Premiums should be iconic in nature (we'd like to create walking billboards).
- MusicFest is going green this year. Tunes would like to participate and kick off our environmental awareness campaign here using elements of our on-site presence — for example, by using eco-friendly giveaways and premiums.

Budget: Range is $250,000 to $350,000, including transportation costs, premiums, and data collection.

Present budgets based on the following scenarios:

- Everything including a wrapped tour bus
- Everything including some alternate method of transportation

Timing:

- April 12 and 13: Pitch meetings
- April 19: Agency assigned
- June 28: Event begins
- June 30: Event ends

Asking for references

Whether you take the time to issue an RFP (see the preceding section), or simply reach out to several agencies, when you've narrowed your list down to one, two, or three agencies that are viable choices for your campaign or initiative, request references of past or current clients. You want to talk to people who can speak to the agency's skills, services, and capabilities.

Turning Your Attention toward the Cash

After all your researching, it's time to talk turkey and see how much this investment is going to cost you. Obviously, the costs will vary depending on the complexity of what you're asking of the agency. Having someone scale a skyscraper dressed in your brand will be a lot more expensive than sending out street teams of people all wearing T-shirts with your company's logo on them.

In order to make sure that you and your agency are both speaking the same language, you need to agree on a bill of services and sign a services agreement before the project begins. These agreements will help outline main costs, as well as any additional costs — such as messenger service, shipping, setup charges, or other little expenses that may pop up along the way.

As you get closer to the launch of your campaign, the costs may be refined or outright changed. Make sure you and your agency agree with how these "corrections" will be handled so that you can both adapt and produce the best initiatives possible.

What to pay

What you should pay depends primarily on what you're asking for. If all you're looking for is the execution of one element of a guerrilla campaign, the cost will be less than if you're having an agency complete a year-long campaign.

Two of the primary ways that guerrilla agencies are contracted are by retainer or on a per-project basis:

- **Retainer:** A *retainer* is a monthly amount paid for goods or services rendered. Retainers can range from small to large, depending on the scope of the project or campaign. For retainer agreements, what you're really paying for is having this agency's ear and ideas for a set period of time. *Hard costs* — such as buying media or executing campaigns — are not usually covered in the retainer fee.

The retainer fee will be affected by the numbers of hours the agency plans on devoting to the project, as well as the resources that the agency needs in order to get the job done.

✔ **Per project:** A *project-basis account* is a predetermined payment to cover the entire project from beginning to end. As long as no additional items have been added or amended, it's okay to expect that the price agreed to at the beginning will be (and should be) the price paid at the end. This is the more common method of paying a guerrilla marketing company. This type of account works well for smaller organizations in particular, because you're paying for exactly what you're using, and no more than that.

Depending on the scope of the project, and agency practices, it's not uncommon to pay 25 percent or even 50 percent upon signing the contract. The balance is then due either when the project is complete, or 30 days after the project is complete. The percentage you'll be asked to pay upfront varies from one agency to the next, as does the deadline for the final payment. Just make sure you and the agency are clear on the terms of payment before you get started.

Like all things in business, agencies and clients can be cautious when working with each other for the first time. As you develop a relationship with an agency, the terms can be negotiated on a case-by-base basis, with less formalities and hesitation. However, in your first encounters, creating a hard and fast framework for payment will help put both parties a bit more at ease.

What to expect in return

By bringing in an agency to execute your guerrilla efforts, you're essentially saying, "I'm trusting you to make me look brilliant!" With careful planning and coordination with your agency, there's no reason why you *shouldn't* look brilliant.

Some clients who are working with an agency for the first time may be unsure what they're going to get. Make sure your guerrilla marketing agency provides you with the following key components:

✔ **Whatever services you agreed to at the outset:** This is why getting it all in writing is critical.

✔ **An alternate contact person:** You need this in case you have to speak with someone about your campaign or initiative and your main contact is out office.

✔ **Guidance and insight if requested and/or needed:** Inside expertise and advice on how to best design and execute your campaign. Things to consider might include timing, locations, legality, and known obstacles to avoid that will help ensure a smooth and successful campaign.

✔ **Photo and written documentation recap report:** This gives you the opportunity to review the highlights of the campaigns and ways it might be improved in the future. This should include written reporting, color photos and in some instances video reel.

Saying Goodbye

Businesses part ways with guerrilla marketing agencies for a variety of reasons:

✔ **Cost:** Marketing dollars can be tight, so one of the most common reasons for parting company with an agency is that the money dries up. Agencies know that this is the way of the world, and as long as you're upfront about the situation they'll look forward to working with you again, when you have the money.

✔ **Dissatisfaction:** Another reason for bidding your agency *auf Wiedersehen* is that you're dissatisfied with the experience. Although most guerrilla agencies work conscientiously to make their clients as happy as possible, sometimes things just don't work out. You may have had creative differences or miscommunication — whatever the case, there are other agencies out there, and another one may be a better fit for you and your brand.

✔ **Project completion:** The most common reason for saying goodbye, for the time being, is that the project is complete. When you've hired an agency on a per-project basis, after you've executed the campaign, received your recap report, and had a post-initiative wrap-up call (if you've previously agreed to have one), that's the end — for now.

Coming from an agency background, our hope is that, after reviewing your work, you may find that it was a positive experience and you have yourself a new promotional partner!

Part II
Marketing at Street Level

"It's a PR campaign, right? What better costume to wear on the streets for a restaurant called Hooters?"

In this part . . .

Sometimes, alone on Friday nights playing Dungeons & Dragons online, one of us (we won't say which one) likes to pause for a little game he likes to call, "What Would I Stop For?" The game is relatively easy: In cities flooded with spectacles, entertainment, and visually stimulating ads, you simply have to come up with something so dynamic, so cool that you'd just have to stop and take it in.

If you chose to join this game, what would your answers be? How can you use this insight to benefit your brand? Essentially, this part explores the "What Would I Stop For?" game as it pertains to street teams, marketing events, and publicity stunts. We detail the essentials to design and execute each of these outlets perfectly.

Chapter 6

Hitting the Street with Street Teams

"**I**'ve got next to no money to spend, but I really need to get the word out. Help!" This plea is frequently shouted from the rooftops (or at least internally screamed, in silent desperation) by everyone from small-business owners to heads of marketing. Sometimes the answer to your marketing woes can be summed up in two words: street teams.

Street teams are trained brand ambassadors who are placed in targeted locations to engage your audience for the purposes of distribution or acquisition. These street-level efforts have proven very effective in raising awareness for a product or service and acquiring information (such as e-mail addresses) that you can then use to generate future business. We often sing street teams' praises because street teams allow for one-to-one communication — the purest form of direct marketing. It *literally* puts your product directly into the hands of the consumer — letting them see it, touch it, try it, even taste it!

When street teams are used correctly, you'd be hard pressed to find a better way to talk to your target audience, deliver a marketing message in an unexpected way or place, avoid or even eliminate waste, and steer clear of being seen as obtrusive. To an astute marketer, street-team methods are a godsend. And when you take them seriously and don't abuse them, they can truly provide a mutually rewarding marketing experience for both brands and consumers.

Another reason we find street teams a particularly effective tool is because they can be executed on nearly any budget. For resourceful business owners looking to make a genuine connection with their consumers, street teams get the message out in a targeted, personal way.

In this chapter, we cover the basics of creating an impressive street team. We get started by giving you some pointers on how to select the shining faces to deliver your message. Who are they and what will they be saying? From there, we discuss effective distribution pieces to give your message legs. And finally, as the saying goes, "It's all in the timing" — we fill you in on timing and locations to make sure you're presenting a campaign that sticks!

Coming Up with a Budget

Street programs can be scaled to meet almost any budget. But just because they work even if you're living on a shoestring doesn't mean you don't have to take a good hard look at what you want to spend. Before you can close your wallet, you need to budget for the following:

- ✔ **Staff pay:** If you go through a staffing agency, you can expect to pay $25 to $45 per person per hour. If you hire staffers directly, you can cut this cost dramatically (see the "Hiring the right staff" section, later in the chapter).

  Don't forget to include an extra hour or so for training (Check out the "Teach your staffers well" section, later in the chapter.)

  Life happens, be prepared. If you have some extra money, you may want to consider hiring an alternate for your street team. The morning of your campaign, someone may get sick, stuck on a train, or not be dressed acceptably when he arrives on-site — having someone ready to replace that person can be a huge help.

- ✔ **Attire:** For a basic printed T-shirt and a non-branded hat or cap, plan on spending at least $25 per staffer. If you want someone dressed as the San Diego Chicken, you need to budget for extra feathers. (See the "Finding the right clothes" section, later in this chapter, for more information.)

- ✔ **Materials:** Depending on what you choose to distribute, these costs can be as low as the cost of printouts at your local copy store or as high as the cha-ching of high-value premiums. Plan on at least $50 — and possibly a lot more. (See the "Creating the Right Distribution Piece" section, later in the chapter.)

- ✔ **Transportation expenses:** If staffers are traveling a great distance or require a vehicle for the purposes of the campaign, be sure to figure this into your financials. It could be as little as the cost of subway fare or as much as the cost of a plane ticket, depending on your campaign. Plus, take transportation into account with your premiums. Do you need a car, van, or reserved parking space to store materials, supplies, or staffer belongings?

✔ **Contingency fund:** Depending on the complexity of your campaign, you should leave a little extra money for unexpected costs, such as the cost of shipping materials, parking costs, or coffee for your staff. Set aside at least $150 for this, more if you have it.

You've started your budget and you've discovered that staffing costs are going to be a little higher than you'd like to dole out. Look to the products or services that your business offers and see if you may be able to trade your company's products or services for street-level efforts. For example, say you own a tanning salon, and you want to distribute postcards to people on their way home from work encouraging them to take advantage of your special happy-hour tanning specials. Why not trade your staffers 30 minutes of tanning for every hour they work? This way your branding gets into the hands of potential customers and your staffers are able to preserve their delightful, golden glow.

Building a Winning Team

You've decided to assemble your own personal A-team to spread your message, but you're overwhelmed, tense. How many people do you need? What do you tell them when you find them? And, perhaps most daunting, how much is all this hullabaloo going to cost you?

In this section, we answer all these questions. Here you find out how to select, train, and outfit your staffers — and in such a thorough way that you'll be saying, "I love it when a plan comes together!"

Hiring the right staff

When you're selecting staff for a street campaign, ask yourself, "Would I want to take something from this person?" You don't just need a warm body standing on the street — personality and appearance matter. Tailor your staff to project the image of the message you're trying to communicate.

When selecting your staff, you want to choose street-team members who best resemble the people in your target audience. No matter what product or service you're marketing, you want to make sure that the staff you hire to relay your message to consumers has credibility and will be respected by the audience you're trying to reach. If you're promoting the opening of a new skate park and you're trying to reach teens hitting the half-pipe, your team probably shouldn't be made up of 40somethings dressed in button-downs and khakis. Aside from creeping out your boarders, the likelihood of those 40somethings being able to connect with your edgy skater kids is exceptionally low.

Often, street teams are assembled from actors, models, and college students looking to pick up some extra cash. Actors and models, in particular, are exceptional resources, because they're usually already trained in how to properly project to an audience and present themselves in the public eye. With those pluses, however, come a variety of temperaments, from the agreeable young ingénue to the jaded diva who's "over it," so be aware of who you're adding to your team.

When interviewing candidates, spend time talking to them and get a sense of their demeanor. If you can't quite get a read on someone (or don't like the read you're getting), chances are your consumers won't either and you should probably pass on that person. If the person is friendly and communicates in an articulate, agreeable manner, that's one to hold on to! Taking the time to hire the right people can be the cornerstone of a successful campaign. **Remember:** They're your mouthpiece when you're not there.

You should be able to say the following about every person you hire:

- ✔ This person strikes me as friendly, attractive, and outgoing.

- ✔ This person can relay my message confidently and articulately.

- ✔ This person's demeanor and attitude is in step with the image of my company and brand.

- ✔ I can see my target audience spending a few minutes chatting with this person on the street.

- ✔ This person understands the elements of my campaign and feels comfortable with what's required.

The people you hire for your street teams will be representing your brand to consumers. The way that they present themselves in your interview will give you great insight into how they'll present your message.

You're a busy person. You've got acquisitions to acquire, sales to solidify, and expense reports that to be filled out. Because you can't be everywhere all the time, consider hiring a project manager to oversee the execution of your campaign. The project manager will ensure that everyone is on message, take pictures to document your efforts, and act as your eyes and ears on the ground. Even if you hire a project, check in whenever possible — that's not micromanaging, it's being responsible and involved.

Determining the size of your team

As you meet with staffers and start seeing some you like, you'll probably find yourself getting more and more excited about the campaign — so much so that you'll want to send out an army of people to help spread the word . . . until you start looking at the costs.

Although hiring a large number of distributors to "own the city" sounds like a great plan, most campaigns don't warrant this sort of conquest. Instead, take a look at which locations you think are most important for you to hit first (see the "Identifying the Best Time and Place for Your Campaign" section, later in this chapter).

After selecting some tentative locations, create a team of two individuals for each chosen location. We've found that teams of two work well for a number of reasons:

- ✔ Staffers are more energetic and outgoing when another person next to them shares the enthusiasm of the product or brand they're promoting.

- ✔ A team of two adds instant credibility to a campaign, especially when compared to the lone soul standing on the corner across the street.

- ✔ Having a second staffer ensures that you'll always have someone there doing the distribution and gives each person the chance to take a break or step away for a minute.

Finding the right clothes

The clothes (or lack thereof) can be the element that makes the campaign. People are generally receptive to distribution campaigns if they can size up what they're walking into before they're in among it. Outfitting your team in branded gear can provide instant credibility and association with what they're promoting.

Branded hats and T-shirts are relatively inexpensive and go very far in putting a polished finish on your guerrilla campaign. It also gives you a chance to make an impression on consumers who may not be interested in taking a distribution piece, but still notice the name of your company or Web address as they walk by.

If you've got a little extra money and you want to amp up your street teams, dress them like bunnies! Okay, maybe not bunnies, but you may want to try some brand-related costuming. To encourage consumers to set sail on a cruise ship, the national cruise industry trade organization dressed up several brand ambassadors as ship captains and dispatched them throughout New York City. This unique twist on a distribution program not only put a professional finish on the campaign, it caused consumers to approach the staffers on their own accord. This led to questions, interactions, and, ultimately, trips to Fiji!

Don't scare 'em: Healthy skepticism from the public is understandable. So don't make choices in your costuming that turn a skeptic into an outright adversary. Keep your costuming as close to your brand as possible and in line with local tastes. If you're using costuming that covers your staffers' faces, have another branded team member there to reassure consumers of the legitimacy of the campaign while at the same time keeping your own costumed dynamo safe!

Teaching your staffers well

After you have your team, it's time to train them to take the field! Taking the time to train your crew can take a campaign from "eh" to outstanding.

The most efficient way to ensure that your goals are effectively communicated to your staffers is to hold a training session. In order for your training session to be effective, you need to prepare for it and plan an agenda. Here are the main steps you want to include in your presentation:

1. **Start by introducing all team members.**
2. **Distribute the branded gear and sampling materials.**
3. **Communicate the program goals.**
4. **If possible, give the team members the opportunity to sample the product or service they're promoting.**

5. **Give the team members talking points and frequently asked questions (FAQs) about your product or service so they know what to say and how you want them to say it.**

   Include additional information such as a Web site or video that will better inform your team. Be sure to take the time to instruct your team as to how the material should be presented in a straightforward, uncomplicated way.

   Simply saying, "Good morning!" goes incredibly far! Especially when juxtaposed with some disheveled schlub standing expressionless and motionless trying to distribute similar items.

6. **Delegate individual duties.**

7. **Walk through the timing and scheduling of the campaign.**

   Make sure that you build breaks into your schedule. Doing so will help keep your staff focused, energized, and effective.

8. **Address what staffers should do if there are problems or hiccups in the campaign.**

9. **Open the floor for questions or clarification.**

10. **Provide and review a *one-pager* (a single sheet given to staffers that includes all the aforementioned information; see Figure 6-1).**

    Don't forget names and phone numbers of all parties involved (managers, staffers, van drivers, and any vendors who may be involved). Make sure you can easily get in touch with your managers via cellphone, to maintain a steady flow of communication.

Taking the time to hold this training session will help everything come off exactly as you've envisioned. It gives you the chance to make sure they know how they're supposed to be dressed, who they should approach, what they're saying, and how they're supposed to be saying it — and a clear grasp of all these points is key to effectively getting your message out there.

Grandma Selma's
Homebaked Muffins

Postcard Distribution One Pager

Staff Contacts:

Manager:	Benny Salvatore – 555.5555
Staffers:	Stew Frankenfurter – 555.5555
	Margo Magarigold – 555.5555

Event Date / Hours:	June 8; 12pm – 4pm
Meeting Location:	Grandma Selma's
	42 Tasty Lane

Attire:

Manager:	Khakis and a polo shirt
Staffers:	Grandma Selma's t-shirt & jeans

Duties:

• Be presentable at all times

• Appropriate demeanor around consumers & guests at all times

• Distribute postcards

• Communicate reactions, comments and problems to the manager.

Run of Show:

11:30 am	Arrive on-site, dressed and ready to go
11:45 am	Pick up postcards from Grandma Selma
12:00 pm	Begin distribution
2:00 pm	Staffer One Break (15 mins.)
2:15 pm	Staffer Two Break (15 mins.)
3:45 pm	Clean-up materials and prepare for wrap up
4:00 pm	Event conclusion – END OF DAY

Talking Points:

• Get a FREE muffin today only with coupon!

• Try Grandma Selma's new tropical flavors!

Figure 6-1:
A one-pager
prepared
and
distributed
to staffers
helps get
everyone
on the same
page.

Crafting Your Message

Whiz-bang! That sound you're not hearing is brand messaging flying about your ears! Every day, people are bombarded by millions of suggestions to buy. Chances are, as you sit at your desk and look around your office, you can find ten brands staring back at you — and that's without even trying! With all that brand saturation, it's even more challenging to make an impression that lasts.

The secret to creating great street-team messaging is keeping it simple. Giving your staffers all the information about your product or brand is great, but don't expect them to share every detail with every consumer. Keep your talking points clear, concise, and intriguing.

You've got less than 15 seconds — make it count! Nothing kills a street campaign faster than overly detailed or diluted talking points. The following message:

> Good afternoon! Check out a *free sample* of Skull Crusher Energy Drink's new flavor, PAIN!

is far more intriguing than:

> Hello, I hope you're having a great day. Skull Crusher Energy Drinks, the maker of quality caffeinated beverages since 1986, has long been an innovator in personal fuel. Our techniques have often been imitated but never duplicated. Well, we've done it again with our newest flavor, PAIN — on sale here today at Sal's Sporting Goods. So please, stop by and ask for a can of PAIN!

The second message is highly informative, but by the time your street team starts telling them about personal fuel, the consumer has already popped into the deli for a Red Bull. All the while, they could have experienced your quality product for free!

If everyone tells you they think you should be a standup comic or write for a TV sitcom, why not try your hand at some clever copy for your street team? Sometimes a funny line can shake a morning commuter out of her drone as quickly as a can of Skull Crusher Energy Drink! But be careful: Just because you think you're funny, doesn't always mean the public will. When in doubt, run some lines by a colleague or friend — and as always, keep it short and sweet.

Creating a Distribution Piece

You assemble a crack team of distributors. They're all on message. Now, what are they giving out? Although your well-trained staffers will, no doubt, make a resounding first impression on your target audience, the distribution piece is what the consumer takes away from the experience.

The exciting thing about guerrilla marketing is that there are no rules — just creativity and sensibility! If you can create a brand-related distribution piece that's clever, funny, and maybe even a bit shocking, you may have created not only a successful distribution campaign, but also a press opportunity as well. (For an example of a distribution piece that, arguably, fits all three of the criteria — clever, funny, and shocking — check out the "Barf bags, anyone?" sidebar in this chapter.)

There are no hard-and-fast rules for creating distribution pieces, because each campaign should be unique. But in this section, we give you some things to consider before you spend hundreds or even thousands of dollars on items that, in the end, may fall flat.

Keeping your brand or business in mind

You work very hard to produce a quality product. Every day, consciously or subconsciously, you diligently make numerous decisions that tailor the perception of your product. When choosing your distribution piece, you need to maintain this same sense of brand integrity.

Say you found a talking keychain and you think it would make an incredible distribution piece. But when put into practice to promote your upscale flower shop, the appeal and relation to your brand may be lost on some of your more well-heeled clientele. Not only will this cost you the $5 a pop for the keychain, but it could cost you potential business as well.

Barf bags, anyone?

An irreverent fashion blog recently distributed branded airsickness bags to consumers outside the upscale New York Fashion Week tents, making a point to offer them to the emaciated fashion models as they entered the event. In poor taste? Perhaps, but the pieces were small, cost-effective, and very unique distribution items that amused most New Yorkers enough to take and share them with their coworkers — all the while, painting a very clear image as to what the blog is about and garnering a lot of press along the way.

Instead, maybe you should go for a custom half-dollar-size coin, which can be redeemed in-store for one of your prize roses. This classier branded piece is much more synonymous with your posh shop. Ultimately, this better-related premium not only reinforces your brand image, but may also bring in new, affluent, male patrons looking to play Casanova or get out of the doghouse.

Even if you don't have money for a fancy keychain, make sure that every component you select reflects positively on and directly connects back to your brand. Consider this in every element of the piece that you craft, whether it's a high-value premium or a printed piece. From the images selected to the tone of the copy to the quality of the finished product, make sure that the finish screams, "This is my brand!"

Reviewing the key sample specs

Whatever you do, make sure it's brand related, small, cost effective, and has a shelf life. Otherwise, you'll find city sanitation workers cursing your company name, as unwanted materials clutter up their streets.

What kind of sample would *you* take from a street team? Maybe you don't normally take materials from people on the street, but the other day you found yourself graciously accepting the complimentary breakfast bar with a small coupon attached. What was it that intrigued, excited, or piqued your interest? Chances are it was one or all of the following:

- ✔ **The size of the piece:** When it comes to samples (and a few others things in life), size *does* matter. The smaller it is, the easier it is to put away in a pocket or purse. We can't tell you the number of times we've seen people try to hand out full-size, 8^1/$_2$-x-11-inch flyers on plain white paper, only to be shocked that no one was taking them!

  In an average day, a person carries around keys, a wallet, a cellphone, pens, lip balm, and a myriad other things. There isn't a whole lot of room to take on any additional baggage unless that item is easy to stow away and interesting enough to not only keep around, but use and share with others.

- ✔ **The cost of the piece:** Just because you want to make a splash with consumers doesn't mean you need to mortgage your beach house in Maui — or not pay rent this month on your studio apartment. Take a look at your budget and get creative! Whether you have less than a dollar or more than five to spend on each premium, there are a wealth of sampling opportunities that won't break the bank. From low-cost pens, key chains, and refrigerator magnets to higher-end premiums such as flash drives, T-shirts, and beach blankets, there's almost always a premium and price point to match your product or brand.

✔ **The shelf life of the piece:** Why hand out something that gives people no reason to hold onto it? With people on every corner handing out *something* these days, it's crucial to make your distribution piece something they may actually *want* — and something they may share with a colleague or friend.

To jazz things up a bit, you may want to create a special offer or come up with an enter-to-win component. Or create an item that will be useful to consumers for months or even years. One such piece we like is the *Z-card* (a credit-card-size piece that unfolds to a full 8½-x-11-inch page). When fully unfolded, one side is used for the branding or marketing message, and the other side is something functional like a subway or city map, thereby giving recipients a reason to hold onto it.

In Table 6-1, we put these three categories to work in relation to common distribution pieces. Use this type of checklist when evaluating your own ideas. Hitting at least two of these three qualifiers will put you on the right track.

Table 6-1	Selecting an Effective Distribution Piece			
Item	*Small?*	*Cost-Effective?*	*Long Shelf Life?*	*A Good Distribution Piece?*
Postcards	X	X		**Yes!** These inexpensive premiums are easy to throw into a pocket or purse and the thicker stock keeps them around a little longer than a regular piece of paper. An enter-to-win contest or useful information will help give your postcard a longer life.
Large stuffed animals			X	**No.** Although people love winning a big ol' stuffed animal at the county fair, it's not always practical for the everyday. Better to save this kind of money for incentives to consumers who have purchased your product or taken the time to visit your store.

Item	Small?	Cost-Effective?	Long Shelf Life?	A Good Distribution Piece?
Foldout maps	X	X	X	**Yes!** Quick and easy to pick up, these premiums are useful to both tourists and natives alike!
Chocolates	X			**No.** Most people love chocolate, but its properties make it a temperamental distribution piece. Size is also an issue — too small and it's lost, too big and it's a cumbersome choco-mushy-mess.
Button pins	X	X	X	**Yes!** Get your message out quickly and cheaply in a premium that can live in or on your target audience's bag, jacket, or bulletin board.
Wall posters				**No.** Unless they're looking to land something to accompany their *White Snake* posters, most people on the street aren't excited to receive a huge piece of paper. The large size makes it too big to carry and, as a result, your creative energies (and distribution dollars) end up in the trash.
Scratch-'n'-win cards	X	X	X	**Yes!** How many times have you bought an instant lottery ticket just to do the scratchy bit? Small and cost-effective, when paired with prizing incentives, these little pieces work wonders when it comes to driving traffic to a Web site or storefront for redemption.

If you're still stumped on what you want to give away, reach out to promotional-item vendors. To get in touch with them, start by talking to colleagues and industry contacts for leads. Chances are someone had something produced before. If not, a quick online search for "branded *[name of product]*" (branded key chains or branded tote bags, for example) will help you locate those who specialize in the product you're looking for or general premium providers. Many vendors are eager to work with you and your budget to help come up with some great ideas. And the best part? The ideas are free!

Making sure you don't run out of samples

Avoid running out of materials — plan ahead! In a high-traffic location (such as a mall, transportation hub, or tourist hot spot), you can distribute 200 high-value premiums per person per hour and/or 125 printed pieces per person per hour.

If you've done your calculations and you've still run short, it's time to get down and dirty! Go to your nearby copy center and have copies of your piece printed four times on bright colored paper. A few swings of the paper cutter's arm and you're back up and running. Oh sure, it may not have the same polish as your glorious, glossy postcards, but it's better than leaving your staffers twiddling their thumbs.

Identifying the Best Time and Place for Your Campaign

The context in which you present your message to the masses can make or break an initiative. If you want something from a significant other, you know better than to make your "ask" when he's have just crashed on the couch to watch *The Golden Girls*. The same rings true for your potential consumers. Be smart about when and where you choose to snuggle up and ask for your proverbial pony. Your distribution efforts can (and should) vary depending on the product or brand you're promoting.

Before dispatching those friendly, attractive, outgoing staffers dressed and trained in your brand, ask yourself the following questions:

- ✔ Who is my target audience?
- ✔ Where do they live, work, and play?
- ✔ When is the best time to speak to them?

For example, maybe you've just created a revolutionary purple ostrich that teaches kids ages 2 to 5 their ABCs. After going through the preceding checklist, you've deduced the following:

 ✔ Your target consumers are moms ages 30 to 50.

 ✔ They congregate at playgrounds, malls, and science museums.

 ✔ They're usually out and about by 10 a.m., but home by 4 p.m. for naptime.

By answering these questions, you have all the information necessary to stage your strategic staffing assault. You know that you're not going to get anywhere by putting your street teams near the local playground between 5 p.m. and 8 p.m., and you're not going to get anywhere by putting street teams in front of city hall from 10 a.m. to 1 p.m. — at least not with this audience and this target audience.

Mornings are often better for a call to action that requires high-speed Internet, because consumers are heading to work where they'll have access (and time) to log on and visit your site. Evening rush hour is better for products or services that call for conversation and a decision from spouses or partners.

Keeping Your Team out of Trouble and Your Image Untarnished

Every day, literally hundreds of street campaigns are being executed to promote a variety of initiatives. Unfortunately, the ones you usually hear about are the ones where a company, "thinking outside the box," sent out street teams dressed in some horrifying costume and frightened a poor old lady to death. It's press like this that has a tendency to give street teams a bad rap.

The fact is that most campaigns, when executed conscientiously, realize brand goals without incident. Still, executing an effective campaign involves tempering creativity with discretion. Here are a few tips to keep you and your staffers out of trouble:

 ✔ **Keep an eye on your staff.** It's your name they've got on their shirt. Make sure that your staffers are presenting the material specifically as you requested. Staffers who are rude or inappropriate around consumers, smoking, swearing, talking on cellphones, or doing anything else inappropriate should be pulled immediately. Good word of mouth can cause your business to catch on like wildfire, but bad word of mouth caused by rude staffers will burn it down.

✔ **Be safe and sensible.** Make sure that the elements of your campaign are safe for all involved — don't distribute any materials that could be toxic or dangerous to consumers. Make sure that the pieces you're giving out are in step with local standards of taste. Stay away from items that directly address sex, religion, or politics — it'll help stave off angry calls and negative press.

✔ **Be aware of your surroundings.** Distributing materials is okay in most places throughout most cities, but avoid private property, as well as city and government buildings and commuter stations. Distributing inside train stations and bus depots without a permit is illegal, and the person doing the distribution (not the company he's working for) will most probably be fined for doing so — trust us.

✔ **Know when to say when.** If you're told by business owners or local law enforcement that you can't distribute at a particular location, don't get into a shouting match with them. It ain't worth it.

The best way to handle this kind of situation is to take a brief pause and regroup your team. If you haven't done so prior to the launch of the campaign, select an alternative location and introduce your efforts there.

As a savvy guerrilla marketer, make friends with the locals. If you're handing out a desirable sample or an interesting distribution piece, go out of your way to befriend the powers that be near your location. By plying them with product and charm, you increase the likelihood that your campaign will carry on uninterrupted and may even pick up a few new customers along the way.

Chapter 7

The Spectacular! Publicity Stunts

*A*round the turn of the 20th century, showmen like Harry Houdini and P. T. Barnum achieved great success, all built on their shrewd understanding of the power of the publicity stunt. Today, stunts may have grown grander and, in some cases, more expensive, but a few core ideals remain the same. By applying your own creativity and resourcefulness, you can produce a publicity stunt that creates a little magic for your product — a stunt that would make Houdini and Barnum proud.

In this chapter, we give you the tools you need to create a publicity stunt that will have 'em clamoring for more. We begin by detailing the pieces that go into the creation of a stellar stunt. From there, we show you how to design and craft your own PR coup, making a colossal impression with a pint-size price tag. Then we help you get the pressmen there to help spread the word. Finally, we look to the blooper reel to show you a few stunts gone wrong and tell you how you can avoid a similar fate.

Defining the Elements of a Sensational Stunt

You're big time. You know it, we know it, and creating a publicity stunt gives you the opportunity to let your *consumers* know it — in a big way. *Publicity stunts* are highly visible brand-related spectacles crafted to promote a product or service through concentrated press coverage and heightened consumer awareness. Stunts are arguably one of the most fun and exciting tools in the guerrilla's tool kit, because it gives you the opportunity to reach many consumers at one time, in a fantastically theatrical way.

Whether you're daring to escape from a straightjacket or attempting to set the record for World's Largest Sculpture Made Entirely of Pork 'n' Beans, a few basic elements are the foundation for a successful stunt:

- **Message:** All blood, sweat, and tears that go into the creation of an impressive stunt will be for naught, unless you're able answer the simple question, "What do I want consumers to take away from this experience?" In other words, what is the message you want to convey? Are you touting a new product or service, declaring your dominance in an industry? Whatever the case, make sure your efforts effectively communicate this message. There's too much involved in the creation of a stunt to not have a clear and concise declaration.

- **Location, location, location:** Yeah, yeah, so it may not be the most clever or profound statement ever uttered, but selecting a prime location for your stunt can make the difference between people seeing it or not. Be sure to secure a venue that's in keeping with your brand, easy for the press to find, and easy for consumers to experience.

- **Timing:** Beyond morning, noon, and night, there are a variety of timing variables to consider when you're putting together an impressive marketing stunt. If you're creating a large ice sculpture outside in the heart of the city, you probably don't want to do it in Phoenix in the July. Common sense might clue you into this, but other timing considerations (such as those related to your choice of venue and target audience) may not be so obvious. Does the location you've selected have peak foot traffic times that can be used to your benefit? Does your target audience only come out at a certain time of day? You need to take into account all these factors.

- **Stagecraft:** This element involves making like a director and setting the scene. You do this by fashioning a stunt that is both visually thrilling and capable of being instantly associated with your brand.

    Imagine your stunt through the lens of a camera. In a quick snapshot, do you know what the event was about? What it was for? If you don't, then the press may not either and that snapshot will never make it to the cover of *The New York Times* or the town circular.

- **People:** After dreaming up your masterpiece, you need to identify your people involved in your stunt. Sometimes the "who" is just as intriguing as the "what." Who's participating? Who's emceeing? Who's judging? Placing that call to an ex-reality-TV star to judge your pie eating contest may be just the hook the press needs to cover what would have been an otherwise overlooked event.

- **Giveaways:** Creating some sort of reward — whether for personal or altruistic gain — helps put a nice finish on your spectacle (see "Leaving a lasting impression," later in this chapter).

✔ **Press:** Reaching the press is the main reason behind producing a publicity stunt. A truly successful stunt reaches out to the press, cultivates their participation, and, when appropriate, follows up to ensure the stunt gets the ink your marketing dollars paid for.

Knowing the essentials going in will help you cover your bases and design a stunt that not only will be unmissable, but will live on long after you've cleaned up the mess from your pork 'n' beans sculpture.

Crafting a Cohesive Stunt

You've decided that you're ready to do something extraordinary. You've tried traditional methods and maybe even a few nontraditional ones to attract attention to your product and, for one reason or another, it just isn't sticking. (In retrospect, maybe branding your grandmother wasn't such a good idea.) This is your opportunity to capitalize on your boundless creativity and finally apply the knowledge you've gained from watching all that reality TV to design an exceptional publicity stunt.

Producing a stunt can be a little overwhelming, because a stunt has so many moving pieces. But by taking the time to consider each piece, you make sense of the puzzle in front of you.

Choosing and planning your stunt

Parading an elephant through the center of town in a pink tutu may be a funny visual, but if your business has nothing to do with elephants or ballet, that's a pretty expensive chuckle. By taking the time to consider your brand and the sort of impression you want to make, you put yourself in a position to get noticed in a way that will have you laughing all the way to the bank.

Matching the stunt to your brand

Designing a stunt begins at the brainstorming table. So grab a big pot o' joe or other vice of choice, assemble some co-workers and those kooky friends you keep around for just such an occasion and get creative. Start with a dry-erase board or a big pad of paper, and ask yourself a few questions:

✔ **What are the symbols or immediate associations consumers may have with my brand?** Let your imagination go wild and write down every association that pops into your mind. For example, say you own Hercules Tire Shop. As the wheels get to turning, you pump out: tires, rubber, gods, wings, roads, super-human strength, road trips, and power ballads. The key at this point is to not judge anything. Make it outlandish and ridiculous and messy, but always keep thinking of the brand.

✔ **Of these associations, what can I take to excess or place on a grand scale?** Take a handful of the associations that you like best, and go to extremes. For example, if copy paper is your business, how about producing a custom "airfield." Invite the public and press down to hold a paper airplane contest to see who can craft a plane that can travel the farthest.

Don't judge any of your wacky, wild ideas just yet. Write down every crazy stunt that you can possibly come up with based on your associations. Some concepts may be too outlandish to execute entirely, but what you're doing is creating a virtual smorgasbord from which you can later cherry-pick pieces to fashion a delectable feast.

You may want to consider setting or breaking a world record, because they're usually covered by the press. A word of advice: Setting a record is easier than breaking a record. If you're setting it, all you have to do is complete the task (and check with Guinness World Records to make sure it covers the category). If you're attempting to break a record, you've got to get up over the initial stunt before you've achieved your greatness!

To break or set a Guinness World Record, you need to apply. If you have more time than money, you can wait the four to six weeks (or longer) that it takes Guinness to reply to regular, free-of-charge applications. If you have more money than time, you can submit a Fast Track application, pay the approximately $600 (the official price is £300), and get a response in just *three days*. For more information, go to www.guinnessworldrecords.com/member/how_to_become_a_record_breaker.aspx (or just www.guinnessworldrecords.com/default.aspx and click on Break a World Record).

✔ **Of these larger-scale concepts, which one is most visually appealing and clearly indicative of my brand?** As you look over your concepts, one or two will pop out at you right away. This is one of those "go with your gut" moments. If you can see one concept becoming synonymous with your brand, that's the idea you want to pursue.

If you're undecided and/or obsessive compulsive (that is, if you're anything like us), you've probably spent countless hours of time brainstorming ideas and, frankly, you're a little impressed with yourself. You've got quite a few ideas that are your babies. At this point, it's time to shed those parental instincts and think about your ideas more critically. Play devil's advocate for each stunt. You can do this by making sure your stunt *really* relates to your business. A stunt enables you to share your brand's message with your consumers and press who attend. Make a mental the snapshot of this event. Is this how you want your company to be perceived in the press, the trade, and (if you're lucky) the world?

Brainstorming and refining your stunt ideas allows you to think big with the scope of your stunt, while keeping your brand and the message you're looking to convey as focused and precise as possible. To put it simply, it's the flash and pizzazz that brings them in, but it's that clear-cut message that you want them to walk away with.

Creating and enforcing the rules

With most stunts, especially contests or world records, it's all about the rules. Crafting definitive rules for the stunt will help quell the cries of, "That's not fair" or, worse yet, "I'll see you in court!"

The words "Well, I didn't know that" should never be uttered during the course of your stunt. Switch over to your focused, Type-A personality and create rules for every possible scenario. Here are some questions to get you started on your way towards covering your hiney:

- ✔ Who can participate?
- ✔ What is the objective of the stunt? How will you know when it is completed?
- ✔ What can disqualify a person from participation?
- ✔ Is there a time limit?
- ✔ What if something goes wrong? What happens?
- ✔ If there is a prize, when will it be awarded? What if there is a tie?
- ✔ Who has the final say?

By answering these questions, you'll get a clearer sense of the specifics of your stunt. Make like Milton Bradley and write up those rules. Be as specific as possible. The clearer comprehension you have of how the event should go, the more foolproof you can make your stunt.

Your rules are made, now it's time to get a little legal smarts. You need to plan for the worst so that you can enjoy the best. After you've given all your participants the chance to read your rules, they need to sign their lives away. You need them to sign a document saying that they'll abide by the contest rules; agree to not hold you, your vendors, or anyone else responsible if something goes wrong; and concede that the decision of your contest judges is final.

Especially where there is prize money or the participants are engaging in some activities that could be potentially dangerous, having your participants sign all your documents certifying that they understand everything and are willing to play by your rules is critical. Their John Hancock on all documents must be a condition of play — no exceptions.

If the idea of drafting rules and composing waivers has you in a tizzy, there's an alternative: Hire a lawyer to alleviate that stress. Taking a first crack at it will help your esquire get started — and, with any luck, bring down the costs a bit. If your attorney doesn't feel comfortable with creating your rules (this would be rare), there are companies that exclusively handle contest rule creation and fulfillment — but you'd better be prepared to pay big for their services.

Selecting the venue to present your masterpiece

At this point, you're well on your way toward producing a nontraditional work of art. Now it's time to select the wall upon which your work will metaphorically hang.

When picking your venue, two considerations need to be on the top of your list: the press and the public. The primary focus is making sure that you select a location that is appealing and easy for the press to cover. Plus, you want to select a site that is engaging to consumers who happen to be out and about while your stunt is going on.

Whenever possible, strive to make your stunt not just an exciting *visual* but something that attendees can *experience* as well. By considering both of these elements, you'll be set on the path toward mounting something remarkable.

Power of the press: considering the media

Think about your day. You roll into work and scarf down a yogurt-and-granola parfait and some coffee. You listen to your messages and decide which ones you can passive-aggressively ignore and which ones you actually have to answer. Then you look to your calendar, only to discover you have a meeting all the way across town. You launch into a series of expletives because you know that the cross-town meeting is guaranteed to eat up the greater part of your day. Now imagine you have three to five across-town meetings that day. *That's* a day in the life of the press.

Why not make it *easy* for the press? When considering your venue, take note of the media outlets you want to reach. If there's a central location where most of your press works, head down there and do a little reconnaissance (camouflage garb and face paint optional). Walk around the area. Is there a parking lot, a park, or an abandoned storefront that will work for your purposes? Discovering a new venue or reinventing an existing location can become another hook to your story. Take pictures and make a list of potential locales around the area, being sure to jot down phone numbers to follow up later. These notes and photos will give you something to refer to and make your decision easier.

The real purpose of producing a publicity stunt is to attract press and, in turn, raise awareness for your product or brand. The first step toward getting the press to cover your event is choosing a venue that they can step outside their doors and cover.

Power to the people: Considering your public

Having your stunt end up on the five o'clock news and plastered across the Internet is pretty wonderful, but never underestimate the power of word of mouth.

While traveling to Houston from New York, one notable guerrilla marketer engaged in the somewhat tricky task of explaining to a stranger exactly what he did: "Well, we do a wide array of things, from producing publicity stunts to sending out street teams to promote a number of products and brands."

Suddenly, the questioner's ears perked up. "You mean like dressing people up like zombies and having them invade the city?"

Surprised, the marketer responded that he had worked on that very campaign, and asked how she had heard about that particular example. The questioner said, "My sister happened to be visiting New York that day and she had her picture taken with one of the zombies. Made her day! She was so tickled, she e-mailed the picture to everyone she knew!"

And such is the way with word of mouth. Think of ways you can maximize this sort of exposure. It may be done through online infiltration (see Chapter 12) or on-site distribution efforts (see Chapter 6). Regardless of the route you chose, make sure you're taking advantage of every opportunity to get your public talking. Getting the press to your event is crucial, but you don't want to overlook the public. Word of mouth can facilitate success, especially when consumers carry your messaging in concert with media efforts.

Much like your press-geared location scouting (see the preceding section), take a city tour again, but this time look for high-traffic locations instead. In most cities, one or two central locations are constantly busy. Maybe it's the town square or the multiplex or the hairdresser's. While you're scouting out the area, list any locations that would serve as a good platform for producing your stunt. Take some pictures and make notes to refer to later.

Also, be aware of potential problems around the venue — a train passing every 30 minutes, light posts that don't turn off at night, a public area within your venue that may wreak havoc on your stunt. Any environmental elements that could cause problems should be factored into your decision.

Tackling permits and permissions

When you're executing a guerrilla event, such as a stunt, don't be surprised if some nosy person decides it's his duty to saunter over to "find out who's in charge" and pose the question, "Do you have a permit for all this?" When this happens, kick him in the shins and run away.

Okay, maybe that isn't the best route, but it *is* one option. The *better* option is to actually seek and attain permission and permits.

Unlike some of the other activities that are outlined in this book, where permission is optional, when you're producing a PR stunt, you need to play by the rules. There is far too much involved to risk having to cancel your stunt because you didn't have permission to build an ice sculpture in the center of Main Street.

Permission to use your venue

Depending on the venue you've selected, you may only have to talk to the person in charge of the venue itself. However, if you're conducting an event outdoors, some more players may be involved. For example, city property is usually approved by the town hall or mayor's office, and parks are run by local, state, or federal parks agencies. Find out who has jurisdiction over your venue before you start making calls.

Regardless of whether you're indoors or outdoors, be completely upfront about what you're looking to do. Make sure everyone you're seeking permission from has your timelines for load-in, a complete plan for the day's activities, and the time you'll be checking out. Nothing sours the day's festivities faster than the plug getting pulled prior to the thrilling climax of your event. Ensuring everyone is on the same page will help you avoid surprises.

What if you've made some calls and the venues you had in mind just will not give you permission to hold your stunt. The nerve. Why not bring your stunt home? Local ordinances very from state to state and city to city, but if you own your property (or can sweet-talk your landlord into giving you permission), you usually own the first few feet of sidewalk from your property. Typically, this is the first 6 feet away from your building outward toward the street — the perfect amount of space for a smaller stunt.

Although doing your stunt at your house may be a nice way to sidestep getting permission, be sure to double-check with your local city officials to make sure that this is allowed in your area. Otherwise, you could find yourself in a sticky situation.

Additional permits

If you've gotten permission to conduct your stunt at the venue, your permision-seeking may not entirely end there. Depending on how strict your city is and how many extras you're including, you may want to check to see if you need one or more of the following (keep in mind costs vary from city to city, from $25 application fees to permits costing upwards of $1,000):

- **Sound permit:** If you're producing any form of amplified sound, you should check whether a sound permit is required. If you're holding a stunt for the World's Worst Karaoke, bank on needing a permit.

- **Parking permit:** Just because you've secured permission to be at a venue, that doesn't mean a meter maid making her rounds won't ticket your car while you're loading and unloading your vehicle.

- **Street activity permit:** In many smaller stunts, you may find you just want to set up your spectacle right on the street or sidewalk. Well, the city may have a few other thoughts about that. If you're planning to conduct your event on the street or sidewalk, check with city hall to see if you need a street activity permit — and check early! Permit offices generally do not have the same sense of expediency that *you* may have, so you want to get this taken care of as soon as possible.

- **Water and electricity permit:** If you're planning to tap into the city's water or electrical supply, it isn't as easy as calling up your Uncle Sal, the retired electrician, and plugging in. You're going to need a green light from the city.

Making nice

According to an old saying, "The squeaky wheel gets the grease." We say, "Grease the wheel before it gets squeaky." Playing nice with the neighbors is crucial to the success of a stunt. Bring them into the event and make them feel special.

If you have a cordoned-off VIP section, give them prime seating. If you're offering light catering, make sure you set them up with a doughnut and a cup of coffee. If you have a celebrity on hand, get them an autograph. You get the picture.

This kind of local outreach is very important to maintaining good relations. When your stunt is a staggering success, you may want to do it again next year. If you ticked off the neighbors, a grassroots letter-writing campaign demanding that you never return can quickly halt those plans.

Finding the venue to fill "the bill"

Just like that piece of swampland that you purchased in the bayou, spending money to rent a piece of real estate for your stunt can illicit a fair share of buyer's remorse — especially when the price is tens or even hundreds of thousands of dollars. Although the venue is key for drawing in your press, you shouldn't spend so much money securing the venue that you can't afford to do anything else.

As you do your research, you'll find that the range of costs is huge depending on where you're looking to go. For example, if you can stage your stunt in a public park, it may be as inexpensive as simply paying the permit fees. On the other hand, if you want the unequaled visibility of Midtown Manhattan or Hollywood Boulevard, you could have to pay tens of thousands of dollars.

If you've looked at your books, and spending thousands of dollars on a venue just isn't going to happen, consider the resources around you. Does your brother have a vacant storefront? Do you have access to a large balcony overlooking a high-traffic area? Sometimes the right venue is the one that doesn't cost anything. Cutting this expense can free up the cash needed to purchase more cats that jump through fire — you know, the essentials.

After you've surveyed the venues, what if you find that either you can't afford a place to stage your stunt or you don't like the places you found. Answer? Find religion. As long as they don't object to the content of your stunt, houses of worship are occasionally open to accepting a donation in exchange for the use of their parking lot on a day it's not in use.

And the venue is . . .

Upon completion of your stealthy recon outings, you should have two lists of venues: one that's great for the press, and one that's great for passersby. Much like your own personal Venn diagram, when you stack these two lists up side by side, with any luck, one or two venues will overlap. Venues that are on both lists should be bumped to the top for your consideration.

If you don't have any venues that are on both lists, look at your lists and see which locations can best serve both considerations, placing slightly greater value on press accessibility. After you've narrowed down your options, take your top three and start making calls to the powers that be. You may want to see if any of them can add anything extra to sweeten the pot (see "Getting a little more out of your venue," later in this chapter). This will be the moment when you balance your wants, the venue availability, and your budget, and make your choice.

As long as you're under my roof . . .

As a guest in someone's home, you don't walk in, move all their furniture around, create a ruckus, and then leave the mess, do you? Of course not. The same holds true for holding your stunt at a selected venue.

Many people who manage venues oversee their location with an inherent sense of pride and trust. They're giving you the opportunity to come into their "home" and hold crazy shenanigans. You need to respect that and keep in line with the rules set forth by the venue. You paid your money to be there, sure. But in order for that spot to be successful, they need to be able to hold many another events there long after you've pulled up stakes.

Keep in mind that there may be some extra expenses associated with your tenure. Venue deposits and insurance fees for your time there are not unheard of, so be prepared if this comes up in conversations and contracts.

Remember: Playing by the rules at the venue may help cut costs — or allow you to get the joint for free — for future functions.

Choosing the time to reach your target

Producing a publicity stunt is primarily geared toward getting the press to cover your event and spread the message for you. If you schedule your stunt at a time that's easy for the press to cover, you put yourself in a position to get the greatest amount of coverage.

Two times are particularly successful when looking to attract press:

- ✔ Between 7 a.m. and 9 a.m., for morning-show coverage and print media
- ✔ In the evening — traditionally from 5 to 7 p.m., in order to get the channel to do a live remote during the weather forecast

We usually opt for the earlier slot, because you have the entire night before to set up and put out any fires that may flare up prior to the launch. Plus, you get two shots for exposure — even if a network or other outlet isn't able to do a live shot, they'll probably be able to send someone down to get some footage, take a couple of shots, or interview participants. These captured sights and sounds can then be released later in the day.

When you're looking to reach the consumers at large, a slightly different set of rules apply. Most people work all day during the week, and when they get home they want to crash. Think about the weekend instead. If you're anything like us, you use the weekend to sleep in, catch up on chores, and dust your pristine action-figure collection. All these things take time, so if you're gearing up to reach out to the public on the weekend, shoot for early afternoon — most of your public will be out and about by then.

Bells and whistles: Production elements and more

Production elements are all the extras that add a professional polish to your stunt. Here, we outline some of the components that can help beef up your presence. Some of them are must-have's, some are just little touches that help to draw attention to your stunt. In most cases, the stunt you select will help dictate the trappings you need and those you don't.

On the day of the event, don't forget some light catering. Providing coffee and doughnuts for the neighbors that helped schlep the giant cutout of you from your truck, or the local town official who agreed to stop by for the photo-op will not only work to keep everyone happy, but increase the likelihood that they'll help again in the future.

Setting the stage

You choose production elements from the following laundry list to craft your spectacle! So grab a bib and get started!

Figure 7-1 illustrates many of these staging elements. **Remember:** You don't have to use them all — you can pick and choose which ones you need.

Figure 7-1: Staging involves several elements, but you can choose the ones you need and forget the ones you don't.

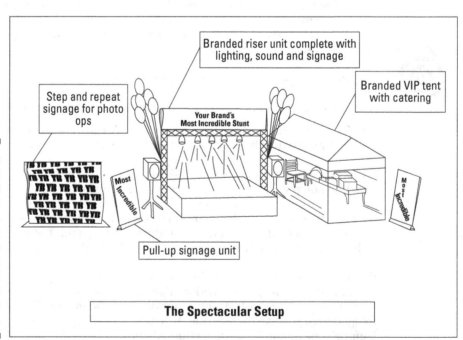

Regardless of which elements you chose, you're spending the money to produce a stunt, and you need to document every element of it — from the first truck arriving to the last bag of garbage hitting the can. On a budget you can do this using your family camera and camcorder.

If you have a little extra loot, you may want to consider hiring a professional photographer and/or videographer — you'll get a better quality of footage and images, plus these professionals often have the media contacts to release the materials directly to the press.

Rates for photographers may vary from city to city, but you can expect to pay between $500 and $1,000 for a four-hour shoot. Expect a videographer to charge upwards of $1,500 for shooting your event and doing some edits to help transform it from raw footage to something you can show at your company picnic.

Some people can understandably get upset if their image is used without their permission. If you're shooting video footage (after receiving permits from the venue to do so, of course), display several bold disclaimer placards, clearly stating that, by being on-site, they understand that their image may be captured and used for commercial purposes.

A riser for the main event

Setting the stage doesn't get more literal than building an actual stage (refer to Figure 7-1). If we've learned nothing else from professional wrestling, we've learned that elevating your stunt raises the visibly and heightens the drama of the exhibition.

You can rent risers from most audiovisual production companies. Or, if you're particularly crafty, build a custom stage using two-by-fours, plywood, and stage skirting. Also, don't forget the stairs.

Sound and lighting

Nothing says showbiz like a little light and sound! You don't need to hire Rolling Stones roadies, but you may want to consider elements that will help your event pop — things such as a microphone for your emcee, speakers to play fill music during dead air, and lights to throw some color on your stage all help tell the public, "Hey, we've got something going on here!" (refer to Figure 7-1).

Tenting

You can make plans till the end of time, but the one thing you can't control is the weather. If your event is outside, plan for the worst weather and hope for the best. Clear rain ponchos for branded staff or branded rain ponchos for unbranded staff can create a silver lining if dark clouds appear. To avoid having to cancel the event, try to have a tent or tarp on hand (refer to Figure 7-1). Also, have a "war room" tent where you and your team can congregate — plus, you've gotta keep the coffee somewhere.

Signage

Signage (refer to Figure 7-1) is a crucial component to any stunt. You can craft the most messy, clever, hysterical, emotional stunt ever, but if there is no branding attached to it, it's just a messy, clever, hysterical, emotional stunt. You're spending too much money to let that happen. Instead, research signage opportunities. Some options include

- ✔ **Step and repeat:** This is a backdrop usually measuring 8 feet high by 10 feet wide, which simply has your logo (and co-sponsors' or partners' logos if applicable) repeated over and over again. This layout ensures that, when photographers shoot your event, there's no way they'll miss your branding. (For an example of this kind of signage in action, check out the photo in the "Herding the high-maintenance" sidebar, later in this chapter.)

- ✔ **Banners:** These are usually made of vinyl or mesh and contain event messaging. They're usually hung horizontally throughout the event from grommets that have been riveted into the banner corners.

- ✔ **Pull-up banners:** These are self-contained units typically measuring 3 feet wide by 6 feet high, containing signage in the base. An extendable pole is placed in the base and the signage is pulled out of the base and attached to the top of the pole, much like an inverted world map from your elementary-school days.

- ✔ **Balloons and blimps:** Highly visible — and usually relatively inexpensive — branded helium-filled balloons or mini-blimps work to put your brand right at your guests' eye level. Plus, the balloons make for a nice give-away for the kids.

Crowd-control barricades

If there is the potential for consumers to get hurt, use police-style barricades to cordon off your stunt. This will also help to define your space, and deter a visit by an overzealous lawyer.

If you have a stunt that could be potentially dangerous or harmful passerby, be sure to include warning or other cautionary signs around the venue. Although you'll have worked diligently with safety in mind, these signs will help cover you if problems arise.

Determining the participants

Imagine yourself back in high school, except with better skin. Now, in this seen and be-seen culture, you're invited to a party or major event by someone outside of your clique. What's your first question? "Like, who's gonna be there?"

In a lot of ways the press and the public at large have maintained a bit of this high-school-clique mentality when it comes to attending and covering stunts. Who's going to be there is a fair consideration, because the participants' flavor help to inform the overall feel and purpose of the event.

In an era obsessed with being a voyeur, the contestants who will carry out your zany ideas can have as great an impact and be as informative to the public as the activity itself. In this section, we tell you how to determine who should participate and where you can go to find them.

Matching your participants to your target

You've crafted your stunt and you're determined that it's going to knock their socks off! The only thing you're missing is the ethos to give your spectacle the human touch. If you're so inclined, you could always dust off that old copy of Aristotle's *Poetics* that you've been using to prop up your sofa, and flip to the chapter about knowing your audience — because knowing your audience is key to finding the right participants.

To give your event that personal feel, you need to have a razor-sharp grasp on who you're trying to reach by executing your stunt. For example, if you're trying to connect with the retired Southern yachting set, selecting extreme skateboarders to participate in your stunt probably is not the route that you want to take. Instead, select participants who are most like them or reflect what they would most likely want to be.

The stunt will evoke far more excitement and be a greater success if your audience can picture *themselves* participating in the event or activity.

I know who I want — now where the heck are they?

You've considered your target, and you've decided who you want to participate. Just one problem: You don't know anyone who fills the bill. What to do?

This is one of those moments where you need to switch hats from logistical guru to guerrilla mastermind and use the tools available to you to help track down your guinea pigs, er, participants. Here are some ways you may be able to bring your participants to you:

- ✔ **Send an e-mail blast.** So maybe you don't know any rodeo clowns to participate in your stunt. You know who does? Your Aunt Rita, that's who. Why not drop her a line?

    You may have outstanding connections to people that are easy to over-look at first glance. Try sending out a mass e-mail to all your friends, family, and associates outlining who you're looking for. You may be sur-prised by the response.

Include as much information about participation as you feel comfortable releasing prior to the event. Don't forget to include the benefits of participation (international notoriety, cash prize, lifetime supply of shoe polish, and so on). Although people may not initially be willing to climb a gym rope in their tighty-whiteys, they may change their tune if there's $25,000 at that other end of that rope.

✔ **Take to the interweb.** In this age where people are practically glued to their computers, reaching a select audience online is easier than ever before. By posting bulletins and creating online groups, you can attract your participants quickly and directly. (For more about targeting Web sites, creating postings, and developing online communities, check out Chapter 12.)

✔ **Develop a contest for participation.** Make your event something your target is clamoring to participate in by creating a contest to select your stunt candidates. This can be as simple as producing an enter-to-win component where each entrant must explain why she's the ideal person to participate. Once again, having a potential monetary or other high-value prize goes a long way toward drumming up entries.

Securing a media sponsor such as a local radio, TV, or print outlet can be a great tool to extend the reach of the contest. We know what you're thinking: "Mainstream media? Pricey." Not necessarily. First, see what you may be able to barter to create a partnership — maybe you can give the media outlet exclusive access to your participants, offer them an on-site presence, give them billing in all signage and press materials, and so on. If you don't ask, you don't get. If you can't barter with the media and get coverage of your contest for free, you may want to consider cracking the piggybank for a small media buy.

Herding the high-maintenance

A major cable network, WE tv, was looking for a dozen or so demanding prima donnas who were engaged to be married to participate in a cake-eating contest in Times Square to promote their show about difficult brides-to-be. To enlist these persnickety participants, the network partnered with a local radio outlet who encouraged their listeners to have fussy ladies e-mail in the ways in which they were "strongly opinionated" when it came to the planning of their nuptials. The response was outstanding. The network was able to secure some ladies with a multitude of demanding back stories that were used in press materials as well as adding yet another facet to what turned out to be an incredibly successful (and messy) stunt. The $50,000 in prize money didn't hurt either.

Tapping into talent

Admit it, when you're in the line at the grocery store, you take a second look at the tabloids to see who's dating whom, or who just named her baby after a piece of fruit. We love celebrities! You can decry the culture's obsession with celebrities all the livelong day, or you can make it work in your favor. Depending on your stunt, you may want to add a local or national celebrity to help raise the visibility of your activities.

Before you go phoning up agents in L.A., consider who you want to select and in what capacity those people will contribute to your event. Do you want them to judge some element? Do you want them to emcee? What will they be doing during the course of the event? Answering these questions will help you home in on who you want and enable you to explain to them or their representatives exactly what you want them to do. Clarity in these early stages helps to avoid miscommunication that can dampen the finish of your extravaganza.

Going big: National talent

On numerous occasions, we've had clients call us up and ask, "Can you get so-and-so to participate in our initiative?" The short answer is, "Of course, we can get so-and-so." The bigger question is, "Can you *afford* so-and-so?" Any way you slice it, talent ain't cheap. National talent rates for two-hour programs can begin around $10,000 and go up from there depending on who you select. Knowing this going in will help you make reasonable choices.

If you decide you want to go this route, it's time to make some selectively placed calls and e-mails. It's surprising (or frightening, depending on how you look at it) how easy it is to track down talent and/or their representatives. Many times, you can simply do an Internet search for "representation for *[insert starlet here]*," and the person's talent-agency contact will pop up.

If a simple Internet search doesn't yield results, go to the Internet Movie Database (www.imdb.com), sign up for IMDb Pro (which at the time of this writing offers a free 14-day trial) or WhoRepresents.com (which charges a membership fee), and search for the talent of your choice. In the listing for that person, you'll find his representation and, in most cases, the direct line for his agent.

So you've got your top choice's agent's number scrawled on a piece of paper grasped tightly in your clammy hands. Be cool, baby. If you've never done something like this before, remember: Much like anything else, talent and entertainment is a business. Clearly outlining for the agent what you're looking to do, what his client's participation would involve, and what you're prepared to offer will help expedite negotiation and acquisition.

Having talent appear at your stunt doesn't always end after you cut the check for his fee. National talent can have riders that may include some of the following perks that you should consider when fashioning your budget:

- ✔ **Travel:** If your stunt is occurring outside your talent's point of origin (usually New York or Los Angeles, unless you're flying Demi Moore in from Idaho), most agents insist on first-class round-trip airfare plus livery services to and from the airport. If your event is being held in the city of origin for your talent, you can expect to be chauffeuring your star around via an upscale livery service or other comfortable mode of transportation.

- ✔ **Hotel accommodations:** Once again, look to drop a pretty penny, because your talent will be looking for first-class accommodations, not a night at the no-tell motel.

- ✔ **Per diem:** *Per diem* is a fee paid to cover miscellaneous expenses when a person is out of town (such as food and entertainment.) Make sure both parties are clear on what you're paying for and what you're not.

- ✔ **Agent fee:** The going rate for agents is 10 percent of the fee. Normally, the talent will pay the agency out of his take, but in some cases, agents will ask for "plus 10," meaning that you'll be paying an *additional* 10 percent of the total amount. Avoid this if you can.

- ✔ **Talent staff:** Some stars travel with staffs of assistants, stylists, makeup artists, dog walkers, and more. Be sure both parties are clear on who's paying for this — and if you're responsible for it, make sure you know what you're paying for and what it'll cost.

Don't have the budget for national talent? You can get that star appeal by just facing reality — reality TV stars that is. With reality TV shows popping up like weeds, there is a large crop of talent that's less inexpensive than major national talent to secure for an event. And they still carry decent name recognition.

Thinking local

Travel? Per diem? Agents? This isn't what you signed on for! That's okay . . . it's time to think local. Often, there are great opportunities for talent as close as next door. Every town has local celebrities who seem to have the gift of gab: the mayor who knows every constituent, the local weatherman, the star of the local community theater, or the hot radio DJ. Look around you and capitalize on the stars of your everyday life.

Selecting talent

Sometimes securing talent is an expense you may not want to incur. It's time to do some soul searching. Although it may be fun to fawn over your favorite movie star for a few hours, your stunt may not need it. Can you execute this stunt and get great press without the star? If the answer is yes, scrap it and cross the task of securing talent off what is an inevitably long to-do list.

If you decide that having the First Action Hero preside over your festivities is essential, make sure you milk it for all it's worth. During talent negotiations make sure to secure permission to use the talent's name, likeness, and, if possible, endorsement in your pre-promotional activities. These assets are ones that you need to exploit to the best of your shamelessly self-promoting abilities. Engaging talent is an investment in your stunt; your duty is to make sure that this investment reaps dividends in the form of media coverage and word-of-mouth buzz.

We've had a lot of success using radio personalities as hosts or judges for stunts. They work well because the public feels a certain rapport with them and they're exceptionally skilled at narrating and "filling" as needed — after all, they've spent years conducting one-way conversations on the radio. For the budget-conscious, local radio personalities are also much less expensive than national talent and you may be able to leverage their involvement for on-air mentions to help pre-promote your event as well.

Leaving a lasting impression

If you want your event to make a mark, consider including

- **Giveaways:** Giveaways are small, often brand-related items distributed to those who attend the event. They work great as little reminders, so that when people arrive at work, they can share their giveaway with a co-worker and say, "You'll never guess what I saw today."

- **Grand prizes:** You may consider having a winner or some sort of prize that's awarded at the conclusion of your stunt. The winner may get $1 million, or you may donate a certain amount to a charitable organization. Creating some sort of reward — whether for personal or altruistic gain — helps put a nice finish on your spectacle.

Although they aren't always essential to the success of a stunt, if you're creating some sort of contest, they make an impressive (potentially press-worthy) addition to the activity.

Show us your hands

One car dealership, eager to raise its visibility, decided to produce a stunt. What did the dealership have at its disposal as a giveaway? A truck. Using this spark of creation, the dealership produced an event where contestants had to keep their hands on the vehicle at all times without leaning on the truck. The participant who kept her hands on the longest without falling over won the vehicle. The human drama of endurance captured the imagination of the press throughout the course of the contest and even went on to inspire a documentary, *Hands on a Hard Body*.

Bring in the originality, bring in the media

The press love to cover stuff that hasn't been done before, so whenever possible do something unique and original — or put a unique and original twist on something that's already been done.

Publicity stunts may be popular in major markets such as New York, Los Angeles, and Chicago, but they aren't commonplace in most smaller markets. If stunts are rare where you are, make sure you amp up this angle to the press. Presenting a stunt "the likes of which have never been seen in the area before," can help to coax the press down to the event.

Understand, though, that, although you may think no one has anything cooler going on right now, there is a whole world out there, and your stunt wouldn't be the first one bumped for things a bit more newsworthy.

Lay a solid foundation with your targeted press outlets to get the most out of your stunt. To do this, identify the press outlets that'll help carry your message (see Chapter 15). Then make the most out of the groundwork you've done by putting your public relations prowess to work (see Chapter 16), and look to the media to cover your event and help convey your message.

If You Build It, Will They Come? Pre-Promoting Your Event

For all your dreamin' and plannin' and schemin', how awful would it be if no one ever saw your exploits? Pretty awful. Here, we address some tools at your disposal, most of which are cheap or free, to help get the word out about, and attract press and consumers to, your big event.

By this point, everything is well in place to make a huge impression, now it's time to let the cat out of the bag! This is your opportunity to reach out to the press and your target, let them know what you've been brewing, and invite them down.

Getting street-wise

In the days leading up to your stunt, hit the street and get the word out via street teams. It's time to call in all those favors to friends who you helped move and family members who owe you money, and get them to help you chat up locations around the area.

Nothing attracts a crowd like a crowd, so you need to attract the masses to your stunt and budget accordingly. As we say, you can produce the most staggering work of genius ever, but if no one ever knows about it, your efforts are all for naught. Plus, when your press *does* arrive, you'll definitely want your throngs of attendees in the backdrop of your photo or live remote.

If you have the cash, print some flyers that you can distribute to consumers on the street and local businesses. (For a more detailed overview of organizing and executing street teams, check out Chapter 6.) Many businesses such as barber shops, laundromats, and so on have community bulletin boards in their establishments. Ask politely, and if you're nice enough, your flyer may end up on every board in town.

It's cool, I've got a ticket

You're all geared up to distribute materials on the street, but you don't want to just hand out flyers. So don't. Get innovative — try producing a ticket instead. The creation of a ticket creates a sense of exclusivity. Encourage consumers to bring the ticket onsite for entry. Technically, yeah, you don't need a ticket to view a public event, but you'll probably find that the perception that you need one will stir up a little more interest. And, as an added bonus, the ticket can be used as a bookmark afterward, giving it a longer shelf life!

Hitting the computer

Most people spend several hours a day on their computers checking e-mail and social networking sites, and you can utilize this understanding to catch your audience where they play — online.

Send out mass e-mails to everyone you know, saying, "You don't want to miss this event!", and encourage them to forward the message on to their friends. Hit social networking sites — such as MySpace (www.myspace.com) and Facebook (www.facebook.com) — and post bulletins and event invites there as well.

Does your local newspaper have a community forum or do you have a community bulletin board? If so, your event should be all over it. You may even try being tastefully provocative. Are there ways that you can tease and pique people's interest on these formats? "Dude Looks like a Lady: On July 3 at 9 a.m. in Duffy Square, see women's clothing like you've never seen it before."

For more about getting your message out online, plug into Chapter 12.

Getting a little more out of your venue

If you're holding your event at a location other than a place you own, you probably had to pay or barter something for it. Get the most out of it! In the earlier stages, when you're negotiating what you're going to pay and what you're going to get, ask for some onsite advertising from your venue. Some great things to ask for in advance of your event include

- ✔ Signage in and around the venue
- ✔ Mentions on the venue marquee (if applicable)
- ✔ Access to the venue's e-mail list to send out a mass e-mail
- ✔ The opportunity to distribute materials onsite at events prior to yours

When Good Stunts Go Bad

Stuff happens. When executing a stunt, chances are, you're producing something that has never been done before, so there is no obvious path you can tread to avoid trouble. Unforeseen hiccups and obstacles will, no doubt, come up on the day of your event. Consider it your personal charge to anticipate problems so that you can quickly identify and fix them on the big day.

Before launching into producing what you think is the most ingenious publicity campaign ever, carefully weigh the ramifications of your actions. Can what you're doing be seen as dangerous or in bad taste? While getting extensive local and national coverage is excellent, if the coverage results in your target audience grabbing pitchforks and torches or launching a boycott, you'll be wishing all that amazing publicity would just go away.

Perhaps one of the most gleaming examples of this situation is one from very recent history. A cable network, in an effort to promote it's adult, male-centric cartoon programming, decided that it wanted to generate some attention by hanging 2-foot square light boxes featuring one of the characters from the program, in a variety of locations in major markets.

For weeks, these light boxes resided in their positions undisturbed and unnoticed. When they finally *were* noticed, it wasn't by their selected audience; it was by the Boston bomb squad. These simple light boxes had enough power to shut down the entire city for several hours, and resulted in some $2 million in fines, and just as many wagging fingers.

Publicity stunts can be seen as a double-edged sword. When executing these initiatives you want to challenge yourself to do things that haven't been done before, because that's what people (and the press) want to see! However, because it hasn't been done before, it simply isn't possible to be armed with everything that could possibly go wrong. For example, a major vendor of refreshing beverages and icy treats decided that it was going to break the record for the World's Tallest Popsicle — a record that up to the point stood at 21 feet. Before the sweet confection could be raised, the 80°F summer heat swooped in, melting the insides of the treat. As it was being unloaded from the truck, it broke and flooded the streets with kiwi-strawberry-flavored fluid. Instead of the front-page photo being 25 feet of frozen deliciousness, it was of firefighters hosing down pink streets and pedestrians fleeing the venue. Not the kind of impression you want to make.

Is there such a thing as bad press

"I don't care what the newspapers say about me as long as they spell my name right."

Oddly enough, this quote has been attributed to P. T. Barnum, Mae West, George M. Cohan, Will Rodgers, and W. C. Fields, masters of the publicity stunt all. Even today, the debate as to whether there is such a thing as bad press remains an open question. As it pertains to the examples in the "When Stunts Go Bad" section of this chapter, you could make the case that even the bad press that was attributed to each of these stunts helped to spread the word about the product or brand it was meant to promote.

During the course of the light-box outrage, the network involved had its name and clips of the program broadcast on every major media outlet. Granted, the things they were being associated with that brand weren't all that positive, but who's to say what consumers retained? Would they remember that everyone was talking about that brand or that it was connected to a bomb scare? Furthermore, could the outrage from city officials and other authority figures actually appeal to the edgier male target by further illustrating that parents just don't get it, man?

We don't have any easy answers for this question. In fact, we squabble over it with each other whenever the topic come up.

Take your plan, tear it apart, and have a strategy for everything that could go sour. What could possibly go wrong? What if someone doesn't show up? Are all of your production materials and crew prepared to do the job they've been assigned? Have your planned for the role that weather could play?

After you've thoroughly analyzed your plans and entertained every possible situation, make a contingency scenario for these situations. If your co-workers are helping you execute your program, let them in on the plan as well. A plan that only you know about isn't going to be of much use if no one else can help you carry it out.

Back in the planning stages you shared with your venue your plan for the day. Do the same with everyone involved. Make sure every staff member, caterer, and dancing-bear handler knows the schedule and his involvement in it. If you're bringing in outside vendors to help you with your stunt, remember they've based their day around your activities — respect their time as you want them to respect yours.

Chapter 8

Events and Experiences

"**S**o listen, see, I want to give consumers the opportunity to experience my product in a way unlike any other. I don't want to just put up some posters — I want something aces, ya see? Okay, marketing genius — go."

Not all business owners sound like 1920s mobsters (though we've had our fair share of ones that do), but in many cases the desire is the same. How do you give the public, either en masse or targeted, an exciting way to not only see, hear, or sample your product, but *experience* it as well? One way to do this is by producing an event.

An *event,* as it relates to guerrilla marketing, involves reaching out to your target consumers by producing an experience that is involved, educational, and entertaining. For the purposes of the organization of this book, we're addressing publicity stunts (see Chapter 7) as spectacles geared more toward attracting media coverage, and in this chapter, an event as primarily focused on drawing in consumers and giving them a personal, experiential engagement with your brand. But we openly acknowledge that there will be some crossover. Hey, if you produce a great event that consumers love, why shouldn't you get some press?

More to that point, when we refer to events, we're looking to address things like a grand opening of a spa or beauty salon, open house enrollment for a health club, or after-work wine tastings at the local spirits store. These are brand-related experiences that can be tailored to give consumers the opportunity to be introduced to, or better informed about, the product or service you're offering.

This chapter outlines exactly what goes into pulling off an event and how your brand can get the most out of doing so. To get you started, we tell you the integral pieces that help make an event a unique experience for your consumers. As your creative juices help motivate you toward constructing your event, we walk through some popular events such as meet-and-greets, performances, casting calls, and on-air events, and investigate how each of these concepts can be tweaked to benefit your business.

"So if you got the moxie, to put your ideas to work, you'll quickly find yourself made, ya dig?"

Knowing What Makes a Good Event

If the idea of putting on an event strikes you as a little foreign, don't worry: Chances are, you have far more experience planning an event than you may think. For example, let's say your birthday is rolling around and — congratulations! — you're turning [cough, cough]! That's great news! With this new age, comes a new dawn in your life and you've decided to take matters into your own hands and plan your own perfect birthday party — something uniquely fitting your personality that will have your friends commenting for years about how that birthday party was just so undeniably "you."

To get started, you write down a list of the people who just *have* to be there. After reviewing your list, you choose a restaurant that's close to where all your friends live and is famous for that dish that you're notorious for picking — you know the one. . . . Then on to entertainment. Known among your friends for starting your day with a full-throated classic-rock anthem, the big-hair '80s tribute band complete with dance floor and pyrotechnic show is an absolute must. As the *pièce de résistance,* on display at the gift table, you lay out signed 8-x-10 pictures of yourself for your guests to take home and mark this magical night as the best birthday party ever — or at least one that had "you" written all over it.

If you were a product or service, you would have just laid out a basic (albeit arguably narcissistic) brand-related event. How did you go about producing such a brand-centric experience?

✔ **You were audience-specific.** Although other patrons at the birthday party may appreciate what you've created and tell their friends about what they saw Friday night, you targeted your immediate social circle first and provided them with an unparalleled experience, which ensured that your name was on the lips of the people important to you.

This is an opportunity to utilize your guerrilla targeting skills. Starting out of the gate, decide who your ideal event attendees are and build outward from there.

✔ **You entertained and engaged your guests.** As it pertains to your penchant for '80s tribute bands, you created something that was flashy and fun, and that gives insight on who you are. The degree of participation for your guests here can be as simple as rolling their eyes at the lead singer's spandex pants or as involved as rockin' the casbah on the dance floor. Either way, you've presented something a little different.

When you're planning the event for your product or brand, think about what you can do that's experiential and informs your guests about your product or brand. What can you provide them that will bring them in for your pitch? What will be the degree of their involvement after they're there?

✔ **You provided a clear takeaway.** Although distributing your headshot at your own birthday party may be considered a bold move, you did it with the right intention and put a smile on your guests' faces. Plus, you left them with a reminder of a truly remarkable party and, in your case, an amazing person.

What's your audience taking away from your product or brand event? Are they walking away with a sample of your product, a printed piece, or simply a clear, concentrated message?

These three elements — choosing your audience, entertaining and engaging your guests, and providing a takeaway — will help give a framework to start working through the kind of event you'd like to carry out, but you can further clarify your event by taking a few other items into account. We cover these in the following sections.

Being the only game in town

When you hear stories about prosperous businesses, often the simple explanation for their initial success is that, at the time, they were the only game in town. In order for your event to be well attended and for you to get the full value of your efforts, you want to put yourself in the same position. Do yourself a favor and steer clear of potential conflicts that could have your consumers saying, "Oh, I would totally go if it weren't for. . . ."

Take a quick spin through your 12-month calendar and make note of national holidays around your projected event date. If a major holiday (such as New Year's) or event (such as Election Day) will monopolize your consumers' attention, you may want to change your date accordingly.

Locally, you can avoid being overshadowed by doing a little legwork and seeing what's shaking in your neighborhood. Find the resources in your community that will help you tap into the pulse of your area. Start by checking out local calendar listings, neighborhood papers, community bulletin boards, and Web sites.

After you've made your initial surface sweep, it's time to dig a little deeper. Place some calls to various civic organizations as a "curious citizen" or a tourist seeking more information, just casually wondering what's happening the week of (projected event date). Outlets that are particularly helpful in this realm include the visitors and convention bureaus, local business improvement districts, and parks and recreation offices. Most of these organizations will have public affairs departments whose sole job it is to make sure the public is aware of upcoming events.

Scoping out the competition is a great idea as well. If you own Otto's Auto Emporium and you want hold an event at your dealership, look around and see what other car sales locations are doing. If you discover that your rival, Crazy Carl's Cars, is having its Once in a Millennium 50 Percent Off Sale on the same day you were planning to hold your event, you may want to consider rescheduling — or step up your plans to make sure your event trumps Crazy Carl with the "Twice in a Millennium 75% Off Sale!".

Doing all this conflict research may not sound like a lot of fun. What's worse, though, is spending all that time and money to produce your event only to be upstaged by the local popcorn festival — a mistake you could've avoided by making a few phone calls and doing a quick search online.

Making it easy for your target to attend

Say you own a wine shop, and you want to reach out to upwardly mobile 30-somethings and turn them into regular customers. To do this, you decide to hold a series of fun, hip, wine tasting events featuring a noted area sommelier and a local DJ spinning some ambient, atmospheric jams — something that's fun and educational without being pretentious.

You have your plan and you know the consumers you'd like to reach. Now you need to clear the way for your ideal consumers to participate. What can you do to make it as easy as possible for this target audience to attend? Start by putting yourself in their shoes and considering which day of the week works best for them. These are busy people, and you know you're not going to be able to catch them early in the week. They've got deadlines to meet. So try later on, maybe Wednesday or Thursday. Your event may be a little too posh for weekend craziness, but just right to help welcome them to the week's end.

So now that you've got a good sense of what day you want to hold your event, it's time to pick a time. Prior to setting your time in stone, consider your target and put some initial feelers out there (conduct a straw poll) to see if this works for your target audience. If the overwhelming answer to your proposed time is "no," ask this cross section what time would best work for them instead.

Talk to your 30-something friends, and maybe you'll find that they enjoy a nice happy hour after a long day of work. Later on in the evening, plans may involve dinner or a movie or some sort of sporting event, but right after work — say, 5 to 7 p.m. — they're available.

Finally, make your window of participation as wide as is appropriate. Someone won't show up for an event if, by arriving 10 or 15 minutes late, he's missed the greater part of the experience. He'll be more likely to show up if there are two or three hours during which he can swing by. Try, as much as possible, to arrange your event so that guests who arrive at the beginning, middle, or end will all get the same experience.

Providing a unique experience

The cliché that you only get one chance to make a first impression is a cliché for a reason. When you turn on the news, all you hear are stories about how people are busier and more productive than ever before. With all that people have going on these days, the burden is on you to produce something that's unique, something that will make your guests happy they took the time to stop by. Whether you hold an event for ten people or a thousand, make it entertaining and personal. In the following sections, we show you how.

Offering the human touch

"They're only doing this so they can make a buck!" Sometimes the public views marketing efforts as insincere, manufactured, and even manipulative — and sometimes they are. So go out of your way to prove them wrong! Anything you can do to overcome this unflattering light and put a human touch on your event is in your best interest.

Little things can make a big difference. Something as simple as having an attractive, smiling person greeting guests as they arrive is more effective than most people realize. You and your team should introduce yourselves (first names only, to avoid the crazies), and chat up your guests. Consumers may not read your printed materials when they get home that night, but a delightful conversation with you and your staff will stick in their heads.

Also, do whatever you can do — within reasonable and ethical bounds — to make your guests comfortable and happy while they're "in your house." Every day, consumers have to deal with a lot of crap (nothing on TV, traffic, taxes), so when they arrive at your event, you should make them feel glad that they got a babysitter so they could attend.

Giving your guests the V.I.P. treatment

Most of your consumers probably aren't Hollywood A-listers, but that's no reason why you shouldn't treat them like they are for a few hours. Reaching out and catering to your consumers is great, but what's even better is giving them an experience that makes them feel like they're on the other side of the ropes.

Some classy touches that will have them saying ooh-la-la may include the following:

- ✔ **Light hors d'oeuvres:** Don't let the French fool you, this can be as simple as a cheese tray, an assortment of small sandwiches, or a plate of cookies. For that little extra *je ne sais quoi*, why not recruit someone to pass your culinary treats around to your guests?

- ✔ **Drinks:** Engaging in a high-class event like the one you're putting on can leave your guests parched. Quell their thirst by making water, coffee, tea, or another event-appropriate beverage close at hand.

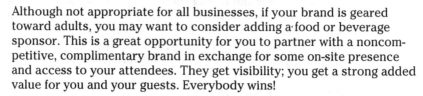

    Although not appropriate for all businesses, if your brand is geared toward adults, you may want to consider adding a food or beverage sponsor. This is a great opportunity for you to partner with a noncompetitive, complimentary brand in exchange for some on-site presence and access to your attendees. They get visibility; you get a strong added value for you and your guests. Everybody wins!

- ✔ **Music:** Have you ever been at a gathering of complete strangers and noted how the silence was just plain eerie? Fill the void with a little music. Consider the tone of your gathering and fill your MP3 player with all the right tunes a week or two before the event.

- ✔ **Photographer:** Having a roving photographer take photos of your guests can quickly give the semblance of a big-time event. Yes, the pictures could be used for the local paper, or it could just be Cousin Ed in a fancy black suit. No one has to know — they'll still stop and smile, we promise. Either way, people feel like they're being admired by the press and you've got great photos to document the experience!

- ✔ **Giveaways:** Whenever you tune into *Entertainment Tonight,* they just love to show you all the goodies that the celebrities get to take away from various events they attend. You probably don't have ten grand to blow on each gift bag, but what do you have at your disposal? Can you offer branded products or samples as a thank-you for attending? If so, add that to a coupon or printed piece in a branded gift bag for a nice, classy touch.

- ✔ **Décor:** The final component you'll want to consider is décor. What can you add to your event that will help people feel more comfortable or involved while they're there? Would some additional furniture, lighting, or greenery make the venue nicer? Maybe a branded backdrop for Cousin Ed to use when taking pictures of your guests as they enter?

You've decided that you want to give people at your event the opportunity to walk the red carpet in style. You may want to try swapping it up and substitute the "red carpet" outside your event for something that relates to your brand, like branded Astroturf for a sports bar, or fluorescent orange shag carpeting for a '70s themed event.

Engaging your guests

Involvement or engagement is the degree of participation required by your guests in order to experience your brand. How much are you going to ask of them? When they stop by, will they be able to simply enjoy the atmosphere or will they be asked to do the chicken dance? No matter which direction you go, in the following sections, we offer some suggestions to get the most out of it.

Limited engagement

If your event requires only limited engagement, all you're asking of your guests is that they come down and check the place out. The idea is that, when they're there, they'll be blown away by what you offer and want to turn to you to fulfill their needs.

While guests are at your event, they should be given the opportunity to see your environment, experience the product, and ask questions of you and your staff. A limited-engagement event is more laid back — it's an opportunity for you to say, "This is who we are. We've got some nifty stuff going on. Check us out."

Even though you're asking little or nothing of your guests, that doesn't mean you should overlook any opportunity to reiterate who you are and what you do. Try employing a few inexpensive add-ons to help your brand stick in their minds:

- **PowerPoint loop:** A PowerPoint loop is just a quick presentation displayed on computer or TV screens throughout your venue that outlines your business and can be looped throughout the course of the event so that once the presentation finishes it will automatically restart itself.

  When many people think of PowerPoint presentations, they think of stuffy boardrooms and mind-numbing, copy-heavy slides of company earnings. For the purposes of your event, you want to turn that association on its ear. Your loop should be as flashy as the feel of your event will allow. Include as many intriguing, colorful pictures of your business as possible. Try some animation. Spice it up by having your logo zoom into the screenshot. If you choose to go this route, do so sparingly. As for the copy, just the facts! What do you do? How do you do it? What's unique about your company? Pages of text won't get read and will leave your guests walking away with visions of yes-men dancing in their heads — not a very positive association.

✔ **Video loop:** A video loop is an edited reel of footage that gives your guests the chance to see what you do. If you have footage that outlines your process, your services, and unique points about your company this is your chance to share it! You may think the history of how your great-great-granddad started the company in 1919, had a lovable Irish setter named Big Julie, and was a big fan of collecting butterflies and mounting them on his wall is fascinating, but if all that information has nothing to do with the drywall you're selling, consumers will press on. Keep your content short, succinct, and, again, as flashy as your brand will allow so that it stands out.

✔ **Enlarged photographs:** Enlarged photos are a great tool to help reaffirm your brand on-site. If a picture is worth a thousand words, how many words is a really, really big picture worth? Enlarging photos of your logos, products, and brand associated images, in addition to adding an atmospheric touch to your event, gives yet another opportunity to communicate your business to attendees. You can hang these images on the wall, or set them on easels (available at any office supply store).

When producing these photos, take your brand into account. Are there different ways to present these photos that are unique to your brand? If you're particularly artsy, you may want to present them in black-and-white or sepia, invert the colors, or create a collage of images. Ask yourself how you may want to tailor these pictures so that your consumers give them a second look.

If you have a few extra bucks, you may want to bring in a graphic artist for a few hours to generate some layout options. Working with a designer to produce these concepts could make a big difference in something looking legit and professional, which in turn will reflect very highly on your brand.

Higher engagement

You've decided you want to involve your guests in your event. You don't want them to just stop by, eat your grub, and go home. You want them to really participate in the event. Going this route involves a higher level of engagement. What this means for you is that you have to craft something that's one of a kind — and if it doesn't fit that description, you'd better at least reward them well for playing.

When you were in school and the teacher asked for a volunteer to come to the chalkboard and explain the Pythagorean theorem, most people stared at their hands and avoided the teacher's gaze, right? Why weren't the kids clamoring to volunteer? Simply put, no one wants to look stupid in front of a large group of people. Knowing this, whatever form of engagement you choose — whether it's some sort of contest, game, dance-off, or what have you — make sure you and your staff are as supportive as possible. You're already asking more of them than just attending, so don't make them feel ridiculous on top of it.

The more you're asking from your guests, the more you need to be prepared to compensate them for their involvement. If your event involves having guests come on stage and make a fool of themselves, they'd better be getting more than a branded pen out of the deal. Figure out what it would take for *you* to participate in what you're proposing for your guests. Would you need a $15 gift certificate or a lifetime supply of product? If you're particularly extroverted, you may want to ask some of your less outgoing friends to make sure that the reward befits the deed. (For more on rewarding your consumers, check out the "Banking on participation" sidebar in this chapter.)

To avoid a case of shy (or no) volunteers, you may want to have a few friends in amongst the crowd as "plants" who can be called upon to get the ball rolling if necessary. Consumers may be able to learn just as much about your product by watching someone else enthusiastically participate in the activities as they would by participating themselves.

Banking on participation

A major financial institution created a unique loyalty program where consumers received more tangible rewards for banking with them. Rewards included things like basketball hoops, video gaming units, digital cameras, golf equipment, and gift cards. Their challenge was to create an event that gave guests the opportunity to experience these various rewards in the hopes that they would open an account with their institution.

The bank's solution was to create an event that engaged consumers in a series of activities involving the reward items in exchange for high-value premiums such as gift cards. To do this they created a large-scale game show that quizzed consumers about the program, a putt-putt course, a video gaming station, a photo booth, and a basketball shootout. Each of the stations was produced using the various rewards available, giving consumers a hands-on experience with each of the items they could receive through the program.

This guest engagement resulted in record enrollment with the bank over the course of the three-day event. Whether guests stayed for one minute or one hour, they were still able to get the same experience from attending. The program was so successful that it was sent on the road to give consumers across the country the opportunity to experience it!

Gathering information about your guests

In exchange for everything you're doing and offering at your event, it's all right for you to expect something in return. This can include building a moment into your event to give your spiel or simply requesting attendees' contact information to keep them posted about your business.

Adding an enter-to-win component can be a great way to get your attendees' contact information while adding another exciting element to your event. An enter-to-win component is an opportunity for your guests to win a prize by virtue of submitting their names and contact information — and it's far easier to execute than you might think.

First, look to your business. Is there a service- or brand-related prize that you can offer guests? Good prizes include month-long (or multiple-month) awards of products or services. When you're deciding what you're going to give away, be aware that the higher the value of the prize, the greater the number of likely participants.

Be mindful of any legalese that you may need to associate with your sweepstakes or contest. Be sure to properly and clearly articulate things like rules, eligibility, and entry dates. Frequently, larger organizations turn to their internal legal department — but you can accomplish the same thing by turning to a promotion agency or group that specializes in this field.

Next up is a trip to your local office supply store. Here, you want to pick up a clear acrylic suggestion box or entry hopper, a few stacks of multicolored index cards — because they just look pretty in the hopper — a few boxes of pens, and some paper. You now have the tools you need to get started.

At the venue, set the hopper, pens, and blank cards on a draped folding table. Include a pre-filled card next to your stack of Technicolor entry forms so that consumers can see all the information you're requesting of them. We suggest the following:

- ✔ Name
- ✔ Address
- ✔ Phone
- ✔ E-mail
- ✔ How did you hear about the event?
- ✔ Can we contact you with news and updates?

Gently inform your guests, either on the card or verbally, that incomplete entries will not be eligible to win your prize. Including these elements will ensure that you get all those important details you can use for targeted mailers or e-blasts down the road. The last question will give you the opportunity to follow up after the event and develop a useful mailing list.

As an additional opportunity to tout your contest, you may also want to make up some signs next to the entry hopper showcasing the prize and drawing details. Make sure this table is manned by a cheerful, outgoing person whose job it is to encourage participation, answer questions, and make sure your consumers give you all those nitty-gritty details you're looking for.

You've scoured your business and aside from some dodgy homemade cheeses your grandmother keeps sending you, you've got nothing to give away as a prize. If this is the case, cut the enter-to-win entirely and opt for a guestbook instead. Guest books can be seen as a classier, familiar way to document all those who were in attendance. Just make sure there are lines for all the information you're looking for to produce your database down the line.

Meet-and-Greets and Performances

Scapes, a luxury landscaping business, is opening up its showroom to unveil its new offering: lawn art — etchings in grass that look like your family members and more! Seeing busts of your family carved in your lawn is pretty impressive, but the folks at Scapes don't want to take any chances. How can they ensure that the public comes to their open house? One option may be to secure a guest for a meet-and-greet, someone who knows the turf. The greens master of the local chi-chi golf course may be just the person to have on-site.

If you're setting up a meet-and-greet or performance for your event, you want to find performers or celebrities who are relevant to the brand and who add value to the event or the experience. The key phrase here is *relevant to the brand.* Having the star pitcher from the local AAA baseball team show up at your event may be kind of cool, but if your brand has nothing to do with baseball or sports, the appearance may seem gimmicky and ultimately confuse your audience.

Before adding a meet-and-greet or performance to your event, you need to evaluate what the celebrity or performer will contribute to your plans. Will adding this element make your event more appealing? Get people to stick around longer? If after your event evaluation you decide that it will, you need to think about who you should get to appear.

Meeting and greeting

What is worth taking the time out of your day to go and see? A panel on horticulture? An interview with the world's premier coffee roaster? Meet-and-greets are effective tools to communicate your messaging and provide your consumers with an experience that may be out of the ordinary.

Such events are exciting tools, but they aren't for everyone. Here are a few quick questions to help you decide if this tool may be useful to you:

- ✔ **Does the guest have something useful to share with my consumers?** If the person is speaking to coffee enthusiasts and doesn't know his Arabica from his Blue Hawaiian, chances are his presence won't prove relevant to your guests.

- ✔ **Is there an item or product of interest from your storefront that can be hyped, promoted, or sold in conjunction with your guest's visit that will generate a spike in sales?** The power of connecting an appropriate face with the brand can have sway and influence in select consumers. For example, when your mom went to the local home store for a meet-and-greet with the inventor of a new high-powered vacuum, she may have become so intrigued and impressed as he displayed its features that she immediately bought one, regardless of the fact there was only one carpet in her home.

- ✔ **Is having this person speak at your event likely to be press-worthy?** Will a person of national repute or a highly respected pro in the industry speaking at your event generate trade, local, or national press?

Securing guests and speakers

After narrowing your list of potential special guests, you begin making calls. Unless you have deep pockets, reach out to the most relevant and local head-liners first. You'll have direct contact, and the possibilities for what you'll be able to conduct at your event will be greater as well.

One school of thought is to bring in someone who can benefit as much from speaking or appearing as you can from having him there to do so. Is there a local author who has a cult following? Perhaps in exchange for appearing at your event, he can be given the opportunity to sell his books on-site. Making the benefits of his participation clear may put you in a position to gain from his appearance with little or no cost to you.

If you look through your list of candidates and decide, "You know what, I really need to get that famous chef with the charming catch phrase to cook a baked Alaska at my event." If so, begin making calls and research his representation. (For more about tracking down elusive celebs, check out Chapter 7.)

Be clear about the degree of participation you need from the celebrity. Also, identify any additional perks (such as being able to hock his wares at your event) you may be able to offer to make your case for his involvement. Most likely, you'll have to pay a fee or make a donation to the celebrity's favorite charity in exchange for his attendance at your event.

If your celebrity performer is coming from out of town, make sure you've nailed down who's covering those expenses. Imagine your horror when you settle upon a price for her appearance, only to have to pay three times that amount for her 4-star hotel!

Family, friends, and associates are incredible, usually untapped, resources. Let them in on what you're looking for in the way of a guest. Sometimes securing the perfect speaker or performance is as simple as a friend placing a call to an old college buddy who's "just what you're looking for."

Having a clear plan of attack

You wouldn't go into battle without a plan, and you shouldn't go into your event without one either. So maybe that analogy is a bit intense, but having a plan sure is helpful! The addition of this special-guest component adds another layer to your event. Don't stress out about it, but the guest is another factor that you needs to plan for. You need to come up with a *run of show* (a one-sheet piece of paper detailing contact information, duties/ responsibilities, and the timeline for the event) and give it to your guest and other involved parties. This document should include the following:

- ✔ Contact names and telephone numbers for all participants
- ✔ The guest's duties, responsibilities, and any other special requests
- ✔ The guest's arrival time at the venue and mode of transportation
- ✔ Timeline for the guest's appearance at your event
- ✔ The guest's departure time from the venue
- ✔ Talking points for the guest, if he has the opportunity to speak with the press

One fun luxury is to be chauffeured around a la *Sliver Spoons*. If you have the extra cash, arrange a car service to deliver your guest to the venue. Aside from being a classy touch that will make your guest feel like a rock star, you'll be able ensure that she's there when you need her to be.

To complement your in-depth run of show, put together a quick *production brief,* a list of all the production pieces necessary for your guest's appearance (table, tablecloth, microphone, a case of Evian, comfy chair, and so on). You may also want to include a simple sketch laying out where everything will be placed in the space.

Making the most out of an opportunity

You've clarified the specifics on an in-house level and briefed everyone on how they fit into the plan. Now you need to make a public schedule of events based on the essentials of your run of show and get the word out! Post your schedule wherever your target audience will see it. Stick up signs around the venue, identify hot spots that your consumers frequent, post messages on community bulletin boards, spend some time online — you know, the usual suspects.

Take advantage of additional opportunities to get the most out of this attraction — both on the day of your event and in the weeks and months to come. Here's how:

- **Offer V.I.P. access before the event.** Most businesses are constantly looking for inexpensive opportunities to thank their customers for their patronage. Why not hold a V.I.P. pre-party prior to the actual event? If you've secured a celebrity, this is an opportunity for your best customers to get autographs and pictures with your guests. Giving special attention to your special customers is a kind of tip of the hat that will, with any luck, come back to you in the form of continued or increased business.

- **When your featured guest is making her grand entrance, make the appearance as accessible as possible.** Make sure that everyone in attendance can see and hear what you've created. That way, you're sure to get the word-of-mouth buzz that you're after.

If you're holding a meet-and-greet, allow plenty of time for autographs and pictures. If you've secured a big star, 30 minutes won't cut it. The last thing you want to do is disappoint her adoring fans — and have them blaming you for it! When negotiating the contract with the guest, make sure you're clear how long the person will be signing autographs and make that clear to attendees. We usually find an hour will suffice.

- **Get a little something to work with later.** Having happy V.I.P.s and wowed masses is great, but why not position yourself to reap the benefits of your guest's appearance long after he's left the building? Here are some examples:

  - Pictures: You should be able to walk away with exceptional pictures of your featured guest with you, your brand, and your guests. If possible, get permission from your guest to use his image for future marketing materials. Verbal agreements to do so may be legally binding, but be sure to get it in writing, too.

- Video: This can be as simple as grabbing the family video camera and taping the event. The footage may end up on the floor of your closet or you may decide that you want to release the video to media outlets, post it on your Web site, or enter the realm of video sharing sites. Not capturing this footage when you have the chance will leave you slapping your forehead later.

- Signed items: Getting a few extra items signed by your guest is likely to prove beneficial down the road. Glossy 8-x-10 photos are a unique opportunity for your guest to create a personalized give-away to attendees. The guest may be able to provide them, or you can easily produce them at your local photo shop.

  You may frame them and put them in a place of honor in your business, or donate the signed items to a charity auction. If nothing else, they'll serve as a personal memento of the experience.

Casting Calls

Looking for a fresh face or voice to represent your brand? Everyone wants to feel like a star, so give your consumers the opportunity to take center stage by holding a casting call.

A *casting call* is usually used by media folks looking to secure talent for things like commercials, TV pilots, and feature films. However, for your purposes, a casting call can also be used as a marketing event in and of itself when it's targeted to consumers. Think about it: When it's held at a storefront, a casting call can quickly lead to buzz, crowds, and maybe even an increase in foot traffic and sales — all key components to a successful event.

When executed correctly, the benefits of holding a casting call are twofold:

- You're given the opportunity to find great talent to represent your brand.
- You're able to meet and ingratiate yourself with potential clients and consumers.

Tracking down your talent

There are many talented folks out there. Who knows, you might even discover the next superstar at your call!

When beginning the search, keep in mind the following:

- ✔ **Have a clear definition of who you're looking for.** Are you looking for a housewife in her 40s or a biker dude in his 60s?

- ✔ **Be clear on what's in it for them.** For participating, will they receive a $10,000 contract to be your spokesperson? A lifetime supply of your product? Or simply the privilege of representing you? The more you can offer financially or personally, the greater the turnout you'll get.

Think about where your target works and lives, and get the word out to them. Don't forget to tell them the benefits of their participation!

Structuring your call

Let the search begin! Now that you know what you're looking for, it's time to structure your call. Here are the keys you need to keep in mind:

- ✔ **Pick a location for your casting call.** If you have the space, you may want to consider bringing the public to your doorstep by holding the auditions at your place of business. If not, you can just as easily book space at a nearby dance studio, recreation center, or place of worship.

- ✔ **Provide a check-in desk.** When people arrive, they may be nervous. Put them at ease by having a smiling staff of people greet them and give them an audition card (as shown in Figure 8-1) and, if possible, a sample of the product with as much information about it as possible.

- ✔ **Assign the order of the auditions.** The order should be decided based on a first come, first served basis.

- ✔ **Give them their lines.** As part of the audition, give them a quick line that includes your brand name — for example, "Fricasee's chicken has me comin' back for more!"

- ✔ **Record your contestants.** When your talent comes in to audition, video-tape them or take a Polaroid and attach it to their audition cards. If you like a person, you'll want to put the name with the face later.

- ✔ **Thank them for attending.** Just coming out took a lot of courage. Be exceptionally supportive and grateful for their having attended. This also creates a positive contact with your brand so that, even if they aren't cast, they'll look upon you and your brand fondly.

In the entertainment business, the casting director is the gatekeeper to the actor's big break. But when it comes to casting for marketing events, a casting director adds authenticity (not to mention the invaluable opportunity for your attendees to get in front of a casting professional), which can lead to bigger draws. Most casting directors also have resources available to help generate interest by performing outreach on your behalf.

Fricassee's Fresh Face Search

Name: _____

Address: _____

Phone: _____

Height: _____ Weight: _____ Hair color: _____ Eye color: _____

Union Affiliation (SAG, AEA, AFTRA, etc.): _____

Past Experience:

Scheduling Conflicts:

Figure 8-1:
Who have we here? Make an audition card to keep track of your talent.

When holding your auditions, you need to know whether your talent is a member of one of the various performing unions, such as the Screen Actors Guild (SAG), Actors Equity Association (AEA), or the America Federation of Television & Radio Artists (AFTRA). If she is, it isn't the end of the world. It just means you may have additional expenses — such as insurance, pension, and other payments — beyond your talent's fee.

If you're looking for talent under the age of 18 or whatever the local ordinance is in your area, make sure parents give written consent allowing their kids to participate and be photographed.

Hiring your star

Through your exhaustive search, you've been given the opportunity to introduce your brand to tens, hundreds, or even thousands of people. More to the point however, you've narrowed down your choices and hopefully found your star! That's great — but before crowning them your fresh face, do a little bit of due diligence to insulate yourself (and your brand).

You just want to make sure that there's nothing about the person's immediate past that could embarrass you or your product. Although we all have secrets, requesting business and personal references, and (if budget allows) hiring a private investigator to perform a background check, are useful tools to find out about your talent. If everything checks out, contact your talent and let him know that he's in the finals but you'd like some references. Call the references and make sure you like the picture they paint of the person you've selected. If all that checks out, call your talent, make sure he's comfortable with all aspects of your campaign, and give him the good news!

On-Air Events

Events are primarily geared toward engaging the *consumers* as opposed to engaging the media. That said, if you can get a local TV or radio station to come down and do a remote from your event, or if you can find a way to be interviewed on-air about your event, well, that isn't so bad either.

Getting on-air

Getting that on-air publicity to reach your consumers either in the lead-up to or during your event can be a tricky proposition. If you aren't doing something stunty (see Chapter 7), arousing interest in your activities can be difficult. Even so, there are ways to help stir up a little free publicity for your event:

- ✔ **Present yourself as an expert.** The best kind of advertising is the kind you don't have to pay for. A free way to possibly get on air is to present yourself as an expert on a topic scheduled to be discussed. If there's a live TV or radio show relating to your field, your expertise and presence could help take you (and your business) far. It could allow you an on-air plug for your services or event — or at the very least, mention your Web site or storefront location.

✔ **Offer prizes.** Radio stations, in particular, are constantly looking for prizing ideas and contests they can offer their listeners as added value to tune in. There are only so many times they can give out free tickets to the county fair. Their need to offer something exciting can be the ticket *you* need to help promote your event. Can you contribute products or services as part of a larger prize package, or perhaps something big enough to stand on its own? If you can come up with something of value, you're likely to score on-air mentions whenever the contest is announced.

✔ **Create an event they can't miss.** Although the preceding two ideas are ways to sneak on air to promote your event, getting radio on-site without a media buy is a challenge. If you can offer the station's demographic a unique event, provide prizes the station can give away as part of a contest, and throw a little something to the DJ to act as the host, emcee, and even the casting director of your event, then maybe, just maybe, you can not only get them to your event, but snag all the on-air mentions your heart desires.

If for all your hard work, you *still* can't get the media to your event, perhaps it's time to bring your event — or part of it — to the media. For more on taking it to them, check out the "Just thought I'd stop by . . ." sidebar in this chapter.

Just thought I'd stop by . . .

A famous immunity booster wanted to grab a little more media attention for their product. So naturally, they dressed an actor up as their iconic germ and took him from radio station to radio station bearing gift baskets full of product. A loony wanting to get on-air can easily be shooed off, but an outgoing germ bearing gifts is darn near impossible to turn away. The unusual visitor, accompanied by a handler from the brand, was granted access to nearly every station they went to, meeting the employees and radio personalities, ultimately resulting in water-cooler chat and the jackpot — on-air mentions acknowledging their visit and the gifts they provided.

Knowing what to do when your press arrives

You've done it, by Jove! By virtue of your tenaciousness and resourcefulness you've managed to get press and media on-site to cover your event. Now you need to get the most out of their presence.

As soon as the media arrives at your event, you need to do whatever you can to make a positive impression for your event and your brand. Here are some pointers:

- **Introduce yourself immediately and provide them with event materials (known as a *media kit* or *press pack*).** To make sure your press is getting the message the way you want it to be represented, make sure your media kit includes a press release (see Chapter 16), bios on all parties involved, high-resolution photos (both hard copies and on CD), and, if relevant, a sample of the product being featured at the event all neatly contained in a branded folder with easy-to-find contact information.

- **Have someone knowledgeable about the event (a friend, family member, or colleague) be available to answer questions, walk them through the setup, and facilitate interviews with any talent on-site.**

- **Don't crowd them, but make yourself accessible in case they have any questions or need some assistance.** They're probably not going to stay very long, so you want to maximize every moment you have them.

- **Give them the best seat in the house.** Providing the best view and/or access will help them experience your event in the best possible way, which will hopefully lead to nothing but positive coverage.

While the media are enjoying the best that your event has to offer, why not give them something exclusive? Light catering and a fun goody bag can help make the best impression. Positive editorial coverage can't be bought, but it certainly can be influenced.

Part III
Opportunities All around You: Nontraditional Media

The 5th Wave   By Rich Tennant

©RICHTENNANT

IN A BIZARRE SET OF CIRCUMSTANCES, DOUG'S FAUCETS BECOMES THE FOCUS OF A SMALL CULT LOOKING FOR ANSWERS.

DOUG'S FAUCETS

PREPARE TO MEET YOUR MAKER

In this part . . .

Marketers live a charmed life. In past centuries, the methods of communicating messages were limited to the reach of carrier pigeons. These days, the marketing world has burst wide open with unlimited options to not just communicate, but connect in direct, targeted ways. Many of these options are readily available, just waiting for you to pick them up and make your unique mark on the marketing landscape.

The media opportunities available today enable brands to reach consumers both indoors and out. The chapters in this part describe and discuss some of the popular and recognizable platforms, craft ways to make your message stand out, as well as provide sample media buys and costs associated with each of them.

Although existing nontraditional platforms will no doubt get you thinking, your inner revolutionary would never be satisfied stopping there. Perhaps one of the most imaginative and exciting elements of guerrilla marketing is the creation of new media. When you're looking to stand out in the mass of marketing messaging, you need to stay ahead of the curve and create new platforms to present your brand. In this part, we discuss the importance of using your own creativity to discover and use untapped resources around you to effectively share your message — and maybe pick up some passive income in the process.

Chapter 9

Out in the Fresh Air

*Y*ou walk to work and see ads glued to scaffolding. You take the bus and notice ads under the shelter while you wait. You drive to the mall and pass by several large billboards along the highway. You hail a cab with an ad on its roof. You ride the subway and see ads overhead. You're stuck in traffic next to a truck that's been plastered with an ad.

If you have even a shred of doubt about advertising outdoors, write down every ad you see on your way from home to work one morning. This little exercise is all the proof you'll need that advertisers are trying to reach you anywhere and everywhere — and that *your* business can get in on that action.

According to the U.S. Census Bureau, the average American spends 100 hours a year commuting. Now, we're not very good at math, but if you multiply those 100 hours times the 300 million people living in the country, that equals, well, a very large number of opportunities to get your message out there.

Today's on-the-go lifestyle may keep people harried and hopped up on coffee, but to the keen marketer this presents a wide array of opportunities to reach consumers out-of-home (OOH). You can select the media that will best enable you to get your message to your target demographic in a direct, highly visible manner.

In this chapter, we explore a variety of options for reaching consumers in the great outdoors. We detail a basic overview of some of the more popular methods, as well as the benefits and downfalls of each. From there, we step into the realm of identifying and contacting the people who will help you get your message out there and creating your ad. Finally, we show you how to take your message on the road, whether you're on a tight budget or you're operating on grander scale.

Whether you're a small-business owner or a marketing manager for a larger organization, if you're thinking about taking your message outdoors, you may be asking yourself, "Where do I begin?" Our answer: with this chapter.

Buying the Outdoors: What's Out There?

Taking your message outdoors can be a great move, but you have lots of options to choose from, and you need to figure out which one is right for your brand. Here, we let you in on some of the more popular options available, and offer our suggestions on what to buy, how to buy it, and who to buy it from. With this information, you can make informed choices about the best options for your business and how to use these options to get your message out there.

Wild postings

When it comes to marketing and advertising, wild posting is the guerrilla's scrappiest tool. *Wild posting,* also known as *sniping* and *guerrilla postering,* consists of posters glued to any wall or flat surface and, in some cases, lamp posts or street poles as well.

The technique itself is nothing new. In fact, it's been around for centuries, used to promote everything from vaudeville shows to boxing matches. Perhaps its most iconic implementation was the ubiquitous Wanted poster. Despite its humble beginnings, over the years, the wild posting has become a popular and somewhat edgy method for national brands looking to raise awareness in the OOH market. It's also been a way for local bands looking to increase ticket sales, boost attendance, and acquire groupies.

Wild postings can be executed in many different ways — from large-scale posters to small handbills tiled across the space. Regardless of the size and content of the postings, however, the two main categories that all wild postings can be divided into are: with permission and without.

Going full-on guerrilla: Wild posting without permission

Although we advocate the medium, we don't always advocate the method. If you decide to go the route of not getting permission, beware: Although posting without permission is guerrilla to the core, this method can leave you with a mailbox full of expensive tickets and some strongly worded letters. Some municipalities have very strict rules restricting, and sometimes even forbidding, wild postings. In some cities, wild postings are lumped into the same category as "quality-of-life violations" (such as in New York City) or even vandalism, especially when executed on government or private property. Because it varies from city to city, your best bet is to start by checking with an agency or wild-posting vendor, then look to police and building departments and see what your options are, and make an educated choice from there.

We advocate going with a vendor for the reasons listed in the previous section. Although we're all too familiar with the expression "Sometimes it's easier to seek forgiveness than get permission," if you go it alone realize that you may have to plan on some groveling if your activities get picked up by the authorities. Fines and fees may result.

The best of both worlds: Permission to post wild

If you're interested in pursuing this media with permission, we strongly recommend working with an agency or vendor that's familiar with wild postings, and that can help you weigh your options about where, how long, and how expensive your buy should be. Working with wild-posting vendors has several advantages:

- ✔ **They can supply you with pre-secured locations that are expected to be available during the time period you're looking to buy.** Most pre-secured locations are on private property — places like construction site walls, scaffolding, parking garage fences, and sometimes even stores or buildings that lease their wall space facing a high-traffic street corner or intersection — which saves you from having to pay those oh-so-unpleasant fines.

- ✔ **They can assist with the production of the posters.** The costs of production, however, will still be on you.

- ✔ **They handle installation and maintenance of the posters.** This varies from agency to agency, but most will repair or replace your posters if they get torn or vandalized during the course of your media buy.

- ✔ **They will (or should) supply photo documentation at the conclusion of the campaign.** Although you may take the day off to tour the city and see your fabulous posters, you can't be everywhere. In light of this fact, ask your vendor to supply photo documentation. This'll give you proof that your posters actually were put up, as well as give you a record of your buy.

Frankly, although we strongly encourage the do-it-yourself spirit, wild-posting vendors already have the contacts and resources to make this approach as easy as possible for you. Plus, with the help of a vendor, you may even be able to do it cheaper than if you took to the streets yourself.

Use the Internet and colleagues to find agencies that include this service in their list of skills and capabilities. Keep in mind that the media is referred to as *wild posting, street postering,* and *sniping.* When you find some agencies you're interested in, ask how they go about executing the media and decide which route is right for you, your brand, and your budget.

When you're talking to a wild posting vendor, be sure to

- ✔ **Explain who you're trying to reach.**

- ✔ **Have a few suggested locations in mind.** The nice thing about guerrilla posting is that, if the location is available, you can pretty much pick the posting sites you want within a ten-block radius.

  If you're working with a vendor, they'll let you know their current inventory of available locations within the market, demographic considerations, and costs for each location (if they vary depending on placement and timing). Finally, they can give you guidance when it comes to selecting your location(s) based on your needs and budget.

- ✔ **Talk to the vendor about how long you want your postings to appear.** Most vendors offer options ranging from one week to several months. You can work with the vendor to tailor your campaign to meet your advertising needs and your budget.

- ✔ **Choose your "canvas".** Wild postings are traditionally sold in three different layouts:

  - Single showing: Usually consists of two posters per location.

  - Double showing: Usually consist of four posters per location.

  - Dedicated board: Exclusive ownership of the space, giving billboard appearance at a fraction of the price.

Make your own wild mosaic. If you have two or four different posters, play them off each other by alternating their placement. A checkerboard or other stimulating layout helps give you a more dynamic presence.

Most vendors want your program to be just as successful as *you* do, so make sure to ask for — and pay attention to — their feedback about what has been effective for their clients in the past.

Unique New York

To comment on New York's notoriously teeny apartments, Absolut Vodka partnered with Ikea to create an actual shoebox apartment, on its side. The ad space used real furniture affixed to the flat billboard space "floor" shaped like Absolut's signature bottle providing dynamic use of the billboard and co-branding for the two participating parties.

In a city where looking up is a cardinal sin (only tourists do that), the unusual sight had New Yorkers in awe as they scratched their heads and wondered, "How *do* they keep that bed from falling down?"

Here, two brands worked together in order to garner a significant amount of visibility, exposure, and press utilizing outdoor billboards in a way that really pops when stacked up against traditional use of this platform. It's also a great example of a mutually beneficial, cross-promotional partnership (see Chapter 19).

Billboards

You probably seen them everywhere you go. And even if you live in a town that bans them (as our editor does), if you've ever taken a road trip, you've seen dozens of them. What are they? Billboards. There are two main types of billboards, and we cover them in the following sections.

Living large: Outdoor billboards

The wild posting's swankier cousin is the outdoor billboard. *Outdoor billboards* are large wallscapes or free-standing structures, traditionally measuring around 14 x 48 feet. They're used to present a brand's message and artwork in a highly visible, unobstructed way.

Billboards are a more traditional method of advertising than, say, wild posting (see the preceding section). They're a very effective way to display your message to specific consumer sets, especially in city and suburban areas, where they enjoy captive audiences as people sit in stalled traffic on the highway. Through targeted placement, billboards allow you to reach a wide audience. Of course, with this higher visibility comes a larger price tag.

The guerrilla take is to look at the tried-and-true method and do it with a twist. In other words, if you're going to go with an outdoor billboard, ask yourself what you can do to make this (more expensive) presence stand out. For example, you may be able to add specialized lighting, video, or three-dimensional relief to serve as a stark contrast to the billboard for that fast-food restaurant at Exit 13. (For an example of a bold billboard, check out the "Unique New York" sidebar in this chapter.)

A moving experience: Mobile billboards

When you've come up with something truly magical for your billboard, the natural progression in nontraditional thinking is to take it on the road! That's where mobile billboards come in. *Mobile billboards* are flatbed trucks retrofitted with large signage units in the bed section, upon which custom advertising can be displayed.

You don't want your message whizzing down the freeway at 75 miles per hour — it'll be completely missed by consumers. So you need to be smart about where you choose to have your placards traveling. For the most effective exposure, target concentrated locations (such as urban areas or large, busy venues) where you can move more slowly and give people the chance to take in your campaign.

If you're interested in mobile billboards, talk to agencies in your area to find one that offers this weapon in its arsenal. Look to traditional outdoor-advertising vendors and see if they include this service in their offerings. If not, search online using keywords such as *billboard trucks, mobile billboards,* and *moving billboards* to find some leads. Ask how they execute the programs and how they prove or document performance; then carefully review rates and costs.

Check with local police precincts to find out about local sound ordinances, and, whenever possible add a sound component to your mobile billboard. Believe it or not, some people may miss a 10-x-20-foot billboard, but if they hear something first, it may be just what you need to turn some heads in your direction.

If your billboard will be traveling in a concentrated area where you know you want to target specific locations, you may want to consider pairing up your rolling signage with brand ambassadors, using the billboard as a backdrop for your street-level activities. (For more on brand ambassadors, street teams, and taking to the streets, turn to Chapter 6.)

Projections

When searching for different methods to display their messaging, some brands have seen the light with projections. *Projections* utilize a high-powered beam of light to throw a brand's logos or content against wallscapes or other flat surfaces. They're an eye catching, versatile way to present messaging after dusk.

More often than not, projections are executed guerrilla-style by an agency with the necessary equipment:

- ✔ A projector with the capabilities to throw the image 20 to 30 feet
- ✔ A laptop computer with the content that you're going to project
- ✔ An auxiliary generator supplying power to the setup on the street corner or out of a vehicle.

Although the effect of projections leaves consumers mesmerized, residents around the projections may be disgruntled by what some see as "intrusive advertising." The clattering of a generator usually doesn't do much to help ease these relations much either.

Recently, we've seen a smart, more-compact way to achieve similar results: handheld projectors, including the PixProjector. A computer and battery pack is discretely contained in a backpack worn by a street-team member, and the street-team member holds a handheld projector unit that throws selected images and videos on the wallscapes. This strategy enables brands to hit a variety of locations, interact with consumers, and press on if a local comes after them with a broom! PixProjector units are not currently available for sale, but you can rent them for your street teams. Go to www.pixman-usa.com/affiliates.html to find local agencies authorized to rent the units.

If you don't happen to have a high-powered projector to go traipsing around the streets, you may want to bring your projections in shop. A simple projector like the ones used in presentations can be set up inside your store or office on a vacant wall (or shot out of a window onto the sidewalk at night) to communicate your message at the speed of light!

Taxis, train stations, phone booths, and more

Earlier in this chapter, we cover many of the major media forms to present your message outdoors, but to the nontraditional thinker, the world is your oyster — or your ad space. In the following sections, we provide an overview of a few other popular outlets to reach your target as they're out and about.

There are several ways to go about advertising in (or on) these locations. In most cases, the agency holding the advertising rights will clearly tag the frame holding the ad with its company name, it logo, and maybe even its URL. If not, then a simple online search including the specific advertising platform you're interested in will no doubt yield a slew of results and opportunities.

Just because there isn't advertising on something doesn't mean there can't be. It may just mean that no one has picked up the phone and asked before. If you see a place around town that would be perfect to present your message, seek out the person who owns it and see if you can make a deal. Who knows? You may end up creating new media! (For more about creating new media, check out Chapter 11.)

Shelter for your message

Bus-shelter advertising is usually large-scale ads posted at bus shelters in locations selected to target a certain audience based on location. Bus-shelter ads are effective in reaching consumers because of their high visibility. Plus, the length of engagement with the waiting public is higher, enabling you to provide a little more copy with your message.

Busing your brand

Another way to get your message rolling is by advertising on the sides of buses. *Bus advertising* is the placement of branding or signage on the exterior of buses traveling targeted routes. Particularly in densely populated areas, bus advertising is an effective tool for sharing your message because the ad is on the street as long as that bus is in service, giving your brand repeated exposure as it makes its loop around town.

Taxi!

During rush hour, late nights, or lousy weather all eyes turn to the tops of taxis to see which ones are occupied and which ones are available. With all this attention, taxi tops make for an ideal surface to advertise. *Taxi-top advertising* is double-sided signage running the length of the taxi cab roof. Available in most markets, taxi tops can be adorned with catchy graphics, illumination, and digital video and sound (a recently added feature). Although the locations aren't as targeted as buses, because the taxi is required to go wherever the passenger requests, it ensures that your brand is constantly moving.

Going underground with subways and trains

Train and subway advertising is very loosely defined as branding within train and subway terminals. Depending on the rules set forth by local transit authorities, if you can afford it, you can brand it. Here are some examples of terminal advertising:

- ✔ **Train and subway platforms:** Ads can be placed on the walls or columns on the platform where passengers wait for the train.

- ✔ **In-car branding:** This can be as simple as strategically placed signage or completely branding the inside of the train car — by creating custom-themed wall-to-wall (and floor-to-ceiling) graphics that are applied to the inside of the car.

✔ **Terminal "ownership":** Not as final as it sounds, this involves complete branding of sections of train terminals. It includes — but has not been limited to — waiting benches, floor graphics, pillars, all traditional signage in a selected terminal, and so on.

Get trucking

Truck-side advertising, much as it sounds, involves the branding of the sides of large box trucks. Although you can execute these buys through media agencies, more and more independent owners (such as moving companies) are offering up their fleet of trucks for ad space as an additional revenue source.

If you notice that a certain company seems to frequently have its trucks in the neighborhood of your target, you may want to place a call and see if they can carry your message while they're at it.

Calling consumers who care

Although most Americans seem to rely on cellphones as their lifeline to the world, phone booths are still commonly seen on city street corners. This street-level presence makes for an ideal opportunity to reach consumers. Phone-booth advertising uses the panels making up the "booth" as surface to present brand messaging.

Pedal to the metal

With a raised awareness for environmental concerns, many businesses are looking for eco-friendly options to reach their demographic. Branded pedicabs and bicycle signage fill this need. *Pedicabs,* also known as *rickshaws,* are bicycle-powered taxis, the "cab" of which can be completely wrapped with custom branding. *Bicycle signage* consists of a tricycle design that pulls a 5-x-5-foot billboard; you can have the bicyclist target selected locations. Pedicabs are in business for themselves and carry your advertising as a source of additional revenue; bicycle signage is something that exists solely to display advertising.

Choosing the Form of Outdoor Advertising That's Right for You

You've made the calls, you've got the info, you're aware of the costs. Which form of outdoor advertising should you go with? After considering all your options and setting aside your knee-jerk reactions, it's time for a quick guerrilla checklist:

✔ **Does one form of outdoor advertising relate to your brand more than the other?** For example, if your brand is particularly aligned with eco-friendly initiatives, using pedicab advertising reinforces your commitment to the environment. Or if your storefront requires that consumers take a shuttle bus or train to visit you, advertising on or in these modes of transportation is an obvious choice.

✔ **Does one form of outdoor advertising work better to display your existing message over the others?** You need to select the medium that gives you the size and scope to best relay the message. Some forms of advertising allow customization that simply isn't available in other platforms. For example, if you want to present your message using lights or enhancements (see the "Unique New York" sidebar, earlier in this chapter), a billboard will likely be a better fit than a heavily trafficked subway car.

✔ **Is there a particular form of outdoor advertising that will bolster brand awareness within a select neighborhood or geographic region?** For example, you may want to consider advertising on buses with routes that you know will hit targeted neighborhoods and demographics at select times.

✔ **Perhaps the most important question: What can you truly afford?** At the end of the day, what you chose will likely come down to the price tag. Don't think of your budget as an obstacle — think of it as an opportunity to be creative with the platforms that you *can* afford. For example, maybe you can't afford that enormous billboard, but you *can* afford tiled wild postings in your demographic's backyard. Maybe you can't afford to post on the side of the city bus, but you *can* afford a few stickers placed on the local pedicab.

The big question is, "What do you want to achieve?" And the answer lies in finding cost-effective ways to get there.

We recommend that you shape what we refer to as a *strategic media mix,* where you combine selected initiatives with a street-level distribution campaign or event, so you can take the reach that these buys provide and bring it into a more personal, one-on-one interaction with your consumer.

You can use a variety of media platforms to reach a desired audience or overall goal. For example, say you've purchased a billboard space that you know will be seen by a certain group of people but that will miss another group. What other form of media can you use to catch those who may have fallen through the cracks of your billboard buy? To shape a media mix that's right for you, turn to Chapter 21.

Putting Rubber on the Road: Marketing Your Business Everywhere You Go

Getting your motor running, and hitting the road with your message can take on many forms. It can be as sweeping as wrapping a fleet of custom-branded luxury vehicles or as simple as slapping a sticker on the family minivan. Either way, mobile marketing gives you one more opportunity to reach a wide number of potential consumers while you conduct your daily business. In the following sections, we cover various forms of mobile marketing and how to get the most out of these opportunities.

Before you go spending tens of thousands of dollars to buy that urban assault vehicle you've been longing for, first take a gander at the vehicle potential already available to you. Do you have a company car that's synonymous and available for your brand? A cargo van? An SUV? An RV? A delivery truck? Or better still, a fleet (of three or more) of any of them? If so, you may have a platform to present your brand via your existing business resources.

Always look at the resources you have on hand before you think about spending more money.

If you've looked to your existing vehicles and the old jalopy is just not how you want to be perceived, it's all right — she's served you well. At this point, consider what vehicle may be a good fit for you and how you'd like to brand it.

Make sure your mode matches your message. If you have the resources, work to best match your mode of transportation to your brand's message. For example, if you run an organic tomato farm, using a hybrid SUV or biofuel vehicle to transport your veggies to market will keep your brand message consistent, and maybe even create something that's immediately identifiable with your brand.

After you've decided on which kinds of vehicle you'll use, you need to select the branding. The most popular form of vehicle branding is called *wrapping.* Wrapping a vehicle involves creating custom vinyl branding that's adhered to sections of the vehicle or the entire vehicle. Depending on whether you own the vehicle, this wrapping can be permanent or temporary for a specific campaign. And if you have a campaign for which you want to do something special, you may want to consider renting a unique vehicle and wrapping it specifically for the occasion.

If you wrap a rented vehicle, you'll want to be certain your vendor can take the wrap off when the campaign is complete. If it can, make sure you let both the car-rental agency and the wrap vendor know your intentions. Not all rental companies are okay with wrapping vehicles — even if the wrapping is completely removable.

If you decide to wrap your vehicles, you need to hire a wrapping professional to produce a template, design the artwork, print and produce the materials, and apply it to your vehicles. (Contact a nontraditional agency [see Chapter 5] or do a simple online search for vehicle wrapping to find someone who can help with this.) You can expect to spend $5,000 or more per vehicle for complete wraps, depending on the size of the vehicle.

Wrapping can be cost-prohibitive and, in some situations, downright unpractical. If wrapping won't work for you, you may want to look to custom magnets, decals, or roof toppers, which are far less expensive to produce and can be removed when it's time for the family's cross-country vacation. Your local printer should be able to do this for you or at the very least be able to put you in touch with someone who can.

The traveling strange: Rolling environments

Sure, wrapping vehicles and adding magnets are nice, but what if you want something *outstanding?* If you have the money to execute it, you're only limited by your imagination and local road rules (such as height clearance for interstate travel and other safety considerations).

In the past, the streets have seen horror-themed restaurants touring the town in ghoulishly outfitted hearses, large glass trucks with custom environments contained in their beds, and large trucks traveling with enormous LCD screens running brand content.

Some of these items are altered rentals and some of them are custom jobs produced for various companies. Although there are manufacturers who produce these tailored units, you may be just as far ahead by calling up a buddy who owns a body shop and is skilled with a welder.

Any way you slice it, the more unique your vehicle is, the greater the likelihood of turning a few heads and perhaps picking up some press along the way.

Chapter 10

Going Indoors

*Y*ou go to a movie with a date, and you see ads before the previews begin. You go for drinks with a pal, and you see an ad in the john. You go to the gym for a workout, and you see ads on the screen in the cardio theater. You buy groceries for Friday's party, and you see an ad on the grocery cart.

In order to reach your audience, you need to know who they are, what they do, and where they do it. Indoor marketing gives you the opportunity to select specific locations tailored to reach your consumers — and, if you're clever, you can do it in an innovative way.

Nontraditional marketing and media have transported us from advertising on the outside of a building to advertising inside that building's bathroom. You're able not only to show a commercial on someone's TV, but to show that same commercial inside that person's elevator at work and on a movie screen at his local theater. You can cherry-pick from the various forms of indoor media (perhaps complemented by outdoor media — see Chapter 9) to create a *strategic media mix* (the combination of various forms of available media to reach your target audience where they live, work, and play).

In this chapter, we identify some of the more popular indoor-marketing options available and fill you in on their effectiveness in reaching various demographics. Then we cover methods for shaping your indoor marketing to make it as specific and focused as possible.

Getting the Most Out of Advertising Indoors

Hitting them where they live, work, and play isn't the half of it when it comes to indoor advertising. Unlike advertising outdoors, which may be seen only in passing, indoor advertising often has the benefit of a stationary or captive audience.

Think about it: You're sitting at the food court of your local mall, and you can't help but read those little table tents as you scarf down your General Tso's chicken. Do you read those ads because you really, really need to hear about an upcoming event at the mall? No, you read them because they're right in front of you and you're looking to read *something*. The captive nature of this encounter enables the advertiser to form a longer connection with its target and the opportunity to present its target with more detailed information.

You know those days where you say to yourself, "I'm stressed — I need to go shopping" or, "Man, I need a laugh — I'm going to the movies"? The power of these impulses is far more effective than most people realize. You can hit consumers when they're in a shopping state of mind or a relaxed state of mind, and leverage their state of mind to promote your product or service by owning the consumers' attention in a unique space.

The venue creates a state of mind for the consumer. Shopping in a mall, socializing in a bar, enjoying entertainment-oriented content at a movie theater — just being in these spaces triggers certain associations in the consumers' minds. Use this information to present your product most effectively.

When you're looking to reach consumers indoors, you can do so in a variety of ways. Each of these platforms for indoor advertising is like another tool on your very own marketing tool belt. Need to reach teens? Pull a little mall advertising off the old belt. Really want to reach busy executives? Then it's time to snag that helpful elevator advertising to fix your message up and send it on its way.

In the following sections, we cover the major methods of indoor advertising, so you have the information to decide which methods are right for you.

Bar, restaurant, and restroom advertising

Another stressful week comes to a close and you've decided to treat yourself to a night on the town. So you call the usual suspects to meet up with you at the local watering hole. While you're out, your drink is served to you on a branded coaster, you place the branded swizzle stick on a logoed cocktail napkin, and the bartender is wearing a T-shirt promoting a noncompetitive brand. Feeling nature calling, you head to the loo. Once you arrive in the restroom, you see a large poster of attractive folks having what looks like an unreal amount of fun.

These are just a few of the ways that the marketing world has chosen to reach out to you — the consumer — while you're enjoying yourself at your local bar.

Advertising in bars, restaurants, and restrooms is nothing new. Back in the day, savvy salesmen left free newspapers above the urinals opened to their ads on the page. Over the years, the media has evolved — now those same ads talk, release cologne, and dispense samples.

In the following sections, we fill you in on the myriad ways you can reach your target audience in bars, restaurants, and restrooms.

Bellying up to the bar

Reaching consumers in bars and restaurants is a unique form of engagement, because the guests are usually relaxed and in the mood to have fun. When you're looking to produce marketing materials, this atmosphere offers more freedom to explore a variety of onsite possibilities and ad copy that may not be as well received in other venues.

Here are a few of the more popular ways to get yourself noticed:

- ✔ **Coasters:** Coasters are two-sided pieces of thick paper or cardboard that you can emblazon with a logo or brand. These inexpensive pieces are a great way to put your brand where your target has his eyes — on his drink.

- ✔ **Cocktail napkins:** Cocktail napkins are thin paper napkins, usually around 5 x 5 inches in size (when folded), which you can emboss with a company logo or ad copy.

- ✔ **Drink stirrers:** The plastic sticks used to stir drinks usually have a charm or brandable space at the top that you can use to share your logo.

✔ **Posters:** The prominence of posters has grown recently to the point where they're featured as part of the restroom and bar décor. The ad space is usually a 2-x-3-foot poster space sold through a network of restaurants or bars.

✔ **Table tents:** Table tents are small, 3-x-5-inch, two-sided cards placed on tables (much like a greeting card opened and placed on it's side). Consumers sit in front of them for a good length of time, so you can use a little more copy on them than you can on some of the other media.

Table tents generally aren't available in swankier establishments, so keep that in mind if you're trying to reach an up-market target audience.

✔ **Free giveaways:** Prominently used by liquor companies, this involves having brand ambassadors on-site in bars, giving out premiums (such as hats, towels, or T-shirts) and even free drink coupons in an effort to drive sales of a particular product. (For more on brand ambassadors and street teams, check out Chapter 6.)

After printing up your coasters, cocktail napkins, or drink stirrers, you may be able to negotiate with bars or restaurants to have them use them at no additional cost, because that's one less thing they have to pay for.

Although these are some great ideas for getting your brand in the minds of consumers, you may want to think about other opportunities to complement your advertising. For example, you may want to create a brand-centric game show that could be conducted at bars or restaurants, or you may want to arrange for giveaways at these establishments. Or perhaps tie into existing efforts at bars such as trivia contests, game nights, or other themed evenings. Bars in particular are open to these sorts of initiatives, as long as they don't hurt business and are enjoyable to patrons.

Hitting the john

The average person spends in the neighborhood of 40 minutes a day in the bathroom. It stands to reason that restrooms may be an ideal location in which to advertise.

According to a study conducted by Audits & Surveys Worldwide, and published in *Media Life* (April 28, 2003), 78 percent of consumers (in 14 locations in four major U.S. cities) recalled one or more restroom ads, 75 percent thought restroom advertising was "a good idea," 75 percent thought the ad was more noticeable than or equally noticeable to other forms of media, and 24 percent viewed a brand more positively after viewing a restroom ad.

Here are a few places to promote your business while your consumers are doing theirs:

- **Stalls:** Stall ads are exactly what they sound like: advertising placed inside restroom stalls. Although you may be able to enjoy your favorite tabloid rag on your throne at home, when consumers are out and about, they're looking for something to read. Why not give them your logo and messaging?

- **Urinals:** Urinal ads are placards placed at eye level above the urinals.

  Marc Miller, former president of New York–based InSite Advertising, said it best: "In a restroom for one to three minutes we own you. It's a liability to turn left or right at a urinal."

- **Urinal cakes:** Yes, you can even brand those. These are branded frames that hold deodorant urinal cakes. The frames can even be produced to "talk" when wet or tripped by a motion sensor, providing an audio opportunity to share your message.

- **Posters:** These are 2-x-3-foot posters usually placed next to the sink of the restroom. You've got to wash your hands and fix the coif, and this presents yet another chance to communicate your brand to the consumers.

Most (if not all) of the various media addressed in this section are brokered through a media agency that has exclusive deals with a network of bars and restaurants. The best thing to do is to choose a few bars and restaurants where you'd like to advertise and see what their existing opportunities are. One way to do this is to approach the venue directly to see if your desired opportunities are available; if they are, ask whether you can work with them directly or if you have to go through their preexisting media partner.

Now boarding: Your message

An airplane-themed restaurant created a new form of restroom advertising to help advertisers take off. As bar patrons entered the single-occupancy bathroom, they tripped a motion detector that began a looped audio advertisement mimicking an airplane safety demonstration. The announcement came complete with jet-engine sounds, pilot banter, and cleverly-slipped-in advertisements: "If you look to your left you'll find the sink, and if you look to your need for fashion you'll find Brand X clothing." The audio advertisements were amusing and unique, creating the opportunity to place a bug in the ears of bar patrons, even if they didn't get a fluffy pillow and salted peanuts out of the deal.

In-theater advertising

In-theater advertising is ads inside movie theaters, used to promote anything from a major studio's new film to a telecommunication provider's new cellphone. On a more local level, this media is particularly attractive to businesses trying to reach their local neighborhoods. Real estate agents, restaurants, and local service providers have been particularly effective in using this format to reach the locals.

Smartly, theaters have found a way to sell pretty much every inch of their space. They realize they have a captive audience and can offer advertising opportunities to their customers without infringing on or compromising the movie-going experience.

A recent Arbitron Cinema Advertising study found that most moviegoers do not mind the advertising that appears in the theater before the movie begins.

Some of the popular formats to reach cinephiles include the following:

- ✔ **Popcorn bags and concessions:** What would going to the movies be without a bucket of popcorn, a vat of soda, and your brand! Although costly, you can advertise on the soda cups or popcorn bags. The minimal runs are very high, so this technique is usually used by movie studios or other big spenders.

- ✔ **Lobby displays:** Theaters have a wide array of advertising opportunities in their lobbies — everything from cardboard cutouts, to banners, to enter-to-wins.

- ✔ **On-screen slides and videos:** Whether it's a preshow slide for a local service or a quick trailer, on-screen advertising provides you with a captive audience for your brand.

Brands like this in-theater advertising for a number of reasons. You can target the neighborhood you want to reach, and depending on the style of theater, it's pretty easy to see if the demographic matches the brand or product you're promoting.

Who to call usually depends on which theater you want to advertise in. Many of the larger chains have their own in-house sales teams, while some of the smaller chains or independents work with a variety of vendors or handle the sales in house. The first stop is to go to the movie theater's Web site and contact the marketing department. You'll be able to quickly find out whether you can work with the venue directly or need to speak with their media agency.

You may want to do a tie-in with in-theater advertising. For example, say you own a nice Italian restaurant a few blocks from a popular theater. You may want to create your own dinner-and-a-movie campaign in which your ad informs consumers that, if they show their ticket stub, they'll get a free glass of wine with their dinner. Adding this call to action also provides an opportunity for you to measure your campaign see just how effective your ad really is. (For more on calls to action, turn to Chapter 6.)

Commuter stations and more

Whether you're looking to catch the business traveler or a busy mom, looking to locations where these people spend their time can be the key to the success of an indoor marketing campaign.

Commuter hubs

Travel hubs often make for perfect locations to reach your target demographic. Why? A few reasons:

- ✔ **Specificity:** You already know whether your messaging will be effective in your area because you know their destination. If you want to target people who are going to a specific suburban area for example, simply pick advertising at the terminal that takes commuters to that location.

- ✔ **Frequency:** One of those silly marketing words people like to toss around, *frequency* is the number of times your message will appear before consumers. If you're presenting your message at a commuter hub, you can bet on the fact that your consumers are going to experience your brand at least twice a day, coming and going. Multiply that times the number of months that your ad stays up, and you've made quite the impression.

- ✔ **Engagement:** With delays, connections, and so on, the amount of time that consumers have to experience your brand is higher. For this entire time, you've got your captive audience and you have the opportunity to tell them a little about your service or product.

For these reasons, airports, flights, trains, buses, and light-rail terminals can make for perfect platforms for advertising opportunities. The forms of media vary from hub to hub and market to market. At this level, most if not all of the advertising is handled by a media agency that takes care of sales on the terminal's behalf.

Tapping into these platforms can be much easier than you may think. Sometimes it involves just looking at the small print. Most of these platforms feature the name of the media agency's name and the contact information right on the ad. If you can't locate it, reach out to the venue's marketing department and they should be able to steer you in the right direction.

Health clubs

Maybe you're looking to reach the sporty, the health conscious. It's time to get physical and place your message where your fitness fanatics reside: gyms and health clubs. Brands that can be easily associated with the health, fitness, beauty, and fashion industries can benefit from a presence at these locales.

The opportunities available depend on the gym. With mom-and-pop gyms, you may be limited to only a few postering opportunities. Larger chain gyms may be able to provide you with more opportunities, such as advertising on screens in the cardio theaters, hosting events in the gym, providing samples of your product to members, and so on.

The first step to seeing what's out there: Walk up to the front desk of the gym where you want to advertise and ask to speak to someone about advertising there.

Supermarkets

People have to eat, so eventually they're going to end up at the grocery store. Many businesses overlook how effective advertising in supermarkets can be. Supermarkets are locations where consumers are already in a shopping state of mind, which means they're open to brand messages.

Aside from a general receptiveness, you're also directly reaching out to the people who make the day-to-day choices in household purchases. Winning over the person with the pocketbook could earn you a customer for life.

Some ways to get your message to your target include the following:

- **Leaflets, magazines, and circulars:** You may curse all those circulars you get in the mail or dropped at your doorstep, but you receive them for one simple reason: They work.

- **Displays:** One of the most prominent ways to expose shoppers to products is in-store and aisle-end displays. With this footprint, you're able to share messaging and display your product at the same time.

- **Shopping carts:** Although not always as effective as other methods, another way to reinforce your brand is by advertising directly on shopping carts.

✔ **In-store TVs:** In many of the newer supermarkets, TVs have been installed in aisles as well as the checkout lines as yet another platform to make shoppers aware of sales or featured products.

✔ **Product demonstrations and samples:** In-store product demonstrations have proven to be effective in reaching older demographics. This opportunity is also extremely effective when sampling food. Really, who's not going to stop for free pigs-in-the-blanket samples?

✔ **Checkout counters:** You ever notice how all the good candy bars are placed right there at the checkout lane? This is a last-ditch effort for the impulse buy. Signs placed at the checkout counter are part of the same school of thought. This is the parting shot, one final opportunity to persuade your target to purchase a specific product. You may consider branding cash-register receipts and maybe even the shopping bags themselves.

Shopping malls

Shopping malls are not just the spot where teens go to hang out and discuss the latest school gossip. Shopping malls are an outstanding platform to reach out to specific communities at large. Once again, most people come to the mall because they're looking to spend some money, and are open to hear about the latest and greatest your company has to offer.

Advertising opportunities that are available within the venue include, but are not limited to:

✔ **Large backlit panels:** These large backlit units are usually located around the entrances of the mall. They're conspicuous structures, creating a nearly unmissable first impression as consumers enter.

✔ **Monitors:** The availability of monitors running commercials varies from market to market, but they're commonly seen at the information desks of most malls.

✔ **Graphics on floors, doors, elevators, and escalators:** Much like movie theaters, malls have become quite adept in making nearly every surface a branding opportunity. Custom graphics placed in a variety of locations are extremely effective tools to help raise awareness for your business.

✔ **Tray liners and napkins:** While you're enjoying the gooey deliciousness of your seven-layer burrito in the food court, you may not notice that there are branding opportunities all around you. The tray liner (which caught that extra guacamole) and napkins are additional opportunities to get your message in front of consumers.

Most malls have done much of the market research for you. Call the marketing department of the malls you're interested in to get the inside scoop on the daily foot traffic for that mall, the gender breakdown, the average household income, and other factors. This information will help your choose which malls to advertise in and the methods to use there.

Choosing the Option That's Best for You

Before you select your method of delivery, take a critical look at your product or service and narrow your vision of how you'd like your brand to be perceived. Because indoor advertising offers the potential for a longer period of interaction with your consumers, you want to make sure that the way you're presenting your message is as effective as what you're saying.

Consider the following questions:

- **Is there a venue or locale that is particularly relevant to your brand? What locations can be directly associated with your product or service?** For example, if you're marketing your own homemade energy drink, you may want to start by reaching out to gyms and health clubs to explore advertising and sampling opportunities.

- **What forms of media have piqued your interest in the past?** If in the past a form of media has caused you to do a double-take and think to yourself, "That'd be the perfect fit for my business," honor your own good advice and throw that format into the mix.

- **Are there noncompetitive brands or venues that you can partner with or that you'd like to be associated with?** Partnering up with a brand that isn't in competition with you but has access to your target consumers is always a good idea — especially if that brand makes yours look a little more impressive. Partnering up gives you the opportunity to double your exposure and your resources. (For more on partnering, see Chapter 18.)

- **Are there media platforms that you *don't* want to be associated with?** There's a somewhat snobby expression in the marketing world: *down brand.* In plainspeak that means that the concept or form of media is not in step with (or is beneath) the brand. If you own a jewelry store, advertising with talking urinal cakes probably doesn't reflect the luxurious impression you've worked hard to create. You're far too classy for that. But if you're trying to promote an anti-DWI campaign, talking urinal cakes may be just perfect for you. The key is looking over all the opportunities — both novel and more traditional — to make sure that they best reflect the image of your brand and reach your potential clientele.

- **How long do you want your messaging to appear?** The effectiveness of your ad can definitely be shaped by the amount of time it appears. Do you want to have weekly, monthly, or yearly exposure? Do you want to do seasonal ads?

- **What forms of advertising are within your budget?** You may have come up with some incredible ideas for various ways to use indoor media, however if your eyes are bigger than your budget you may end up disappointed. Just keep that in mind before you plan your entire campaign around a piece of media you may not be able to afford or execute correctly.

Producing Location-Specific Artwork

You've surveyed available places to advertise, and you've decided on one or more locations. Now it's time to have some fun!

If you have the resources, try to produce media that is as specific to each location as possible. Nail down a few of your given circumstances and your goals. Where are you presenting your message? Who do you want to see it? Ultimately, what do you want the ad to motivate them to do? What state of mind are they in when they view it? What kind of tone do you want to take with your ad? Is there something unique about the venue (for better or for worse) that you can play off of?

In the following sections, we give you an overview of some thoughts to consider when creating your indoor campaign. As always, we hope this ignites a spark of creativity that you can maximize when considering the platform and location of your message.

Considering your surroundings

Some ads and copy are better suited for certain types of media. Chances are, you're not going to present the same ad in a restroom at a male-centric bar that you would produce at a more family-friendly mall. Considering the location will help to inform the tone of your ad.

We're always fans of using humor as often as possible. Is there something unique about where you're positioning your ad that can be related back to your brand? Is there a common frustration that you can commiserate with your consumers over? Is there something about the venue that is famous that you can play off of when presenting your brand? Keep your brand in mind through this process and it'll help steer you in the right direction.

For example, you may want to play off the close proximities in train and subway advertising: "Work may stink, but it's got nothing on the guy next to you who isn't wearing Smells Fresh deodorant." In bars, you can play off the fact that libations are involved: "He'll look cuter after another Amber Ale."

Acknowledging your target

As you come up with clever, location-specific copy and ads, keep your target in mind. Although we're fans of using laughs to communicate your message, if your joke is at the expense of the very people you're trying to sell to, your ad is no good.

Depending on which location or form of media you use, you may have the opportunity to share more copy or more involved messaging. If this is the case, be smart about how you make the case for your brand. What is your target's state of mind at the moment? Put yourself in the shoes of your target, and this will help inform what type of ad or offer they'll respond to best.

Getting crafty

A few of the outlets we cover in this chapter (specifically travel hubs and certain theater advertising) can have hefty sticker prices. If this is the case with some of the media you want to use, consider it a challenge!

Your challenge is to find other ways to go about getting in. Approach the venues about producing the materials and providing them for free in exchange for saving them production or purchase costs. This could be applied to things like after dinner mints at restaurants or baby booster seats at a movie theaters. What can you produce at a relatively low cost that alleviates one of the venue's expenses and simultaneously gets your message out to your consumers of choice?

If you're working on a tight, tight budget and you just don't have the funds, another way to leverage some on-site awareness and exposure is to produce window cards. Many local vendors such as eateries, barber shops, laundromats, and so on see these posters as added value to customers and the community.

Come together, right now, over your brand. The most effective messages are the ones placed in locations your consumers congregate. Consider places where potential customers in your own backyard gather and approach these venues to create one-of-a-kind marketing opportunity.

Chapter 11

Using and Innovating New Media

Guerrilla marketing requires you to wear many hats. All at once, you have to be a logistics engineer, a covert operator, a production supervisor, a location scout, a number cruncher, a partnership diplomat, and more. Perhaps the most challenging and creatively involved role of all is that of the innovator.

In this chapter, we help you find your inner innovator by using the latest and greatest approaches to reach your consumers. We offer our own ideas to keep you sharp and ahead of the curve. We do this by sharpening your senses so that you notice opportunities around you — opportunities you haven't explored — as well as new twists on media that you may think of as commonplace. From there, we play a matching game to see if what you want to do fits your product and message. Finally, we step into the world of owning new media and techniques, and making it work for you. Creativity has its benefits and you should be able to enjoy them all. In this chapter, we help you do exactly that.

Staying Competitive by Staying Ahead of the Curve

Throughout this book, we tell you that being an effective guerrilla marketer involves approaching, presenting, and connecting with consumers in a fresh and unexpected way. This ambitious charter is quite the challenge! With everyone pursuing essentially the same goal, how do you make your brand or service stand out from the crowd? The answer lies in innovation.

Often, when people hear the word *innovation,* their minds jump to images of lab-coat-clad researchers tinkering away with steaming beakers, just a few steps away from shouting "Eureka!" Fortunately for the scientifically-disinclined among us, the power of innovation doesn't usually lie in beakers and Bunsen burners — the *real* power is in the idea. Coming up with an original way to get your message across, or just a clever twist, is the key to discovering a marketing breakthrough.

One of the things that makes us get out of bed in the morning and into those early brainstorming sessions before the java kicks in is the idea that we could very well create a brand-new form of media. *New media* is a new platform or approach that effectively connects with consumers.

To think that all those crazy ideas you had swimming in your head, when applied appropriately may just be "the next big thing" is uniquely inspiring. The potential is there — it really is all about harnessing your creative energies to effectively serve your brand in a way that has never been done before.

Guerrilla marketing and nontraditional media give advertisers great flexibility. In fact, advertising has become so flexible and diverse that using existing media to present yourself is difficult, let alone endeavoring to create something new.

This is the challenge of guerrilla marketing —how clever can *you* be to stand out amongst your competition? Do you want to create something as tame as branding a unique structure or get wacky and design "interesting branding" on the torso of your buddy, Ted? Because they're both doable and if clever enough, potentially press-worthy. Doing so also allows you the chance to put your message in a completely uncluttered medium that your brand can dominate and own.

You can't create anything new if you don't know what's been done. When you're trying to adopt a new approach to share your product or service, look to your industry and related industries for hints about what's worked. Take in competitors campaigns and analyze what knocked your socks off, what was okay, what bombed, and why. Then look outside your industry. The stickiness factor with marketing campaigns really depends on whether the efforts matched the brand. Sometimes a business will create some messaging and present it in a truly clever way, but the association is lost or doesn't seem to gel with consumers' impressions of the brand. This may be an opportunity that you can capitalize on, by taking the creative germ, tailoring it to serve another brand or product, and earning those accolades your rightly deserve.

Making Your Mark on Existing Media

We don't mean to give mixed messages, but sometimes it's not about reinventing the wheel — it's just about steering the car in a completely different direction. Often, the most effective nontraditional media efforts make the greatest impression by taking existing media that's been seen as ho-hum and finding a zippy, clever way to reintroduce it.

If you decide to go this route, you'll be entering into the exciting realm of media one-upmanship. May the best idea win! One of the reasons that guerrilla marketing and nontraditional media have thrived is that this healthy competition has created a vibrant environment where media is constantly evolving to meet advertiser demand and fickle consumer interest.

You only need to look to a few of the major forms of existing media to see the progression from small brand tadpole to upright-man-media:

- ✓ **Print:**

  - Infancy: Newspapers and magazines begin running ads. The audiences are wowed by the latest fashion, but picture-quality black-and-white images leave much to be desired.

  - Adolescence: Printing technology improves, presenting consumers with glossy pages that shimmer, images that are crisp and appealing, perforated tear-off pages and sub cards that fall out at inopportune times reminding you to subscribe to the magazine or take advantage of the sale at Waustrom's.

  - Adulthood: Complete and utter brand immersion. Fragrant pages delight the senses, branded bands hug the outside of the publication, and logo-emblazoned sealed poly bags shield the magazine and the free advertiser CD/DVD contained within.

- ✓ **Billboards:**

  - Infancy: The basic board along the side of the road featuring minimal color and basic brand messaging.

  - Adolescence: The colors become more vibrant. Messages on a roll shift to give the messages movement and make them eye catching.

  - Adulthood: Full-blown LCD screens able to showcase messaging, video clips, focused consumer-specific audio, and cellphone messaging communicated through infrared technology.

Have magazine will travel

One crafty car company wanted to give away its cars, but that's no way to run a business. So instead the company took out ads in select magazines. Readers could tear out a perforated piece of cardstock that could be folded to build their own little car. The tiny auto could then live on their desk at work or placed over the mantle at home — thereby giving the magazine's readers an experience unlike anything else in the magazine and subsequently the distribution of a premium with a long shelf life. (For more on branded premiums and giveaways, turn to Chapter 6.)

✔ **Television:**

- Infancy: Television is created and basic black-and-white commercials are produced to pitch products.

- Adolescence: The screens grow in size, color, and clarity and are placed in homes, offices, schools, gyms, you name it. Consumer reach increases dramatically.

- Adulthood: The message becomes mobile. The screens can now be strapped to the chest or adorned above the head of a guerrilla on the ground, able to share messaging with consumers, engage in onsite acquisition, and give a personal touch to TV marketing efforts.

Although these are common and perhaps somewhat obvious evolutions, the growth isn't slowing. Right now, some ambitious young whippersnapper is dreaming up new ways to reinvent existing mediums. Much like that whipper-snapper, you can examine what you see in the market and think about ways those media can be reimagined or reintroduced to make your message stand out from the competition. (For more on breaking through the clutter, check out the "Have magazine will travel" sidebar, in this chapter.)

Never judge your imaginings or assume they can't be done. Shooting off that e-mail or picking up the phone to inquire about your ideas may end up positioning you to reach consumers in an exciting new way!

Taking Advantage of Your Surroundings: Monopolizing Existing Resources

Reaching your consumers in new ways can sometimes be as simple as taking inventory of the things that you already have at your disposal. Take on the role of the discerning non-traditionalist and see opportunities in the everyday.

What surrounds you, your work, and your customers? Here a few things you may have about your establishment that could be rebranded to help spread your message:

- **Shopping bags:** Brand your shopping bags for impact. If you can't afford custom bags, see if you can drop coupons or flyers in each bag to get the most out of the opportunity.

- **Staff:** If you have employees who interact with the public, they should be decorated in your brand. If appropriate, costume them — but don't go crazy or you may have mutiny on your hands.

- **Property:** What do you own that can be branded? An empty wall? An awning? Can you brand a parking space with your logo and "Park Here for Savings" or some other appropriate copy? The more creative, the greater the impact.

- **Trade-specific equipment:** If your business sells something interesting (or not so interesting) or utilizes equipment specific to that industry, brand it and play off of it. Imagine the fun you could have creating branding for a cement mixing truck! What works for your brand?

- **Sound:** Nothing attracts people like sounds that make them feel like an event or something unique is happening. What resources do you have at your disposal to create this effect? An in-house sound system and phone hold music could be yet another opportunity to reach out in an exciting way. What creative ideas can you come up with beyond announcing the yellow-light special and mind-numbing hold Muzak?

- **Blank space:** What areas do you have available in your store? Floors need floor mats, counters need covers, walls need banners, and all these things need to be branded. After you've explored available opportunities, look into which ones have never been used for advertising before. Of the ones that have been used before, how can you do it differently?

If you're like us, you get the momentum going and everything is suddenly an opportunity. We're not saying go nuts and brand every inch of your store or place of business. What we are suggesting is that you take a look around from the point of view of a guerrilla, and see what, if anything you can do to stand out from your competition and connect with your customers.

Figuring Out and Communicating Your Message

In this constantly evolving landscape of new media, the onus is on you to come up with some exciting, new, and unexpected way to share your brand messaging. Different businesses have tackled this responsibility in different ways. We cover some of these ways in the following sections.

No matter which method you choose, be sure to run through the following quick checklist of things that will help make this message and this media a reality:

- **What would help you say what you want?** What permissions, vendors, materials and other resources will you need to make your new media happen?

- **Are the materials to present this new media available?** If you find you need permission, who do you have to talk to secure it? What's your contingency plan if the materials aren't available (or don't exist)? Can you find an alternative or create your own?

- **Is it legal?** Especially if you're trying to produce something edgy, check in with local law enforcement and see if what you want to do is legal. Producing your new media may only cost you $100, but the fines for violating local laws could cost you ten times that or have you serving hard time instead.

Appealing to emotions

People remember a message, image, or expression if they can connect it to an emotion. The question when figuring out your message then becomes, "What emotion do you want to illicit and how will you go about achieving it?"

There's freedom in limitations. Although it's hardly an axiom to start a revolution with, when creating a new way of presenting your message, you need to pinpoint what you have to say, who you want to say it to, and how you want it to be heard.

For example, say you own the quirky Squeaky Kleen Oil Filters Company, which makes oil filters for race cars and other high-performance autos. You need to consider

- **Who uses your product?** Most likely, it's male car owners who work or dabble in the racing or auto industries. They're 30-plus, have an average household income (HHI) of $30,000 or more .

- **Where are the people who use your product?** Catching consumers where they work and play is a great place to start. So you may decide to look to auto shops or — to reach the greatest numbers at one time — racing events.

- **What do you want to say to them, and how you can reach them in an exceptional way?** Taking into account the locations and your target audience, perhaps you can call in a little sex appeal. What if you take an attractive female model and, using creative costuming (complete with Squeaky Kleen branding, of course) and makeup, create a walking side-by-side comparison of Squeaky Kleen versus Brand X by visually splitting her down the middle. On one side of her body, you have the picture of clean purity and attractiveness much like the Squeaky Kleen product (white tank top showcasing the brand, shimmering hair, and so on); on the Brand X side, she has messed up hair, oily-looking makeup, and distressed, yucky clothing.

Is it silly or inappropriate? Who's to say? Racing events are infamous for taking advantage of every iota of available ad space. Maybe getting a little silly and creating this unique way of presenting a brand is exactly what's called for to make your message stand out in an environment teeming with brands, all screaming to receive consumer attention.

Flying under the radar: Stealth marketing

Stop us if you've heard this one before: A man walks into an upscale hotel bar. A lone business traveler sidles up, orders a drink, and opens his laptop to study his notes for the following day's big pitch. Across the bar, an attractive young lady is clearly giving him eyes. Confidently, she strides over and asks if she can buy him a drink — but *she* picks the drink. The man accepts and chats up the young lady. She starts telling him about how this particular brand of booze is her favorite. As the conversation continues, she peppers it with how delightful her cocktail is. Suddenly, she's called away by pressing business, but she coyly thanks the man for the conversation and reminds him to enjoy that drink.

Is this gentleman simply irresistible? That could be, but it could also be that this man was the target of *stealth marketing,* creating a personal engagement with a brand through subtle, positive, and usually covert contact. This highly targeted platform involves producing opportunities for consumers to connect with your brand by creating positive associations and experiences with it

Stealth marketing and advertising takes many forms. It can be actresses placed in strategic locations with conspicuously branded shopping bags openly discussing a new brand that's the next big thing. It can be company boxes placed around locations with a "delivery man" commenting on how busy he's been delivering this brand lately. The form of stealth marketing you use is dictated by your audience and the way you want your brand to be perceived.

The debate about stealth marketing is ongoing, even among the authors of this book. There are two schools of thought on this one: The first is that this platform — in whatever permutation it takes — is deceptive, misleading, and a little creepy. The other suggests that it's simply another form of targeted media — no harm, no foul.

Whichever camp you're in, "stealth" as it is commonly referred to, is quintessential guerrilla. It's targeted, relatively inexpensive, and is another way to get your message out. It's worthwhile to note however that many organizations (both in the advertising industry and out) feel uneasy about this method as a means of professionally and ethically conveying a message to consumers.

Stealth doesn't have quite the reach that other forms of media may have. And if it backfires or your cover is blown, the repercussions could be quite serious. For example, if you're outed to consumers for using stealth as a means of marketing, some of them may feel deceived or betrayed by a brand that they may otherwise trust or feel a sense of loyalty to.

In your face: Creating messaging consumers can't miss

When you're trying to come up with methods for presenting your brand, consider where the eyes already are. Is there something unique about your product or service that draws people's attention?

If you own a deli with a "now serving" ticker, that ticker may be an ideal place to tag with some fun copy or branding, such as "Number 41 is now experiencing quality cold cuts." The more creative you can be, the greater impact your messaging will have.

One agency decided to take their clients' message to where guys' eyes shamelessly wander by offering branding on ladies' bums. To do this, the agency hired lovely ladies as ambassadors for the brands, and printed up tasteful custom underwear with client logos on their backsides. Then the ladies took to the field. With a simple, "Look here, boys," the staffers would flip up their skirts and display the branded britches to the delight of male onlookers. The racy platform isn't for every client, but it was something male consumers (and the press) couldn't resist talking about.

Playing a variation on the theme

Whether you're heading up a worldwide operation or a local mom-and-pop establishment, just because you're looking to present your message in a new medium doesn't mean you have to throw the baby out with the bathwater. Many companies have existing marketing and advertising materials that are already extremely effective. You can take what already works and present it in a different way.

Local businesses many times have jingles, characters, or taglines that are immediately identifiable to that company. Play off this regional or national notoriety and present it in a new way. For example, maybe you have a catchy jingle that no one can get out of his head. Maybe you can contract a local ice cream truck to play your jingle on its route as opposed to its usual selections. If you have a mascot or character unique to your brand, you may consider dressing up an actor as your character and sending him out to casually do everyday activities, like enjoying a caramel macchiato at a coffee shop, reading a paper on a park bench, or waiting on the corner for the next cross town bus.

According to that old saying, "If it ain't broke, don't fix it." We agree — but seeing how else it might work can be a fun and effective way of extending the reach of proven marketing resources.

Creating an Ad

If you know your way around a photo-editing program (like Photoshop), you can certainly come up with something for your ad. However, oftentimes for the media outlined in this chapter, agencies or vendors will either help you or ask that you supply art in a specific format, to fit the template of the method you're looking to produce.

Whether you decide to flex those creative muscles or let the vendor do the work for you, avoid small copy and too many dark colors. Depending on the media, you've only got a glance to make your impact — make sure you can get the most out of this exposure.

Trust your instincts. If you're not 100 percent sold on the finished product, take some time to work on the ad. Run it by your colleagues, friends, or family, and refine it until you're happy. You're the consumer in this situation, you can play the "fussy client card" if need be.

Defining your vision

Boring ads? You deserve better. The saturation factor for many of the media formats in this chapter can be very high, depending on the market — consumers are being bombarded with ads, and you want yours to stand out. It's on you to create something unique with a clear objective.

What do you want from the consumers after they view your ad? Do you want consumers to log on, call, visit a venue, or simply have a raised awareness about your product or service?

After you've identified the goal, think about how you'll communicate this in an exciting way. Will you "tease" the consumer about a product to be revealed at a later date? Shock them? Make them laugh? Appeal to a certain sensibility? Be as clever as your brand will allow — it's the only way to stand out.

It's always effective when the creative plays off the media. For example, on a taxi topper, you may have the copy, "This fare longs for heated bucket seats. —LaRouche Luxury Autos."

Working with designers

If you don't have an eye for design, you need to reach out to a graphic designer. Acknowledging that you need help is a good thing — designers can help lay out an image or message, clarify your creative ideas, and then format it to meet specific requirements for your buy.

Ask for steady updates from the designer about the progress of the design, so that if your designer goes off-message, you aren't stuck at the buy deadline with an ad that you hate. Maintaining a free flow of constructive feedback will ensure an outstanding piece of art, produced in a timely, cost-effective manner.

You've wrapped on your art and you're over the moon. Before you bid your designer adieu, make sure you get electronic files of all the versions of your artwork, any fonts (especially if you purchased new or custom ones), and any templates needed to design future materials. This strategy is not ruthlessly preying on the fruits of your designer — this is about looking out for your brand and providing yourself with the information to produce consistent future designs.

Sometimes using a media agency or vendor designers for your ad can cost you beaucoup bucks. Instead, do some research and see if you can find a freelance designer or design student who will do the job for cheap (or free) to help build her portfolio. Be sure to get some samples of the person's work beforehand, though, just to make sure you'll be happy with the results.

Figuring Out the Placement

After examining what you want to say and how you want to present your new media, you need to consider where you want to place it. Sometimes placement is completely appropriate and geared toward hitting your target audience where you know they'll be. Other times, it's all about selecting a venue that has never been explored before for one purpose only: to get some ink.

Dot-com, Oregon

In 1999, one dot-com company was looking to increase consumer awareness of its service. How did the company achieve this goal? By buying the name of a city, of course. That's right, for the price of $100,000 and 20 new school computers the town of Halfway, Oregon, was renamed Half.com, Oregon for one year. The move proved mutually beneficial. Half.com owned the name of a town and garnered immeasurable press and exposure, while the small, rural town came out of the deal with computers and coin in the county coffers.

The key to getting some ink is communicating your message in a form or location that deviates from anything that has ever been done before. Sometimes where it's being presented is the innovation itself.

For example, a software company was launching its new operating system. It was doing a full-scale media blitz and was hungry for exciting platforms to present their messaging. With nearly unlimited financial resources, it was able to "own" most major markets, but it wanted some new media to get the maximum reach out of its efforts. To answer this call, the company took to the fields and had its logo cut into crops fields across the country so that the logo would be visible from the air; then it leaked news of these crop circles, er, logos to news outlets for aerial coverage. This platform has gone on to be used to promote a host of brands since then.

Money talks — and this is especially apparent when it comes to product messaging. Over the past few years, we've seen branding take on a life of its own. Although we'd like to keep with the guerrilla creed that anything is *possible*, the slightly cynical tongue may say it's more fitting to intone that anything is *for sale*. (For more on money talking, look to the "Dot-com, Oregon" sidebar.)

Getting Exposure by Inventing New Media

Let's be honest: There's only so much news out there to cover. There's only so many times you can read about how Old Man Humphries will destroy any ball that comes over his fence. The media needs to share something exciting with their viewers or readers, something they've never heard before.

That something new and exciting may just be your new form of media. The essence of new media is producing effective, interesting ways to increase consumer exposure for your brand.

Here are a few initiatives done to tickle the press's fancy:

- ✔ British college students sold advertising space on their foreheads for a rate of about three bucks an hour.

- ✔ In Copenhagen, for around $750, you could push your product on a baby carriage.

- ✔ Eligible bachelors across the country have utilized billboard trucks to help them find their mates. One guy who had a board outside his home got more than 60 replies within a month.

As we see it, as long as it's consensual, there's nothing wrong with the increased pervasiveness and creativity of advertising — especially when that creativity is rewarded by media exposure that can positively benefit the product or image of the company.

Also, when you think about these new media platforms pragmatically, it's certainly cheaper than other forms of marketing. For example, in that example of the British college students selling ad space on their foreheads, getting access to coveted influencers in the 18- to 24-year-old age group, for $24 for a day of exposure is pretty much a steal.

Bottom line: Getting a little kooky with available places to advertise lets businesses have some fun with the world around them, creates invaluable opportunities for press, and gives people something to talk about other than cranky Old Man Humphries.

Although more "gimmicky" advertising is certainly fun to see, read, and talk about, tread cautiously if you decide to pursue this path to promote your product. Flashy tools may garner press, but you may find that it's the method and not the message that gets the coverage. The travesty would be spending the money, getting the coverage, and never reaping the benefits. Will anyone remember *who* or *what* was advertised on foreheads, baby carriages. and dogs? Plus, although new ideas may generate interest, there can be backlash. What if this new platform is seen as offensive? Is this how you want your product to be perceived?

Take the time to make sure that if you pursue something wacky, the other things they're saying about you and your efforts are nice as well.

Making opportunities for exposure

You've crafted a new form of media. Maybe it's taking advantage of something unique to your business. Or *maybe* it's something so wackadoo that you *know* there's got to be someone somewhere who needs to know about your platform. How can you let other businesses in on your innovation and, in turn, benefit from a new source of revenue?

✔ **Let noncompetitive brands try it for free (or cheap).** You've got to start that momentum somehow. Why not try letting a noncompetitive brand try it at cost or for free. If there's no overhead for you to produce the medium, let them give it a dance on the house. By doing so, you may find a loyal customer. Or, at the very least, you may find a client who you can say tried your medium or partnered with you. Doing so gives you the opportunity to refine the media, get quotes from a "satisfied customer," and gain some credibility in the field.

You've created a medium that you are incredibly proud of. Maybe that sense of pride just won't let you give it away, even for the increased exposure. If so, default to the barter system — exchange goods or services. That way, you get the exposure and some nifty perks along the way.

✔ **Publicize your new medium in trade publications and e-blasts.** People talk. Spread the word to people who may be interested in your new platform. Look to trade resources — advertise in the classifieds or see if you can't convince your trade publication to do a feature on your efforts. Finally, send out a mass e-mail to let people know what you've created! Aunt Sue may have no use for the fact that you can brand alligator tails, but her girlfriend Jean's CEO son just may have a use for such an outlet. You won't know unless you get the word out.

Finally, keep in mind that sometimes this approach is more about being the first to market — it may not be the tool that sustains your marketing goals and objectives for years to come. So don't go planning your five-year marketing plan around a platform that may end up being a flash in the pan.

Owning Your Innovation

You can create the greatest thing since sliced bread, a form of media that has never been done before, but if you don't take steps to put your mark on it, all your wonderfully creative efforts could be in vain.

Inspiration doesn't come easy, so when you produce something truly different, truly exceptional, you need to legally and commercially secure your position as its creator. Here's how:

- ✔ **Check with the patent office to see if your idea exists.** You can find more information on the U.S. Patents and Trademark Office Web site (www.uspto.gov) or call them at 800-786-9199 or 571-272-1000.

- ✔ **If you have a name for your media, trademark it.** You can find out more about trademarks at www.uspto.gov.

- ✔ **Retain a patent attorney to secure your position and protect you in the event of conflicts down the line.**

- ✔ **Secure a relevant Web address.** You can register a domain name (for example, dummies.com is the domain name for the *For Dummies* Web site) for as little as $10 a year. (For inexpensive domain names, try GoDaddy.com.) You may not use it right away, but registering the name helps to secure your position in the market and ensures that no one else grabs your name first.

Congratulations! You're now the proud owner of this brand-new media. Much like a doting parent, there are lots of worries and concerns. Will it succeed in the marketplace? Will business owners and consumers think it's stupid or a passing fad? Whether it be custom bicycle flags or branded urinal mints, don't be afraid to promote and devote resources (such as time and money) to this new media. Use as many of the guerrilla skills outlined in this book (such as online infiltration in Chapter 13), to share this product with relevant outlets. In the early stages. don't feel like you need to blow a wad of cash to get the message out. Look to the resources around you to spread the word first, and build it from there as the demand warrants.

If you're lucky you've created a form of media that people want to use. That's the good news. The bad news, if there is bad news, is that you need to get cracking and hustle to sell your innovation.

The first and best way to do this is to create a sell sheet, also known as a *one sheet* or *one pager.* A *sell sheet* (like the one in Figure 11-1) is usually a singular page upon which you lay out the media, the benefits, the rates, and any noteworthy items to such as artwork deadlines and file formats. This outline doesn't need to have every little detail on it. The real purpose of this sheet is to begin the conversation and give potential clients the basics so they know what's involved in engaging your services.

If potential clients ask you whether the rates outlined in your sell sheet are gross or net, the answer is: All rates are net. That means that, if an agency buys media on behalf of their client, you won't be paying them any commission over and above the price listed — the price they see is the price they pay. (Gross, on the other hand, means that a commission structure has been worked into the total price for them coming to you for this media. Frankly, gross is a headache you don't want.)

Marty's Messenger Service

Picture 1   Picture 2   Picture 3

Bike Messenger "Aerial Advertising"
New York City Rate Card
Effective January 1st, 2008 – March 2008

Benefits of "Aerial Advertising"
- Direct access to consumers living and working in the midtown area
- Opportunity to put your brand's logo eye level
- Bicycles with flags operate daily fro 9am to 6pm and on an average make a minimum of 50 runs each day campaigns
- Costs include production, installation and upkeep of flags

Sample Program
- (5) Bicycles with flags
- (5) Days per week
- (5) Days per week
- (4) Weeks
- Photo documentation of artwork and bicycles in motion

Sample Program Cost: **$2,500**

Notes:
- Artwork for flags to be supplied on disc no less than one week prior to campaign
- Vendor reserves the right to approve all artwork and logos being used for campaign
- Please note all rates are net

For more information on "Aerial Advertising", or to inquire about service rates for messenger service, please feel free to contact us:

T: 1-800-555-1212
E: info@martymessenger.com
W: martymessenger.com

Figure 11-1:
A sell sheet opens the dialogue between you and your customers.

Part IV
Driving It Home: From the Street to Your Site

The 5th Wave   By Rich Tennant

"Okay, so maybe the Internet wasn't the best place to advertise a product that helped computer-illiterate people."

In this part . . .

The World Wide Web. The Information Superhighway.
The Single Greatest Contributor to Endless Hours of
Delectable Procrastination. Whatever you call it, the
Internet is perhaps the most prime real estate out there to
get your message out in front of a choice demographic.

Studies tell us that 18- to 24-year-olds typically spend an
average of 40 hours a month clicking away at the computer. Some may say, "Forty hours? What's the big deal?"
Well, those 40 hours are precious expanses of time in
which you won't be able to reach those consumers on the
street, at the movie theater, or however else you choose
to connect with them out of their homes.

Rather than be frustrated by your target demographic's
cagey elusiveness, you can capitalize on this knowledge to
create campaigns that reach consumers on a personalized
level, and then reaffirm that connection when they log on.
In this part, we help you synthesize with social networking sites, masterfully manipulate microsites, and execute
exciting enter-to-win contests.

Chapter 12

Different Methods to Online Madness

"**Y**ou mean the TV didn't have color at all?"

Growing up, it used to blow our minds when we asked our grandparents what the world was like before so many of the technologies we currently enjoy (with infinite refinements) were invented. What tickles us even further is the idea that someday our kids or our kids' kids will pose the same probing questions about the Internet!

Fast-evolving developments have helped the Internet explode from a fun way to post messages on bulletin boards and search for listings at the library into a fully engaging, interactive experience. The incredible potential of the Internet now provides companies of all sizes with limitless opportunities to craft marketing plans that work seamlessly to go from street team to stunt to cyberspace — without missing a beat.

In this chapter, we plug into the variety of possibilities available to help your brand grow by melding online optimization with existing efforts to produce the greatest promotional punch! We begin by looking at how you can best direct people to your site as result of street-level efforts. After you've planted the seed, we tell you how to optimize your site to make yourself the Web's first choice when it comes to your product or service. Then we get a bit sly by examining online infiltration and see if it's right for you and your brand. Finally, we click onto banner ads and see how they can help promote your brand.

Including an Effective Call to Action

Food, water, clothing, shelter, chocolate — we all have needs. You have needs pertaining to your consumers. At its most basic, you need consumers to buy something. Beyond this, maybe you need them to just try a new product or tell a friend about your business or check out your Web site.

Regardless of your needs, the most effective way to get what you want is through a direct *call to action* (a request by a brand for the consumer to participate in one way or another). The most effective calls to action reward the consumer in some way.

No sales promotion or ad is complete or effective without a well-designed call to action. To come up with a successful call to action online, remember AIDA:

- **Awareness:** Effectively reach out to your target consumers and grab their attention.

- **Interest:** Provide your target with something that arouses curiosity and excites general enthusiasm for the content you're presenting.

- **Desire:** Move the audience beyond superficial interest and bring them into the realm of really *wanting* what you're serving up.

- **Action:** Motivate the target to act upon their desire and participate in your call to action.

When these steps are implemented on a well-designed Web site, they enable you to convert Web traffic from a prospective consumer to an actual customer.

Say you're starting up a new business making crocheted hats, shrugs, and doggie sweaters. You're offering a fuzzy, funky, and unique product, but you don't have the database of clients to market to. How do you get that database? One way is by creating a call to action that simply seeks to get consumers to sign up and supply their e-mail addresses on your site. Here's how:

- **Awareness:** Make calls, send e-mails, and give out postcards to friends, family, and anyone else who wants quality, handmade knitted goods, and ask them to check out your site. Here you're doing whatever you can to get the word out.

- **Interest:** On your site, post pictures of a small sampling of your most exciting creations. Include a brief testimonial and attractive models showing off your latest duds.

- ✔ **Desire:** Tell consumers how you use a rare wool and only produce ten unique creations a month, one of which you give away to a randomly selected valued customer on your mailing list.

- ✔ **Action:** By simply entering their e-mail addresses on your site, consumers enter to win their very own custom creation. They're so impressed with your site and your sweaters that they figure they might as well try to get something for free. They enter their e-mail addresses, and you've got yourself a database of e-mails.

You can't swipe people's contact information to send them follow-up updates unless you give them the opportunity to opt out. The opt out requisite is as simple as a check box that says, "No, I would not like to receive future updates from Crocheted Garments, Inc." — or something similar.

Whether the goal of your call to action is to get people to sign an online petition, enter their e-mail address, or participate in a survey, remember that a clean, smartly designed landing page and an easy-to-use sequence are essential to helping visitors answer the call. Think about how you spend your time online, if you have to jump through all sorts of crazy hoops and navigate from this page to that, you'll probably get frustrated and bag the whole thing. Avoid frustrating your consumers by keeping it simple.

Be smart about what you're requesting from your call to action. Most people aren't likely to turn over their credit card details or other sensitive information unless they're making a purchase (and sometimes even then it can be touchy). To avoid alienating potential customers, only ask for what you absolutely need.

The power of free

Gather round, we're going to let you in on a the worst-kept secret in marketing: The most successful word in the industry is the word *free*. Nothing causes a consumer's ears to perk and his eyes to dilate quite like that little gem of a word.

Think about what you can offer free of charge. Is it free shipping? A free upgrade? A free travel mug? Whatever it is, don't discount the appeal. Seemingly insignificant freebies may be just that little extra thing necessary to tip the scale in your favor.

In the world of customized consumer experiences, everyone wants to feel as though a product or service is tailored just for her. If you have a more sophisticated, database-driven site, where you have details about your online clients, use this information to cater your merchandising to meet the patron. The power of Free aside, remember that what is appealing and worthwhile varies from demographic to demographic and region to region. Make sure how you present yourself on the Web site, what you give away, and every other aspect of your site corresponds with your brand's image and your customers' tastes.

Spreading Your Message across Several Methods

On our way into work, we always see Wall Street types reading finely typed financial trade papers. The information in these papers may seem cryptic to you and us, but one message that we've taken away from peering over the shoulders of these folks is that you have to diversify your financial holdings. The same advice holds true when you're putting together your marketing campaign.

Whether you're using the guerrilla tactics outlined in this book, or you're opting for more traditional methods, you need to weave your online efforts into whatever strategic media mix you create.

Well-designed campaigns are synergistic — the effectiveness of your campaign can be greater than the sum of its parts. By spreading your wealth across a variety of platforms (perhaps a mix of a TV commercials, newspaper ads, and street teams, for example), you increase the likelihood that your target audience will be aware of you before they even get to your Web site, where they can learn more about your product or even buy it.

In the marketing biz, one of the long-debated questions is: How many exposures does it take to trigger a "buy" response. The reason it's long-debated, is that there isn't a hard-and-fast answer to this question — because there are so many variables (such as the quality, length, and frequency of the exposure).

The cost of this cross-platform approach can quickly get costly, so you need to select the platforms that will both reach your public and enable you to get the most out of your marketing budget. Depending on your goals and existing efforts, you may find that you don't need your Web site to work so hard to excite consumers and bring them in, especially if you're using other platforms to help drive traffic.

Formulating a strong media mix involves taking an inventory of what is important to your brand. Is it getting people through the door, or driving them to your site? For tips to start strategizing, turn to Chapter 21.

Getting people to participate on your site

You meet a friend for dinner and as soon as you get to the restaurant, you're bombarded with over-the-top tales, clearly rehearsed obnoxious jokes, and deeply emotional stories that demand not just sympathy but empathy. The evening comes to a close and, drained of all energy, you just want to go home and go to bed. You've just become the victim of an emotional vampire. Just like the shape-shifting Dracula, this same sort of vampirism can materialize on your very own Web site if you're not careful.

One common Web site affliction is the wrath of the creative vampire. This vampire is the result of an attempt to make your site as exciting as possible, with dizzying bells and whistles, overactive graphics, and elaborate animations. The end result: You suck away the site's effectiveness as a marketing tool.

One of the keys to enabling the greatest amount of quality participation is to keep your Web pages clean, logically organized, and easy to navigate. Here are a few basic guidelines:

- Put navigation clusters in vertical or horizontal bars, in places where people expect to see them.

- Try to stick to the rule of five: Have no more than five navigation buttons or links in one location.

- Allow for white space on your pages. Give your visitors a break. Providing some white space gives eyes the rest they need to find the page's most important elements easily. Clutter causes visitors to click off the page.

- Avoid black backgrounds. White type on a black background is difficult to read.

- Stay consistent to reduce confusion. Keep all major elements of navigation, calls for action, and purchasing options in the same relative position on all pages. You don't want your navigation buttons in the upper-left corner on one page of your site, and then in the upper-right corner on another page of your site.

- Make sure your pages load fast. The average site visitor will give a page between 3 and 7 seconds to load the information he's looking for before he leaves.

- Photos and illustrations are great, but use Click to Enlarge links and/or thumbnail photos to give the visitor the option to see your products larger and from different angles.

- If consumers are making purchases on your site, allow the consumer to enter all the information about the product they want before you ask for her credit card information. You don't want to lose your buyer during the purchasing process.

Your site is your calling card, and nothing turns consumers off more than a homepage that looks amateurish or, worse, completely illegitimate. If you don't feel you have the skills to create something you're proud of, it may be good to hire a professional Web designer. Even if you aren't an HTML specialist, you should have a strong understanding of what will help your site and what will detract from it. Use this information to communicate to your designer not only what you want, but what you *don't* want.

Optimizing Your Site for Search Engines

As the owner of Giuseppe's Gelatos & Italian Ices, you take great pride in being the best in the business. Globally, you're an institution — *the* name in gelatos. So why is it that whenever you do an online search for gelato, Francesco's Frost is the first to pop up? What gives?

Although your icy treats may be unrivaled, the likely answer is that Francesco has optimized its site for search engines in order to "scoop" you out of the top position. Before you can take your rightly spot among the tops of the search results, you need to figure out what the heck search engine optimization is, who does it, and how you can get it to work for you. That's what we cover in this section.

Understanding what search engine optimization is

Search engine optimization (SEO) is the technique of structuring and positioning Web sites in ways so that search engines rank them as top among their results. Although it sounds (and actually is) highly technical, SEO has a somewhat sordid past.

SEO was actually invented by the adult-entertainment segment of online marketers. In the early days of the Internet, while the rest of us were trying to figure out what the heck a modem was, the people marketing porn sites were busy coming up with tricks and tools to enable their sites to come up first when certain words or phrases were entered into search engines. During this early stage of the Internet, porn sites were the only ones that were making money (hey, it makes sense — after all, prostitution *is* the oldest profession), so they had the resources to do whatever they could to get people to their sites.

Not surprisingly, their approach (and this unregulated environment) enabled the practice to quickly turn unscrupulous. It wasn't long before the porn kings began optimizing their sites on search engines for seemingly harmless words. For example, a search for "candy" wouldn't take the user to the site for delicious Jujubes — it would take you to a buck-naked woman named Candy (and variations on this theme).

Whether you find this practice laughable or obscene, back in those days, SEO was easy and kind of fun. How easy, you ask? Well, say you wanted to convince a search engine that you had the best darned Web site for garden implements. To make the search engine a believer, all you had to do was type the terms, *garden implements, hoes, trowels,* and so on, a gazillion times in white type on the white background of a web page (so it wasn't visible to the visitors to your site, but it was visible to the search engines) and, sure enough, the search engines would find the terms and decide that you had the best garden-implement site on the Web.

Unfortunately, for the idle business owner willing to spend hours typing *trowels* on their pages, the search engines have gotten far more complex. These engines now implement elaborate ranking *algorithms* (proprietary tools used by the search engine to effectively explore page content and rank its relevance in order to provide the most pertinent information in response to user requests).

Although these algorithms are still searching for those keywords to appear, things have gotten a little more difficult. Nowadays, the algorithms are far craftier at scanning pages, exploring the appearance and context of the keywords, weeding out the rooks that serve to distract them — all in an effort to deliver the most precise response to the person searching.

Knowing when to ask for help

The process of optimizing a Web site is constantly changing in order to keep up with the developments in search-engine technology. These days, search engines battle it out to present users with the best, fastest, and most precise search results. Because this battleground changes daily, the gatekeepers of search engine optimization are SEO professionals who track the trends in order to put their clients in front of the people who are searching for them.

If you're interested in maximizing your Web presence, you may want to consider reaching out for professional help.

SEO has become an extremely complex industry in and of itself, with its own trade shows, manuals, SEO companies, and divisions within large corporations. And because the ranking of a site on a search engine can mean millions of dollars of business for most companies, SEO is something the world has come to take very seriously — which has put this service in high demand.

If you decide to seek the help of a SEO specialist, there is good news and bad news. The good news: By investing in this service, you have a dedicated person working to make your Web site pop when people search for your trade. The bad news: Every Web developer on the planet will say that he can "optimize" a site — and not all of them can — so you have to make sure you're getting what you paid for.

In fact, due to the changing face of the business itself, very few general Web developers really can do SEO effectively. So although they may be excellent Web designers who create wonderful Web sites, they may not be up-to-date with ever-shifting world of algorithms. Be choosy about who you hire for SEO, and make your goals clear and reasonable so that he fully understands what you expect from the service.

Fair expectations might include an increase in site traffic, being able to see where these increases are coming from, and higher rankings among your industry's search keywords. Beyond this, your specialist should be able to help educate you as to why SEO is an important part of any online presence and how it can help your brand stay ahead of this constantly evolving matrix.

Good SEO specialists are rare and dedicated — and they don't come cheap. Most important, these smarties are not likely to be on the other end of a spam e-mail promising, "High Search Rankings! Increased Site Traffic! Fast and Cheap Results!"

If you're looking for an SEO specialist, you may want to start with your Web designer. He'll probably say he can help — and some Web designers actually are able to. But ask for case studies and examples so you feel comfortable and confident that he's familiar with how to go about setting you up. If you feel uneasy about using the same person for your design and SEO, check with colleagues who might be able to steer you in the right direction. For more information, check out *Pay Per Click Search Engine Marketing For Dummies*, by Peter Kent (Wiley).

Maximizing your visibility on your own

Search engines are looking for one main thing when they crawl your page: keywords. *Keywords* are indicative words that tip a search engine off as to the content of a Web site. (Crawling is done automatically by things called spiders — it basically just means scanning your page and looking for certain kinds of information.)

Make a list of the keywords that your target audience might use to find your site. For example, if you sell garden implements, sure, you'd right down "garden implements," but you might also jot down "garden tools," "garden equipment," "gardening," and then all the garden tools you can think of. You can have your Web designer add a keyword tag to your Web site's code that lists all the keywords you came up with. (Even if your Web designer isn't skilled at SEO, he'll know how to do this.) Plus, incorporate as many of these indicative keywords into your content on your Web site as possible.

Another way to make yourself relevant to search engines is to update your site regularly. As consumers surf the Web, they're looking for the latest and greatest information. Search engines know this, so they do their darndest to provide users with what they want: new information. By updating your content regularly — laden with keywords, of course — you're saying to these search engines, "If you're looking for the latest, here it is."

Update your content weekly. You don't have to knock yourself out by overhauling your Web site every week — as a matter of fact, that's an awful idea. But you can do two things:

✔ **Post regular press releases.** Given your trend-setting nature, you probably create regular press releases. (For more on press releases, check out Chapter 16.) You take the time to produce and share them with the press and the industry, so you should post them on your site as well. You can have a section of your site just for press releases if you want.

✔ **Create a blog.** Press releases can be a great way to let the search engines know that you have new material, but most consumers aren't going to want to read a string of them. A blog is a great way to produce weekly (or even daily) updates about your company or the industry at large. Plus, a blog allows you to connect with your customers.

If you want to draw readers to your blog, and make them regular readers, you need to think about what they want. For example, if you sell garden implements, maybe your blog covers the ins and outs of gardening — you might write posts on a variety of gardening topics, like choosing the right plants for your climate, dealing with bugs, or preparing your garden for winter. Of course, in the posts themselves, you can weave in information about the products and services you offer. But think of this more like a magazine — a gardening magazine may recommend certain products, but it doesn't read like an advertisement. That's the tone you should strive for.

Blogging is a huge topic, worthy of entire books. If you're interested in finding out more, check out *Blogging For Dummies,* 2nd Edition, by Susannah Gardner and Shane Birley (Wiley).

One of the greatest benefits of the Internet, from both a personal perspective and a marketing perspective, is the way it connects people from all over the world. You can play up this asset by creating opportunities for consumers to participate on your site. For example, you might offer:

✔ **The chance for consumers to comment on blogs and other content:** You've taken the time to produce a site — why not allow your consumers to throw in their two cents? If you're offering a blog, make sure it allows comments. Although monitoring and participating in these comments may take time from your busy social calendar, ultimately it can be a very effective way of staying touch with your consumers and fans. Even if all the comments aren't positive, you're still creating online chatter about your site for people (and search engines) to take notice of.

✔ **Chat rooms and forums:** We know it all too well — people love to talk business. Give them a mouthpiece. By providing an online chat room or forum, you're not only creating a place for consumers to congregate but also producing current information on your site. Search engines will pick up on both of these things.

✔ **Opportunities to upload photos or videos:** Depending on your business, allowing consumers the opportunity to contribute relevant photos or videos provides something additional for the search engines to pick up.

Another way to land some hits with search engines is to consider search engine marketing or paid inclusion. This practice, offered by some search engines, allows you to have your site listed with the engine so that your site appears when users search for specific keywords. This tool can be an affordable, easy, and impactful way to aid your existing efforts.

Considering Online Infiltration

You're browsing for books at your favorite online bookstore, reading customers' reviews. Every once in a while, you come upon a review that seems *really* enthusiastic. It may just be that the user really likes that book — or it may be something we like to call online infiltration. *Online infiltration* is posting positive reviews or endorsements of a product or service (or denouncements of rivals) for the purposes of promoting your own product or brand.

You can do this on your own blog, or you can go to stores and blogs that are related to your products, and do it there. Either way, it's one more way for you to make the case for what you're offering to consumers.

So, should you participate in these discussions to help promote your company or product? And if so, how overtly or covertly should you participate? No one knows your company or your brand better than you do. Is presenting yourself through online infiltration something that will positively affect your company's image? Some people whole-heartedly shun online infiltration and prefer to spend their time and money elsewhere. Other people who don't have a problem with using it have seen a surge in their Web traffic and general interest in their products by participating in the online conversation.

Tread very carefully. People read and participate in online discussion forums because they provide the opportunity for open, frank discussions — users cherish this environment as a somewhat sacred trust. Participants are highly sensitive to any messages that they perceive as unsolicited promotion (known as *spam*).

Getting in on the inside

We like to look at these online forums, chat rooms, and Web sites as a big social club where everyone has an opinion. Some of the opinions are valid and helpful; some of them are simply opportunities for people to hear themselves type. Either way, many consumers and industry pros look to niche topic discussion sites to help get an "unbiased" overview of the market's landscape. As an enterprising guerrilla, the chance to participate in this consumer dialogue creates an unique opportunity to engage your consumers — and maybe direct some business your way in the process.

As you walk the aisles of the self-help section in your local bookstore, you'll find countless books exhaustively discussing one principal point. If you want people to like you, just be yourself.

Although going into chat rooms covertly is an option (see the "Illusory infiltrators" sidebar), our belief is that the best approach is to present yourself openly and honestly. The reason we say this is basic: No one likes to be lied to. Attempts at cloaking your identity or other forms of deception are likely to backfire and could cause your company a full-scale public relations disaster the likes of which you don't need — especially for the sake of a few online postings.

If you present your information honestly, openly, and with a newsworthy angle, you could make a magical transformation in the eyes of your online audience. By prudently providing quality information, not just abusing the opportunity to talk about yourself, you may begin to earn a reputation for openness and honesty. You may be able to quickly build a good reputation and lift yourself from novice poster to the lauded realm of "industry expert." Once you've achieved this status, *you* have become an influencer, and that feels good.

Here's how to use message boards to your advantage, and still be able to respect yourself in the morning:

- **Find the message boards that are directly appropriate to your industry.** Check out the "Zeroing in on the sites with the most impact" section, later in this chapter, for more on how to do that.

- **Participate in board discussions for a short time before saying anything positive about your company or product.**

- **Only offer information when it's appropriate to the discussion taking place on the board at the time.** Look at discussion boards the way you would a real-life discussion. If you were sitting in a bar listening to the conversation going on around you, you wouldn't jump in and say, "Hey, I've got a great product for you!" unless someone actually mentioned something relevant to your product. The same rule applies online.

- **Test the waters to see whether the people on the message boards are okay with promotional messages from legitimate sources as long as they identify themselves.** You can do this by looking at existing content. Are there similar or related brands that are openly discussing their company's offerings? What is the response among users? Use past attempts by others to fashion your approach.

Illusory infiltrators

Stealth infiltration involves scoping out sites relevant to your industry, and then creating posts endorsing your company under the guise of an independent consumer. Often, you have to create the persona of an average Joe, just dropping a line to share your (slightly to highly biased) two cents.

When executed deftly, this approach can be an effective way to stir up consumer conversation about your product. Unfortunately, many people have executed this tactic so poorly

that chat-room regulars are hypersensitive to imposters and are eager to call them out. To be accused of spamming is to have your cover blown. And the penalty for having your cover blown is becoming banned from the board and being the object of revulsion from the site's membership, which can prove fatal online. As a result, we distance ourselves from this practice because the potential negatives far outweigh the positives — and we recommend you do the same.

✔ **When you're ready to post with something relevant to the discussion, be honest and fully disclose your identity.** You want to communicate in a way that will be accepted by board participants. You'll probably find that people are pretty accepting, as long as you're not insulting them by pretending to be something you're not.

When you meet a new group of people, chances are, you don't begin your conversations by saying how wonderfully smart and attractive you are. When you're participating in online chat rooms, you should have the same sense of respect for the guests. If you sign up to participate in a chat room and immediately post a glowing endorsement of your own company, without otherwise participating in the conversation, your forum-poseur status will be apparent (and annoying) to site participants. Start off slowly and work your way in gradually.

Zeroing in on the sites with the most impact

When you groggily slosh into work, and finish checking your Facebook profile (see Chapter 14), what's the first Web site that you go to in order to get your head back in the game? Most industries have official trade sites. Especially if they have established and busy message boards, put these sites at the top of your infiltration list, because these people are the ones most likely to act on the message you're going to relay.

Beyond these more institutional sites, you'll want to span out. Are there independently operated sites related to your industry that have a large following? Many times these sites earn more respect from consumers because unlike trade sites, they aren't being monitored or censored by a Webmaster. Often, this unrestricted atmosphere allows consumers to get unbiased opinions.

To find sites that have a large following, you can use the free Google Toolbar (`http://toolbar.google.com`), which has a Page Rank section, letting you know how popular a site is.

Although we encourage you to look outside of your immediate circle of industry sites, don't stray too far from home. Stick to sites that are directly connected in some way to the product you're selling.

While you're here, you may as well multitask. These same sites you're targeting for infiltration and participation may also make for perfect locations to target banner ads (see Chapter 12) and other online marketing initiatives such as a contest or another call to action (see Chapter 13).

Reaching the influencers

Remember in high school when there were "the cool kids"? If one of the cool kids wore her hair a certain way, or wore a certain pair of shoes, everyone in the school mindlessly followed suit. The Web has inspired its own culture of cool kids — only online you don't need to be a jock or a cheerleader to attract this adoration. Online, opinions, credibility, and respect in the industry shape the social elites — the online influencers — and you want to do whatever you can to join their gang.

To reach the online influencers, start by researching respected industry experts. Chances are, through the course of your work and your networking efforts, you know who the thought leaders and influencers in your industry are. Start with these people. Once again, set your sites to the immediate influencers you have access to. Well-read bloggers and business contacts you're familiar with are great places to start and then build from there.

After identifying who you want to reach out to, you can start your online conversation by simply introducing yourself and explaining why you're even reaching out to them in the first place. Once you've made contact, you may want to begin an open dialogue (for others to see) on their chat rooms and blogs. Just like suddenly sitting at the cool kids' lunch table, holding conspicuous conversations with this expert can be a highly effective way to market yourself and, ultimately, your product.

By ingratiating yourself in this scene you are connecting with influencers and providing useful information. You may find over time, you have a bit more freedom to present your product or service's benefits, with relatively objective descriptions and news in ways that would have been otherwise perceived as spam.

Avoiding the wrath of the Inter-mob

If your participation online is perceived by the community as violating the code of responsible posting, forum participants can be much like these angry peasants — only meaner.

There's something about the anonymity of sitting behind a computer and using an online nickname that can bring out the worst in people. Because they know there is usually no way they'll suffer any consequences, they may flame you. (*Flaming* is basically extremely hateful and insulting public attacks.)

If you offer your opinions and information honestly, objectively, and in a newsworthy fashion, you generally won't have anything to be worried about. Still, even if you play by the rules, you may be met with this kind of abuse.

The bottom line is, sometimes people can just be jerks and some forums more or less encourage or cultivate an environment that lends itself to petty, childish sniping. This is why spending some time on a message board before you post is a good idea — you can pretty quickly get a sense for whether flaming is the m.o. or whether people treat each other with respect. Obviously, you want to avoid the sites that encourage or allow flaming.

If you find yourself in a situation where you're being flamed, don't even try to defend yourself. Some will attack you just because they can get away with it, even if they don't necessarily feel anything negative about you or your company. Just bow out graciously.

Wave the Banner High: Buying Banner Ads

Any one who's ever been to a commercial Web site knows there's one thing that is a certainty: Oh yes, there will be banner ads. *Banner ads* are dedicated sections of a Web page designated for advertising space. Why are these ads so prominent? Because they're mutually beneficial for all parties involved. For the site owners, they can generate substantial revenues (depending on the site). For the advertiser, they present a message in an exceptionally targeted and occasionally interactive way.

Banner ads come in a variety of sizes, with a number of different options. In many cases, you can select from static or animated; horizontal or vertical; rollover-activated, pop-up, or pop-under; and from a range of different sizes and positions on a Web site. Ultimately, your decisions should depend on your budget, your program goals, and how many prospective consumers you want to reach.

Selecting sites to advertise on

Shopping for Web sites to advertise on can be overwhelming. There are media buying agencies whose sole function is to get out there, identify, and secure the best locations for their clients. Depending on your business, you may be able to take these surveying duties upon yourself.

You probably want to grab the attention of as many real prospects as possible when you're buying an ad. The best way to do this is to go where the people are. Much like selecting sites for online infiltration (see "Considering Online Infiltration," earlier in this chapter), chances are good that whatever Web sites you visit in relation to your business are the same sites that your best prospects are also frequenting, so these sites are a perfect place to start.

Also, put the search engines to work for you. A potential consumer looking to make a purchase in your trade is likely to first look for it by searching using certain keywords. Come up with a list of keywords you think your potential consumers will use when they're looking to buy products similar to your own. Conduct your own searches on those keywords, and note all the top hits for each of these keywords. Then visit the sites that come up, and try to get a sense of the amount of traffic each of these sites receives.

How do you find out about site traffic? The Page Rank tool on the Google Toolbar (http://toolbar.google.com) is a good place to start. You can download the Google Toolbar for free, and it'll tell you how each page of a Web site ranks. The higher the rank, the higher the traffic a page receives.

Sites that sell banner ads should also make available to you, usually in the form of a media kit, statistics about site traffic. Sometimes smaller, niche sites don't have this information readily available — in this situation, you may want to take their claims with a grain of salt. Or you can be proactive and check them out for yourself using online metrics available at sites such as Compete (http://siteanalytics.compete.com).

Knowing when to buy and when to trade

To get the most for your dollar, look for the most cost-effective reach. For Internet advertising, the reach is generally expressed in cost per thousand (CPM). (To break down the buying of CPM, check out Chapter 2.)

The Internet adds a unique twist to CPM rates, however. With print advertising, you can buy according to *projected impressions.* What this really means is that they're basing your rate on the number of people who are likely to see your ad. Many Web site banner ads are available for purchase using the same formula, but some Web sites offer an even more cost-effective option: cost per click (CPC). With *cost per click,* you only pay for the Web site visitors who actually click on your banner ad — and, presumably, visit your site.

Though not all Web sites offer CPC pricing, whenever it's available, go with this option — it's the best way to measure the value of your banner ad on any particular site.

Consider trading banner ads on your site for a presence on someone else's. As long as you're not cluttering your site with large unnecessary images, this kind of deal is too good to pass up! Even if your ad isn't drawing a tremendous amount of traffic from the bartered site, this is just another opportunity to put the image of your brand in front of your target's peepers.

Whether you're buying or trading your banner ads, be sure to track where your traffic comes from, where it goes on your site, and what visitors do when they get there. Many free sites, including Google Analytics (`http://analytics.google.com`), will do this. Analyzing your site traffic will help you make smart, informed choices about future ad buys or swapping arrangements.

Chapter 13

Creating Your Online Presence

*L*iving in New York City has its advantages. Two of its most entertaining pluses are the near endless opportunities for people-watching and catching snippets of candid conversation outtakes. For instance, take this snippet we overheard, between two well-to-do ladies:

> "I think I'm going to see that Off-Broadway show — would you care to join me?" asked one woman.

> "No," replied her friend. "I went to their Web site, and if the show is half as bad as the site is, that promises to be a painful night out!"

Some might say that this is just a conversation between some bored "ladies who lunch" who are being catty — and they might be right. But their comments reflect an important trend: People judge businesses by their Web sites. Fair or not, setting up your Web site is just as important as (if not more important than) setting up your storefront.

In this chapter, we look at the ways in which you can develop your Web site so that it makes people want to come back for more.

Designing a Web site is a topic worthy of many books on its own, and we don't have the space here to cover all the intricate details. What we do cover are the aspects that pertain to marketing in general and guerrilla marketing in particular. If you're looking for even more information on designing a site, go to www.dummies.com, and search on Web design. In particular, we recommend *Web Design For Dummies,* 2nd Edition, by Lisa Lopuck, and *Web Marketing For Dummies,* by Jan Zimmerman (both published by Wiley).

Setting Your Web-Site Goals

You may be the oldest and most respected establishment in all of your industry, but if your business doesn't have a Web site, you virtually don't exist. Although you may enjoy a strong trade reputation, an upstart company with an impressively clean, engaging Web site can suddenly create the impression that they're an industry guru, and you're a dinosaur — just by their having a great site (and your not having one).

But there's good news: By adapting your Web site to fit your brand and your clients' needs, you can enjoy the benefits of both your well-earned reputation *and* the increased benefits of using your Web site not just as a reference, but as a marketing tool.

A marketing tool? That's right: Your site isn't just a nice place to post pictures of yourself standing next to the biggest version of whatever you create — it can and *should* be used to stir up interest, inform consumers about your product, and maybe even give consumers the chance to buy your product online.

The first step toward getting the most out of your Web site is having a heart to heart with yourself and asking the question: "What do I want my Web site to do for me?" Just because you're looking to make a good impression doesn't mean you have to drop millions of dollars on a flashy Silicon Valley designer. Being honest with what you want to get out of your site will help to dictate the features you need to include.

Here are a few of the more common layouts that, when executed properly, can fulfill basic online needs:

- ✔ **Basic development:** "I don't need any of that fancy-pants stuff!" Maybe your industry is a straightforward, uncomplicated one, where your clients simply need to see who you are and what you do. If this is the case a clean, graphically pleasing site with a small online brochure may do the trick.

- ✔ **Intermediate development:** Maybe the Joneses over there have a fancy Web site with impressive graphics and options to buy. You're green with envy, but you just don't have the budget. In this situation, you may want to spice it up with an intermediate design — one that beautifully lays out your product, and then links consumers to an online payment and fulfillment site (such as PayPal) when they're ready to buy.

- ✔ **Deluxe e-commerce development:** Maybe you've attained that level where you just want to simplify your business so you have more time for your ballroom-dance classes. If so, you may want to spend a lot of money on your Web design, focus on sales, and create a sophisticated e-commerce site. Although this kind of site is significantly more expensive (and involved) than the alternatives, it provides users with a near turnkey operation if they want to add sales and fulfillment to their site. Which will give you the time to practice that foxtrot.

Whatever your goals, and whatever you spend on your site, you need to recognize that your site is one the most visible tools in your marketing mix. You have to produce content for your site that is so rocking, so informative, so engaging, so interactive that your consumers *have* to come back to you again and again for more. Use the appearance and structure of your site to drive your strategic marketing objectives and ultimately help build your brand.

Although using your Web site to promote your product or service is essential, only get what you need — to start. You may find that by putting yourself out there on the Web, your sales will explode literally overnight. If you find yourself in this fortunate position, you can re-evaluate how you want to grow your site.

Adding On to Your Site with a Microsite

You've addressed your marketing goals but something is missing. Maybe a certain component of your business, product, event, or promotion just can't be held within the constraints of your core Web site — it's just too important. The solution: Give this component its own space. Give it a *microsite* — a small Web site or part of a Web site dedicated to a specific subject.

Microsites are the latest battleground in guerrilla creativity. A microsite can serve you well — as long as you've built it to serve a specific marketing strategy. Here are a few of the more clever approaches we've seen recently:

✔ **Contests and prize fulfillment:** One of the big goals in online marketing is to drive traffic. And often the best way to motivate those consumers is a contest. A microsite, complete with conspicuous branding, click-throughs, and redirects to your main site, can be a great place to execute a contest, while still preserving the integrity of your brand.

Microsites can also be used to handle prize fulfillment. For example, we recently had cause to do fulfillment for a contest in which the 20 or so winners were given the chance to select their prize online. The catch was that the client didn't want the general public to know about the site since the contest pertained to only a handful of select consumers. So we used existing artwork from a much larger, more public promotion in order to save on costs and create an inexpensive microsite exclusively for the winners to lay claim to their bling!

✔ **Petitions:** Nonprofit organizations, charities, and socially conscious businesses have been especially successful in creating petition microsites to promote political messages and social change. (For more ideas about charitable tie-ins, check out Chapter 20.) For example, one big issue in New York City was whether to allow artists to use city sidewalks to display their art. If you're an art gallery and you want to get behind the cause, you could host a microsite with additional information.

The Internet allows you to spread a message quickly and get people to participate easily. To help encourage participation, keep it entertaining and keep it simple. (To take a look at the entertaining angle, check out "Slainte! I'll drink to that" in this chapter.) Consumers are more likely to participate if all they have to do is log on and type in their information. Petition sites allow for dominance of a brand or a message with the capabilities to link through to the organization's main site.

✔ **Tease-and-reveal and campaign-specific sites:** One of the most enthralling uses of microsites is for a *tease-and-reveal campaign* — in which consumers are given just enough information to pique their curiosity, which in turn motivates them to check out the site to see what the campaign is about.

An example of this might be the creation of a microsite such as `www.whoislarrymcdandy.com`. Any sort of nontraditional (or traditional) media can be used to lead consumers to the site. After being over-wrought with curiosity as to who Larry McDandy is, the consumer logs on to a microsite dedicated to laying out the specs on Larry McDandy, the strapping new hero of the latest action movie.

Tease-and-reveal is very fashionable right now because, hey, everyone wants to be in the know — it's only human. As is the case with most guerrilla tactics, however, only time will tell whether it'll last. If overuse of this tricky tool causes it to become a cliché, the challenge will fall on marketers to come up with something else to tempt consumers with.

No one likes an alarmist. When you're coming up with clever tease-and-reveal or other campaign-specific sites, stay away from names and concepts that could be misrepresented as threatening. You may want your campaign to generate emotion in your target audience, but you want make sure that emotion is curiosity, not fear, or ultimately, loathing.

If you decide that a microsite makes sense for you, and you're looking to drive traffic from search engines to the site, purchase a separate domain name (the Web address — like wiley.com or dummies.com), and build the site around it. For example, if you're building a microsite for a contest, you might register a domain name like thebestcontestever.com.

To find out whether a domain name you're interested in is available, go to any domain name registrar (some popular ones are GoDaddy.com, directNIC, and Network Solutions) and do a whois search.

If the name you're interested in isn't available, you can always build the contest microsite into your company's existing domain name. Instead of the microsite existing as a standalone, it would now appear as a dedicated site within your own. So thebestcontestever.com now becomes yourbrand.com/thebestcontestever.

If bringing your contest to your own site seems like too much for you to take on, it may be time to draw upon the resources of a professional. Any good Web developer will be able to help you do this.

Working Web Addresses to Your Advantage

What's in a name? When so much business is generated through Web referrals, your name on the Internet may just be the thing that helps your consumers find you.

A Web address, technically called a *URL* (which stands for Universal Resource Locater), is the address of each page of your site. The full URL of a typical Web site page is something like `www.yourcompany.com`. The domain name is the `yourcompany.com` part. When selecting a URL try to pick something that can be easily remembered and re-entered by your consumers.

The one thing that is constant with all guerrilla campaigns is that creativity will always be rewarded. Coming up with something fun for people to enter into that `http://` box may be the guerrilla hook itself!

Being precise with the language you use in your URL is key in enabling your consumers to find you both directly and via search engines. Using precise phrasing in your URL will help make your site easier for search engines to find.

Maybe you manage Hector's House of Helium, the vendor of quality helium balloons of all shapes and sizes. After considering your Web results, you've found that you've been getting very poor referrals based on Web searches. These results are not full of hot air — they may be the outcome of poorly entered URL information.

Slainte! I'll drink to that

Guinness, often nearly synonymous with St. Patrick's Day, created a microsite as a tool for change and a vehicle for incredible viral publicity! In the United States, unless you live in Boston, you can expect to schlep into work on March 17. Eager to give the holiday the place it deserves in the national calendar, the company launched the site `www.Proposition317.` `com` to make St. Paddy's an official holiday. Here, users could log on, sign a petition, make comments, and upload pictures of themselves celebrating the date. Aside from being a fun opportunity, the site quickly spread across the Internet as ushered in by revelers the world over.

In addition to choosing the right URL for your site, you have to think in terms of alternate URLs. *Alternate URLs* are other domain names that redirect visitors to another site. For example, maybe your business sells floor lamps made of recycled soda cans, and your URL is www.leslieslamps.com. Now, people may really like your interesting lamps once they see them, but you just can't seem to get people to your site. You may want to consider registering floor lamps.com and setting it up so that every visitor to www.floorlamps.com is automatically redirected to www.leslieslamps.com. (For tips on how to do this redirecting, talk to your domain-name registrar or your Web designer.)

Many companies purchase multiple domain names and use the different URLs either for specific separate marketing offers or to drive visitors to a single central Web site. Either tactic can be effective, but you need to be careful not to create what the search engines will perceive as duplicate content. Duplicate Web sites can cause a search engine to ban all the sites from its index. Talk to your Web designer about avoiding this problem. Or, if you want to know all the technical details yourself, check out the nearby sidebar, "Duplicate content duplicate content."

Playing with Online Games

Every year, over 200 million people saddle up with their keyboards and joy-sticks and play online games. Unlike the unfair pigeonholing of years prior, these players are not kids or unkempt, munchy-eating slackers. These days, online games are for everyone, and even the ladies have gotten in on the action.

You may be interested in getting in on the action and incorporating a game on your Web site. The good news, from a cost perspective, is that there are thousands of games available on the Internet that you can install on your Web site, and many of them are free. But prior to encouraging your site's visitors to engage in mortal combat with their opponents, ask yourself these two questions:

- ✔ What is the specific marketing purpose of the site?
- ✔ How will the addition of this game help further that purpose?

A game may draw visitors to your site, but if it doesn't further your marketing goals, you don't have a good reason to install the game.

On the other hand, if the game keeps your target on your site a little longer in an engaged, brand-related way, we say, add it on! Oh, and we've got next player.

Duplicate content duplicate content

The actual location of a Web site on a particular server is called the *Internet protocol* (IP) address. You can have two different URLs pointing to the same site (sharing the same IP address), but search engines don't want you to have duplicate Web sites, each with their own URLs and their own IP addresses.

If you feel you might be in danger of stepping into the scary world of potentially being banned, it may be time to call in reinforcements. Any Web developer worth his salt can guide you through this situation and ensure you don't find yourself banned from search engines.

To game or not to game? Knowing when adding a game is a good idea

We like to think of this decision in the terms of enjoying a really good tin of oatmeal raisin cookies. You open the tin, take a cookie, and it's all that you hoped for. "I'm going to come back to that tin for another," you resolve. And you do — again and again and again, much to the delight of the cookie company stamped on that tin. You've been ensnared in a "sticky" product.

One of the hallmarks of a successful Web site is what is sometimes referred to as its *stickiness* — the site's ability to attract repeat visits. A sticky site has the type of content that compels visitors to keep coming back.

Web sites often create stickiness on their sites by using online games. The only problem with using the online game is that consumers may begin to only come to play the games and ignore your products and services. You can avoid this fate, by incorporating as much of your brand in the game as possible. That way, even if they *are* using you for your game, at least your brand is getting the exposure it deserves.

Step right up! Looking at the kinds of games you can offer

The best way to prevent consumers from coming to your site, playing the game, and then leaving without so much as a click through to your products and services is to link your game and its outcomes to your products and services. For example, game winners could be awarded a free product sample or a discount.

If possible, give everyone who plays some sort of prize for participating. Some budgets just won't allow for this — and that's fine — but consider where and when you can offer something because it'll help to build a loyal base and ensure that people aren't just using you for your nifty game.

Another, better option is to create a custom game where you build your products, your brands, and some user benefits right into the games themselves, so your brand and its competitive advantages are continually being reinforced. Although this is the ideal scenario, this isn't the sort of thing you're going to be able to download to your site or pick up at your local computer store. For a custom setup like this, you're going to need a professional game designer.

Talk to your Web designer and see if he knows a game designer who can create something compatible with your site. If you don't get any leads, search the Internet for "online game development."

If you decide that putting in some zippy elements is the direction you want to go, you want to make sure that you get the credit for them by getting the attention of the search engines. Make sure that any media you embed on your site is optimized using appropriate keywords for media searches. To make sure you're getting the most out of this investment, make sure that your Web designer has done his part to make sure that your site is optimized. A quick way to check for this is to do an online search using keywords you feel should drive traffic to this media. If your offering doesn't pop up you might want to discuss how you might improve your rankings.

Going easy on the extras

After you've established your basic presence on the Web, you need to make yourself stand out from the crowd. And believe us, there's quite a crowd out there vying (or screaming) for the attention of your customers and prospects. In order to give your site that "it" factor and enable it to stand apart from the competition, you'll want to give that the sizzle it needs to not only attract visitors but to keep them coming back for more.

Despite the temptation to go nuts with numerous, flashy elements, repeat the mantra "How will this enhance my brand, promote my products, or build my sales?" It may be annoying to your friends and neighbors when chanted over and over, but it will totally be worth it when your pages aren't covered in expensive unnecessary extras

Another reality check is to look around at your competitors' sites. See what devices and applications they are using and aren't. Then objectively consider whether they're effective tools to reach consumers or merely a distraction. If they are distractions, then feel free to gloat. The flipside of this of course is to consider things that your competition doesn't have but may fill a need of some sort to your consumers.

Giving People the Chance to Enter to Win

How many times have you heard someone who's just won something say, "I've never won anything before in my life!" And no matter how often the phrase is exclaimed, it still manages to warm your heart a bit, doesn't it? The idea of someone receiving something for nothing still manages to delight our feel-good sensibilities. If you're looking to add a bit of this feel-good response, you may want to add an enter-to-win component on your Web site.

An *enter-to-win* component is exactly what it sounds like — a contest that allows the consumer to enter a contest on your Web site with the promise of potentially winning a prize of some sort. When an enter-to-win is paired up with existing sites or created as a microsite, you can use the promise of riches or at the very least, free product, as a way to incentivize your consumers to come back for more.

Web designers have taken a page out of the merchandising playbook in creating online enter-to-wins. Merchandising techniques that work well at point-of-purchase — such as a gym offering entrants the chance to win a free month's membership in exchange for filling out an entry form — also work well on the Internet, sometimes even better. Whereas the entry box sitting on the counter at the gym may only attract the attention of a handful of brawny types with inflated arms, an enter-to-win on the Web puts your entry box on the counter of the global marketplace.

Enter-to-win contests can generate awareness, recognition, and excitement about your brand and your products, and it can make your site sticky (see the "To game or not to game? Knowing when adding a game is a good idea" section).

Creating a contest is relatively easy (see the following sections). Plus, the interactivity that a contest creates gives you the chance to have an indirect dialogue with your customers that provides you with instantaneous feedback.

Crafting a contest

Nobody creates a contest just to hand out prizes. Although it may feel good to give stuff away, when you look at it from a business perspective, giving away prizes without expecting something in return is not a smart play.

So in order to get something out of your contest, you need to figure out what you're hoping to get out of it from your consumers. What you're asking for could be as simple as their contact information or as involved as actually purchasing something. ***Remember:*** What you're asking looking for should be in proportion however to what you're offering in the way of prizes.

All contests should have a specific, strategic marketing purpose that builds your brand and, ultimately, boosts sales. The simple rule of thumb is that if what you're giving away costs more than what you anticipate in increased sales, it's best to pass on the opportunity.

An online interactive contest can be very easy to craft. Your Web designer can create a form where visitors input their information to enter. Though some larger sites use elaborate databases to organize the information collected from the forms, you may not need to get this extravagant. You can have your Web designer set up the forms so that all the data collected is sent to you by e-mail — every time someone enters the contest, you get an e-mail with his contact information. You'll have to read the e-mails, but it's a simple, easy, and inexpensive way to execute a contest.

If you want something more sophisticated or polished, you can use work with a company that specializes specifically in designing online contests. Although this approach will be more expensive than doing it yourself (with your Web designer), companies like these are likely to offer a menu of options that may include everything from design to data gathering/reporting to complete *fulfillment* (the execution of the contests and the delivery of prizing), taking the burden entirely off your shoulders. Companies who handle this can be quickly discovered by searching for "online contests and fulfillment."

Only ask people for what you need. If all you really need is a name and an e-mail address for your form (and to meet your goals in terms of acquiring people's contact info), then stick to that — don't ask for their mailing address, phone, or other info unless you need it.

Drafting the rules

No one wants to be told what to do, but when it comes to enter-to-win contests, rules are essential. Drafting your online contest rules is an important step to help clarify the goals of your contest. Plus, written rules provide you some protection against some unlucky person crying foul when she doesn't win an enormous stuffed pink elephant or other obviously brand-related premium.

The rules that are right for your contest depend on the sort of contest you want to conduct, and they'll depend primarily upon what you're asking of the participant. Post all rules and restrictions where they're easily accessible and legible.

For example, if you're conducting a contest, you may require the consumer to make a purchase. In contrast, a sweepstakes generally does not require a purchase. The rules and verbiage for executing an online contest varies from state to state. As is the case with legal jargon, the difference lies in the details, if you're executing a major contest with high-value prizes you'll want to source and secure a contest fulfillment house to handle these rules for you.

When you're drafting your list of rules, ask yourself the following questions:

- ✔ **Who is eligible?** Can only left-handed, piano-playing accountants participate? Make your qualifiers as clear cut as possible, but be cautious to not discriminate. The most common restrictions are ones in which entrants must be of a certain age to legally receive the prizing.

- ✔ **How many times a contest can be played?** Is your contest a one shot deal or can consumers come back for more. If they can come back for more, how many times a day can they enter. If you give people the option to enter multiple times, you also have the chance to get them on the site, keep them there, and encourage them to come back for more — in other words, you've created a sticky site.

- ✔ **What are the prizes?** Prizes are the meat and potatoes of the contest. Whether you execute a contest on a street level or online, undoubtedly the first question out of your consumers mouths will be, "What do I win?" So let them know in precise terms: the number of items being awarded, the specific model, and so on. Aside from fulfilling a legal need, providing all the details will make your contest appear splashy. If after making a list of your awards, it doesn't feel splashy, consider what you can do to sweeten the pot.

- ✔ **How will you select the winners?** Will there be a raffle where the winners are selected from a hopper? Do you have a computer that will select them at random? Will the winners be selected from players who answered a quiz correctly? Again, you want to lay this out as clearly as possible so participants know what they're getting into.

- ✔ **How will you award the prizes?** Will they be dropped over the winner's homes via cargo planes? (Hopefully not!) For example, you might say, "After the winners are selected, they will be contacted by phone and e-mail to verify contact information and the prizes will be shipped directly to them."

- ✔ **How many prizes is a site visitor allowed to win?** It's no fun if you're offering 15 prizes and one person wins 13 of them. We recommend stipulating one prize per person so that you can spread the wealth.

- ✔ **If you're running a sweepstakes, what are the odds of winning (if calculable)?** Chances are, if you're conducting your own contest, you won't have this information handy — why would you? Before you press on, however, you'll want to check with an attorney to see if your state or town requires it. If so, you may want to hire a contest designer (as suggested in the preceding section).

- ✔ **Will you have an age restrictions?** Depending on what you're selling, certain age restrictions may be in place. Again, this is usually a consideration when the entrants must be of a certain age to be able to receive the prize.

- ✔ **Are there any proof-of-purchase or other preconditions?** As kids we used to love to snip those proof-of-purchase bar codes off our boxes of Tasty Flakes in order to enter to win monogrammed cereal spoons. In some ways, collecting those proof-of-purchase labels became as much a part of the contest as the contest itself. If submitting a proof of purchase or some other qualifier is necessary, make sure you spell this out.

- ✔ **When is the contest over?** Especially if you're asking something specific of your customers, you'll want to make sure that the window within which they can participate is crystal clear.

- ✔ **How and when will the prizes be distributed?** How long after the contest is over will the prizes be awarded? You want to give consumers a window during which they may expect to hear from you if they win.

- ✔ **Are there applicable federal, state, and local laws that need to be acknowledged?** You may have heard the legal mumbles at the end of a commercial, "Not available in Ohio, Kentucky, Wisconsin, or for people who like black licorice in Mississippi." Legal ordinances serve to protect participants and the contest provider, so before you launch your contest, make sure that what you're doing is, in fact, legal.

If you're holding a contest, your best bet is to consult an attorney. Paying a lawyer (or leveraging products or services) to take 30 minutes to look over your rules can help to avoid potentially endless time in court if someone has a beef with your online contest.

Sending out the prizes

You've created your contest, your site hits have grown exponentially, and now it's time to pick a winner. For most of our smaller campaigns, we select the winners within the comfort of our offices through a basic drawing. Depending on the scope of your campaign, the number of entrants, and the structure of your rules, you may find that you can handle the selection and fulfillment yourself, saving yourself some money that you can use on your next big contest!

If your contest is larger or requires sending out many prizes, you may need to contact a fulfillment house to help you. *Fulfillment houses* are companies that specialize in handling fulfillment for contests, either as part of designing and managing the contest itself or in the separate function of distributing the prizes. If you're distributing more than a handful of prizes, you may want to consider a fulfillment house to handle the additional workload. Your clerical and shipping staff will thank you for it.

On the other hand, if your prizes are your own products, and you don't intend to give away a volume that would choke your shipping facility, then handling the contest fulfillment in-house would probably make the most sense for you and save you this expense.

Making It Personal: Uploads and Customization

Everyone wants to feel important, like everything in the world is created just for them. You can see this in bedazzled cellphones, vanity license plates, and tailor-made clothes. It's all about creating an experience that is particular to the consumer. Nowhere is customization more pervasive than on the Internet, where it's possible with relatively less expense per person.

The model developed by social networking sites like Facebook (www.face book.com) and MySpace (www.myspace.com), which we dive into in depth in Chapter 14, is very attractive for companies, especially companies with consumer brands that are looking to build an online community. Implementing these personalized elements can have great value as a marketing strategy because by creating items to customize content, using picture and video uploads, associated with your brand, you allow consumers the opportunity to do a work of spreading your brand for you.

For example, you may want to allow your site visitors to upload their own content for others to see and customize the look of their personal pages. If your brand has an icon character or mascot — such as a giant man made of tires — you may want to consider giving consumers the chance to upload their pictures and have their likeness shaped into a person made of tires! Recently, several movies, TV shows, and other consumer brands have had great success in using customization to spread their messages and brands; for example, you can turn yourself into a character from *The Simpsons.*

Although customizable applications are delightful ways to waste a lunch hour, unless you're a design prodigy, you'll probably need to call upon the resources of someone who is. Across the board, branded custom technologies and programming require far more work than what's needed to produce your basic static Web site.

On a smaller scale, you may be able to purchase simple programs that allow visitors to upload files, but you won't be able to have an impressive-sounding "fully integrated community experience" where consumers can participate in the customization of these files. For that, you'll need substantial programming resources.

Finding someone to do the work

A plethora of agencies focus is on creating dynamic presences on the Web. Within these agencies exist a multitude of extremely talented designers, Web developers, graphic artists, game designers, database developers, and programmers who can create something exciting. A quick online search for "internet marketing" or picking up *Web Marketing For Dummies* (Wiley) may help open you up to these wizards' capabilities.

Many of these agencies have dazzling skills and award-winning Web sites under their belts. One way to get a sampling of these agencies is to look to friends and colleagues who have had successful working relationships with web designers. Or if you are already working with an ad agency, pick their brains for suggestions. Regardless, the question to ask an agency when you're considering whether to work with them to produce your new customizable applications is

> Does this agency understand how to make my site function as a highly effective marketing tool?

If you're going to spend the money and creative energy to craft and create an exciting addition that allows uploads and customization, it should work beautifully in coordination with your existing site features to produce a lean, mean, marketing machine. Finding a designer who understands your site, how you want these pieces to work together, and where you want to grow will allow for a successful collaboration.

Offering something unique

You know you love to upload your picture to sites to see what celebrity you most resemble or what kind of pixie you are — we know because we do, too. But even as we make this confession, as objective marketers we have to acknowledge that the ability to personalize and customize our own corner of a Web site is not really a new phenomenon anymore — and it's not different enough to elevate your brand. If you want your site to function as an effective marketing tool, you need to bring something *new* to the table.

This is where your inner guerrilla takes flight and you challenge yourself to bring something new and exciting tot the marketplace. Start by considering what attracts your consumers.

For younger demographics in particular, nothing grabs consumers' attentions like things that play to their not-so-guilty pop-culture pleasures. What appeals to your target? Music? Movies? Blogs? Sports? What is the next big thing in pop culture that can be rallied back to your brand? See what original concepts can be added to your site to keep them coming back and hopefully bookmarking your page.

For an older demographic, can you create an impressive new widget or customizable application (read more about this in the following chapter) that tracks the person's financial flow by way of a constantly updating icon? Politics, real estate, dining, and other related topics can serve as great fodder to provide your older consumers with customizable content that is not only visually and personally appealing, but useful as well.

Always come back to the question, "How will this help my brand grow?" While you're ideas are undoubtedly cool, make sure it creates or perpetuates growth for your brand.

Whatever creative twist you add on, you want to make sure that your efforts build *brand equity* (a positive result or consumer impression based on well-received marketing efforts). Increasing brand equity through the use of your custom application differentiates you from the competition, and keeps your customers coming back for more.

Being cautious when releasing control

One of the reasons the Internet can be so appealing is the element of illusion and fantasy. You may be a 5'4", 120-pound claims adjuster from Kalamazoo, but online you're a 6', 180-pound dashing real estate mogul.

Although the creation of custom personas (often called *avatars*) is fun and can help create sites that consumers come back to again and again, as an online marketer it can come with some pitfalls. Although folks on the Internet are a generally amicable bunch, sadly not every Internet user is reasonable, mature, or sane. One bad apple can ruin the bunch, so you need to apply some type of filtering and editing capacity to make sure that nothing goes up on your site that you don't want there. After all, everything posted on that site will be associated with your brand. You don't want someone spewing hate or obscenities right next to your bright, previously peerless logo. Stay on top of your site, and make sure that nothing added by a consumer harms your reputation.

Build an editing capacity into your software and inform your users that content will be screened before being posted. Then task someone with monitoring the content to avoid distasteful consumer comments. This may seem like an extra expense but applying these resources from the get-go can enable you to avoid a PR disaster down the line.

Showcasing and sharing user-generated content

There's an old management axiom that applies well to user-generated content: "People support what they help to create." People enjoy the interconnectedness of participating online, the sense that they're part of something larger. From a marketing standpoint, business owners hip to this phenomenon can utilize their custom capabilities to help build brand loyalty. Directing attention your site by allowing visitors the opportunity to contribute in a way that is meaningful (such as providing a stage for users to add their thoughts and comments, pictures, and video to your Web site) works to your strategic advantage.

Leveraging a sense of community and competition is essential when it comes to featuring user-generated content. One time-tested method of motivating your users to supply fresh, customized content is to recognize and reward their efforts. Holding on-site contests that encourage good-spirited competition, giving awards, and displaying winning submissions prominently will not only keep your users interested in contributing, it'll also help bring the most compelling content out there directly to your site. Say you're running an online fish tackle store — wouldn't it be fun for your customers to send in snapshots of their latest catch? One lucky fisherman could win a year's worth of bait, just for reeling it in.

Chapter 14

Getting Social

- -

- -

C hances are if you have teenage children or 20-something employees (and maybe even older), they'll probably hit some kind of social networking site today, if they aren't doing so right now.

Social networking sites have taken over the popular online landscape and held young minds captive with their interconnected nature. Where else can you leave messages for friends, manage your real-life social calendar, check out the latest single from that irreverent yet oh-so-poignant new rocker, and see videos of your friends acting totally ridiculous? The simple fact is that the opportunities offered online are virtually unparalleled when it comes to reaching younger demographics, making for fertile ground for you to plant your message in the minds of consumers.

In this chapter, we introduce you to a few of the more popular social networking sites, fill you in on the features that make these sites popular, and tell you how you can begin to make an impact at minimal (or no) cost. We also explore the existing marketing opportunities available on these sites and let you know how you can make informed choices if you decide to use them. We explore ways that you can maximize bulletin boards and chat rooms as an extension to your work on sites like the ones mentioned previously. Finally, we help you evaluate your success on these portals and use this knowledge to inform future efforts.

Welcome to the World of Social Networking

Social networking sites are Web sites that allow users to personalize their own pages and create a network, linking themselves to other people's pages. Social networking sites can be a way to get back in touch with long-lost high-school pals, gather people around a common goal, or check out pictures of that cute guy or gal you met the night before. Whatever the reason, social networking has grown into a societal phenomenon.

Although you may have only recently heard people recommending that you check them out on Facebook or MySpace, these sites have been growing by leaps and bounds since 2000. Aside from providing users with the opportunity to instantaneously communicate with one another, social-networking sites allow participants to form connections across the country or around the globe, all the while making the world seem a little smaller. And if that's not enough for you, it's just plain fun!

The customizable options on these sites vary from one site to the next (we get into the specifics in the following sections). Here are a few of the highlights at a glance:

- **Photographs:** Most sites offer users the opportunity to upload and post personal pictures that can be made available to other users in that person's network — a feature that has resulted in the cult practice of the "MySpace arm" picture: the self-portrait featuring the person's smiling mug and his arm holding the camera.

- **Personal and/or professional stats:** The specs featured here vary from site to site. The sites geared more toward younger people (like MySpace) let users list things like their favorite bands or TV shows, whereas the more professionally-geared sites (such as LinkedIn) focus primarily on a participant's résumé, professional achievements, and connections.

- **Comment boards:** These are sections of a user's page where friends can leave messages and post pictures or videos.

- **Personal blogs:** Some sites allow users to post a *blog* (short for *weblog*), which is often the online equivalent of a diary or journal.

- **Music and video:** Some pages allow users to give their pages a soundtrack or embed videos from popular video-sharing sites such as YouTube (www.youtube.com) right into their site.

The reason these features are important is because for certain demographics, these sites provide a completely customizable, brandable opportunity to bring your target consumers into your network at minimal expense. Fully understanding and appreciating (or, at the very least, having a good sense of humor about) the cultural aspects of these sites is tantamount to getting the most out of these cost-effectives options.

Your social networking site is a satellite extension of your online presence, or as we like to think of it, the cocktail party or consumer mixer of the online world. That said, these days, just having a MySpace page does not a social networking marketing strategy make. On the other hand, just running an online banner-ad campaign on any of these sites isn't all you need to do. Both may be helpful to creating online buzz, but creating a healthy mix, in step with your budget, across several of these outlets will help you shape the best online strategy possible.

Looking At Your Options

Using social networking sites as a tool to market your brand allows you to really get in there and mix it up. Sign up for all the sites you've heard of and passively play around for a few days. You'll quickly figure out whether you want to use one site or another to promote your business, just by getting a sense of what the sites are like.

The most successful presences in these networks are the people, places, and brands that simultaneously entertain and educate like-minded people in a targeted way about their brand. Then take it one step further and supply users with unique, viral content that gives them reasons to share with others and return again and again.

To help you begin your expedition into territory you may have otherwise been leery of exploring, in this section we introduce you to a few of the current big players in the social-networking scene and provide you with a few statistics that you might find simply unbelievable. But believe it, because this information will help you make smart decisions about which sites you intend to work on and what you want to do with them. By being choosy with what sites you use, you can reach your audience in an exciting, targeted way.

Facebook

One of the more popular social-networking sites is Facebook (www.face book.com). Created in 2004, Facebook users have customizable profile pages, as well as the ability to add "friends" to their network and participate in networks based on common ties such as locations, jobs, and school backgrounds, among others.

In this section, we give you an overview of what Facebook can do for you. For even more information on Facebook, check out *Facebook For Dummies,* by Carolyn Abram and Leah Pearlman (Wiley).

The details

Unlike other social sites, which allow users to make their pages different colors, Facebook has maintained relatively uniform, streamlined pages. All the pages are essentially laid out the same way. Page users are encouraged to customize their pages by adding applications (known as *apps*). These apps run the gambit from being able to SuperPoke (sending one of dozens of topical predetermined messages) to virtually buying and selling their friends through Web applications. Brands have picked up on the popularity of these apps and have either partnered with social networking sites to produce computer "widgets" or created their own to make the most of consumers' playful tendencies.

When Facebook began, all users were required to have a college e-mail address in order to participate. Over time, Facebook opened its enrollment to anyone over the age of 13. To the clever marketer, evolution in membership practices provides valuable opportunity to reach desired demographics.

Recently, Facebook has enjoyed increased success by sidestepping the stigma that social sites are just for the kids. Increasingly, it seems to be attracting older users looking to stay in touch without all the flashy visual stimulation that other sites, like MySpace, feature.

This amplified appeal can be attributed to the fact that many of the early-adopting college students who used the site to coordinate study groups and *Animal House*–style antics in the site's infancy, have all graduated but still want to use Facebook. What this means to businesses interested in marketing to the 18 to 25 demographic, is that its users are no longer poor college students. Now they're likely to be employed young professionals with money to spend.

Facebook has an extensive reach:

- ✔ It has over 70 million users (and it's growing).

- ✔ At the time of this writing, Facebook is the fifth most trafficked Web site in the world. (Not the fifth most trafficked *social networking site* — the fifth most trafficked *Web site*.)

- ✔ Facebook users view over 65 *billion* site pages per month.

- ✔ Forty-five percent of the Facebook's users return daily.

- ✔ Facebook users keep their common interests connected by over 6 million active user-generated groups.

How to put Facebook to work for you

If you're interested in Facebook, the first step is to create a page for yourself — start by setting up your own personal page, as opposed to one for your brand, so you can get the lay of the land first. Although we can tell you some effective ways to get started, the shape of Facebook changes rapidly, with the addition of 140 new applications added daily. The only way to know what's happening on Facebook is to participate.

You don't have to go crazy and start adding millions of friends (unless you want to, of course), and you may even want to keep your page private so you can explore in relative anonymity. (Go to your home page and click on Privacy. From there, you can decide who can see your profile, who can view your pictures, and who can search for you.) This way, you can get a sense of the landscape, the users, the applications, and see if the site is right for you and your brand, while preserving your "shadowy mystique!"

Creating a company page or group

One option for staking out your space on Facebook is to get yourself some fans! The simplest way to put your brand on its way to rock-star status is to set up a page specifically for your brand.

Another option is to create a group. Creating a group is far less involved than setting up a new page because you can launch it from your existing pages by clicking on the group's icon and then selecting the Create a New Group icon in the upper-right corner. After clicking here, you set up the basics of what the group is about and you can start inviting fans to join your group. From there you can elaborate as much or as little as you'd like.

In this "scene" the most clever groups win out. What can you do to make yours unique? Perhaps a funny name or intriguing catch phrase can be used to attract consumers to join your group.

When they join your "online assembly," the name will appear on their page. Often which groups a member belongs to gives insight into who that person is or how they would like to appear — and people usually carefully consider this information before adding. Consider how you can play off this to make your online community a "must add."

There are several advantages to creating group pages:

- ✔ **You can track the people who are interested in your brand.**

- ✔ **When people join a group or fan page, the respective pages are published on their profile.** Depending on the number of people with whom your group members are friends, the number of impressions you could get is infinite. Cost to you for this exposure: *nothing!*

- ✔ **After people have joined your group, you can reach out and engage them in a variety of ways.** For example, you can send them a message, invite them to a brand-related event, and engage in discussions that happen right on your page.

Although you may quickly become drunk with power by being able to reach so many people so quickly and easily, we strongly encourage restraint. Only send group messages for items of specific importance. If users decide you're sending them too much fluff, they may just walk away from your page or community.

Publicizing events

You may want to hold some consumer events to raise awareness and pick up some press for your brand. (For more on events, check out Chapters 7 and 8.) To get the word out to your Facebook followers, you can create a group-related event and immediately invite all your fans with a few careful keystrokes. It's quick, it's easy and when combined with other efforts, it's a useful tool to encourage attendance.

Sharing videos: Viral content

We love funny videos. And the great thing about social networking sites is your ability to spread your photos and videos in what's known as *viral content* (it spreads faster than a cold, minus the runny nose).

For example, one well-known beer manufacturer created an entire series of slightly off-color Web ads that while, a little "blue" in their skew, were genuinely funny. One involved a swear jar where every time someone swore at the office, he had to put a quarter in the jar toward the purchase of this beer. The ad then launches into a series of profanity-laden (with tasteful bleep-outs) scenarios as the office workers work toward the purchase of the beer. This commercial would definitely offend old Aunt Gladys if she saw it on TV while watching a rerun of *Matlock*. But a video of this nature would probably only be discovered and forwarded on by people who find it funny.

One of the most common ways that viral content is shared is by placing it on friends' "walls"(breaking down the Facebook lingo: a "wall" is a space where friends can post open messages to a comment section of the page) for viewing by all. Facebook takes this construct one step further with its Fast Forward function — if the user thinks a clip is funny, she can simply click Fast Forward and the video is sent to all her friends in a flash.

The creative challenge is to come up with content that is viral-worthy. You need to come up with something that's not only brand-related, but funny enough that people want to post it on their Facebook pages and share it with all their friends?

If the idea of keeping up with all this stuff seems like more than you're interested in handling, you may want to hire a young college student to spend several hours a day on the site and act as the "Webmaster" for your presence there. You can draw on his knowledge of the site to help keep your stake in this space current and relevant.

Wanna have the opportunity for people to play with your brand daily? Create a custom brand widget or consumer page application! If you have some money to spend you may consider approaching Facebook directly to discuss opportunities for the development of such an application. A click on the "Advertising" link at the bottom of each page will give you the contact information to begin this process.

MySpace

Behold the behemoth that is MySpace (www.myspace.com). Currently, MySpace is the largest social networking site in the United States. The site is unique in that it allows for nearly complete customization for its users — and teaches consumers basic HTML coding in the process!

MySpace currently skews a bit younger than Facebook, but that's not always such a bad thing. Kids buy stuff, too!

In this section, we give you an overview of what MySpace can do for you. For even more information on MySpace, check out _MySpace For Dummies,_ 2nd Edition, by Ryan Hupfer, Mitch Maxson, and Ryan Williams (Wiley).

The details

MySpace was created in 2003 and has enjoyed remarkable success in giving its users the opportunity to create pages that are truly unique. When people sign up for the site, they get a very basic layout and one friend, Tom (the site's president), and they're launched into the world. MySpace users can customize their pages through HTML code that's available online.

What's that? You're not an HTML master? Not a problem, here's what the site itself advises:

> If you do not know HTML or CSS, you can reach out and make a new friend by asking someone who has color, graphics, and/or sound on their Profile page how they did it. People on MySpace are friendly and always willing to help, so just ask! This is a great way to meet new people!

It may sound silly or dismissive, but this approach has helped to develop the sense of community within MySpace. The tone of finding commonality and celebrating the things that unite its users has played a huge role in the success of the site. By making these connections, people are given the opportunity to gussy up their pages and make some new friends — or in your case, potential customers — in the process.

MySpace isn't right for everyone (no site is), so the best thing to do is sign up, set your privacy setting on high (which you can do by going to My Account and clicking on the Privacy link), and noodle around to see what's happening.

Here are the stats on MySpace:

- ✔ Monthly, MySpace has more than 110 million active users throughout the world.
- ✔ As of early 2008, it is the highest trafficked Web site in the United States.
- ✔ On the average day, 300,000 new people sign up on MySpace.
- ✔ More than 8 million artists and bands have pages on MySpace Music (`http://music.myspace.com`).

How to put MySpace to work for you

Moving into the realm of MySpace is exciting because it enables you nearly limitless customization options for your page. There's no need to sweat it if your HTML skills are rusty (or nonexistent) — there are numerous sites on the Internet where you can create custom HTML codes for MySpace. If you can copy and paste, you're set.

Creating a company or group page

The first step toward staking out your existence on MySpace is to create a company page. From there, you can create groups.

Say your company makes delicious burritos geared toward kids and teens. Start by creating an initial Myspace page that really drives home the deliciousness of your burritos. *Remember:* You're creating a page that will be viewed by users who will look at numerous pages that day, so you want to make sure that what you're saying is quick, clever, and to the point.

After you've clearly established your home base, you may want to create a group called "Burritos on the Go," where users are encouraged to post pictures of themselves performing BMX bike aerial acrobatics or other tomfoolery while enjoying your exceptional burritos. Your initial page may be about "you," groups make it about "them" — your customers. A group encourages a sense of inclusion and consumer ownership that can serve your brand well.

MySpace encourages freedom of expression, but like all good things, some people take this too far. To avoid problems, such as persons posting lewd or distasteful material to your page's comment section, you can either employ a Webmaster to keep your page clean of Internet debris, or simply set your privacy settings so that all material posted has to be approved by you prior to publishing. Some MySpacers may cry censorship, but we'd rather field these claims than have to answer for offensive, hateful, or obscene material living on our page.

Sending out bulletins

One of the MySpace features that's a great asset for brands is the bulletin space. Here members are able to post "notes" about happenings, funny surveys, or other events. The reason that this function is particularly effective is because, whenever a bulletin is posted, that note is featured on the homepage of every one of your "friends" until time pushes your bulletin further down the queue.

The bulletins serve as friendly, nonintrusive ways for you to stay in contact with your connections. When paired next to friends' posting for sublets or birthday parties, your bulletin doesn't seem like a marketing ploy — it seems like just another update from this bustling community.

Of course, you don't want to abuse the privilege. Posting periodically is totally acceptable, but make sure your postings don't grow from endearing reminders to hated spam. Major announcements of once a month (at the most) are usually tolerated, while once-a-day announcements are despised and can result in consumers disavowing their "friendship" with you.

Writing a blog

TV pundits and other talking heads just love to lament how the youth of today are overweight, videogame-playing illiterates, but we say, "Not so fast!" Literacy has taken a new twist on the Internet. Instead of reading Victor Hugo in their spare time, users are reading blogs — and perhaps more important than reading, they're participating.

Each MySpace page is enabled so that the user can post blog entries. Other MySpace users can read and comment on the posts. In this capacity, reading becomes a dialogue.

When it comes to marketing online, you can use your MySpace blog to post beneficial information in a targeted way to your users — not as a pitchman, but as a participant in the community. This allows your audience to read your updates and become involved in an immediate way. In the end, it helps to generate a greater sense of involvement and overall excitement.

Many MySpace newcomers find creating a blog to be a bit of a puzzlement. The key to writing a blog that consumers want to read is creating something that entertains while still communicating your message. Want a good start? Here's a challenge in creative writing: Take your most recent press release (see Chapter 16) and turn it into the anti-press release. You can do this by writing more casually, throwing in a few tasteful jokes, and finding the most relatable terms to communicate your message. Then — snap! — you have yourself a blog posting. Your consumers will remember the message that had all the important info presented in an entertaining way.

Promoting events

You can create page-related events, which are e-vitations that come from you, to share with your friends. Send out casual electronic invitations to keep your friends in the loop about your upcoming special events.

Less is more. Be selective about when you choose to send out these invites to ensure that people do actually participate when something big comes up.

And beyond

The growth and additional opportunities provided by social networking sites changes just as quickly as the face of guerrilla marketing itself. The site that is white hot today is tomorrow's dated dud. Although the interconnectedness of people through these larger sites grows exponentially by the hour, we predict that this trend will cool and consumers will request more quality, interest-specific content. This desire will result in the increased patronage of stand-alone sites targeted for particular niches — but that's just our hypothesizing.

What we *do* know for sure, is that although Facebook and MySpace are the big social networking sites, there are a host of others. Many of them employ similar features to those offered by Facebook and MySpace. In this section, we give you a sense of some of the other more popular sites, so that you can work as an informed consumer and make the best choices about where to make your appearance on the social networking scene.

LinkedIn

Networking. When it comes to business, this single word can cause some people to cringe, while other people become filled with glee. Whatever your take, you can utilize sites such as LinkedIn (www.linkedin.com) to maximize your contact with people who could help your brand. And if you're in the cringing contingency, you can keep them at arm's length.

Developing strong industry connections and relationships can help to solidify your trade presence. LinkedIn is yet another tool to help you do so. The site acts as a virtual résumé, project update, and endorsement center. It gives partners, clients, and vendors an opportunity to learn a little more about the people they're working with on a (virtually) personal level.

The core concept for LinkedIn is that its users aren't usually looking to have bragging rights for the highest number of virtual friends. Instead, its users are generally seeking to have a way to collect their business and social contacts. To help achieve this, users must know their contact's e-mail address to add them to their network. The result is a network of people who actually *know* each other and use these connections to further develop business relationships.

Twitter

In the past decade, we've grown accustomed to having our cellphones strapped to our hips. Twitter (www.twitter.com) is the natural progression of social networking. It allows the connections that users feel online to be taken with them everywhere, and makes online interconnectedness mobile.

Here's how it works: You can post a message to your Twitter account either on your computer or by sending in a text message or other approved third-party message (such as instant message). The message is posted to your page and distributed via text message to friends who have elected to receive your updates. Twitter has created a culture of microbloggers — so named because Twitter posts are limited to 140 characters.

Cellphones are one of the few bastions of privacy (kept safely away from telemarketers). Even the most loyal fans of your brand will quickly grow tired of hearing from you every time you make a sale. So pick your shout-outs wisely.

Friendster

Friendster (www.friendster.com) scooped both MySpace and Facebook in making its way into the marketplace when it launched in March 2002. The site offers similar features to the more popular sites, such as messaging and comments.

Despite the similarities to those presented by Facebook and MySpace, at least among U.S. users the appeal of Friendster has fizzled, so it doesn't make nearly as ripe a place to focus your marketing energies. This is just our take on it, though. You may find that Friendster is the perfect fit for your product.

Second Life

Second Life (www.secondlife.com) — you've read about it, you've heard about it, now what the heck is it? In the most essential terms, Second Life is an online virtual world, in which participants can carry out a variety of activities. They can meet each other and chat with players online; buy and sell goods, services, and land; and customize their own appearance.

In 2007, Second Life was wildly successful with everyone from politicians to major international brands creating their own stake in Second Life. Since then, much of the buzz has died down. While we don't personally endorse this outlet as the best spot, you may still want to explore your options here — maybe you'll find it's just what you're looking for.

Using Existing Sites for the Good of Your Product

So you wanna be big on these networking sites, do you? Well, good. To help you do this, we've compiled a list of a few tips to help you put your message out there:

- ✔ **Be yourself.** There are a million 15-year-old youngsters posing as 25-year-old Venice Beach body-builders, and it annoys the heck out of site users. Because so many features in social-networking sites can be customized, make sure that what you put out there is as accurate as possible in representing your brand. When it comes to ethical marketing online, honesty is the best policy — and besides, we like you just the way you are.

- ✔ **Protect your stake.** With all this freedom out there in this global community, the risk of unsavory cads hacking into or inappropriately commenting on your site is quite high. To protect yourself, change your password weekly and set your security and privacy settings at a level in step with your perceived risk. An offensive comment or image posted on your page for only a few hours can do irreparable harm to your brand.

✔ **Participate.** It really is a community out there. Although you may roll your eyes at some of what you see out there, participating will help perpetuate your appeal on these sites. Comment on the pages of like-minded artists, athletes, or other brand-related "influencers" (see Chapter 12). Getting a dialog going with your target consumers and thought leaders only helps to further your image online.

✔ **Give 'em something they can't find anywhere else.** What unique content do you have that can keep your users coming back for more? Can you write funny blogs? Do you have a talented nephew in film school who can create incredible 30-second Webisodes? Do you know someone famous who will pose with or endorse your product or service? Use what you've got to create exclusive opportunities to bring traffic to your pages and have them keep coming back to see what's next.

You may quickly find that you've created a cult following for your brand. Unfortunately, their love is not unconditional. In no time at all you may find your most loyal fans swayed by the flavor of the week — *if* you don't innovate. The reason that guerrilla marketing and social-networking sites gel so well is that the success of both relies solely on the ability of their practitioners to innovate from within.

Like any successful community, you need to give in order to receive. Many times brands give increased (and maybe even exclusive) access to their users in order to maintain this hook. Maybe it's access to a blog from band members or cast members, behind-the-scenes video, audio snippets, live chat with fans and customers, and even exclusive performances for members only. The key to building it beyond the basic framework is asking yourself, "What more can I provide to keep what we're presenting new and fresh?"

Simply creating a presence on these sites and not having a maintenance strategy can actually hurt your brand by making it look stale and boring. You have to maintain the integrity of your initial offering, but always be alert to opportunities that could draw one person into your network who can further the buzz for your brand.

Figuring Out if Your Social Skills Are Working

How will you know whether having good social skills pays off? We like to think of participating in social-networking sites as an investment. Most brands won't sell their wares directly off their social-networking sites, so some people may wonder, "What's the point?"

The point is that increasing your social circle gives you the chance to raise awareness of your brand. Then it's just a matter of how many times you have to make an impression before your target makes a purchase. How fun is it that you're making impressions in a relatively creative way, at no cost to you? Plus, you can have direct contact with your audience, without the cost of a pricey focus group.

In the court of online public opinion, the power of the individual is great. The public will quickly let you know what you're doing wrong, but they'll also let you know what you're doing right. Sure, people love to point out the attacks posted by a highly opinionated online blow-hard — but even more powerful is the tremendous sway that positive endorsements hold on the image of a particular brand.

If you're doing it right, you'll reap the rewards quickly. Successful pages will note increased page hits and increased friend requests. Make sure you include site analytics (see Chapter 12) so you can track in concrete terms what kind of bounce you're getting from your sources.

Part V

If a Tree Falls in the Woods . . . The Power of the Press

In this part . . .

If a tree falls in the woods and no one is around to hear it, does it make a sound? Similarly, if you design and create the most unique, exciting event and no one's there to cover it, did it really even happen? Your pocketbook will be happy to confirm that, indeed, it did — but if you don't get a bounce in awareness or sales, you'll be wondering what the point is. To avoid getting all existential, reach for the power of the press.

In this part, we give you the tools necessary to get the airtime and ink crucial to the success of a guerrilla marketing campaign. To help you attain the media kudos you deserve, we begin by unleashing the shameless self-promoter within. To that end, we identify the people who can best carry your message to the public, and arm you with the tools necessary to communicate your objectives effectively.

Suppose you're not one of those people who like to toot his own horn. Don't worry — there are people who will toot your horn for you. We round out this part by shedding a little light on the people whose business it is to get press: publicists and public relations professionals.

Chapter 15

Identifying Your Outlets

*S*ummertime rolls around and you can't help but be filled with feelings of wanderlust as you gaze out the window and see smiling people enjoying the beautiful weather. That's it, you resolve, you're going to blow this popsicle stand and have the best vacation ever!

Before you can attain this lofty goal, you have to identify the highlights that are going to make your jet-setting two-week vacation everything you dreamed.

To get the most out of this exciting summer excursion, you pull out all the stops. First, you drop a line to Aunt Sue in Florida, who it just so happens owns a beachfront condo. Then you place a call to that client in the south of France, who has long encouraged you to come out and explore his factory, which just so happens to be positioned right next to one of the finest wineries in the world. You build this into your vacation, because when else are you going to have the time (and be able to write off a trip to France)? Last, you decide you want the VIP experience, so you pull some strings to get the all-access L.A. experience. You've maximized all your contacts, articulated the goals and booked your ticket to a successful summer.

Getting exposure for guerrilla marketing efforts can be challenging in the same way that slating the perfect vacation is. Pinpointing and courting personal, professional, and media outlets is to successful guerrilla efforts as selecting Aunt Sue, the French countryside, and a red-carpet experience is to your outstanding vacation.

In this chapter, we help you create visibility and exposure for either the product you've created, or the campaign you're promoting, using new or pre-existing contacts in the mainstream media, industry trades, or more generic consumer outlets. We begin by looking to your very own address book. Who do you know that can help you get awareness and coverage? Sometimes all you have to do is make a gentle request to family or friends. Other times, you may need to get your industry onboard to generate some buzz in trade outlets. Or maybe you're shooting for the stars and looking to get some big-time mainstream ink.

Throughout this chapter we discuss these personal and professional outlets that can be leveraged (sometimes to the benefit of media coverage), consider the pros and cons of each, and examine how you can use them to the betterment of your brand. When successfully applied, these outlets can give you exceptional results that may end up entitling you to that incredible vacation after all!

Sometimes It Is Who You Know: Leveraging Your Existing Contacts

Big ideas happen every day, but you may never hear about them without the help of various outlets. Whether you're having a grand opening, offering a new service, overhauling your brand's image, entering into a mutually beneficial partnership, or just jumping off with an incredible guerrilla campaign, you need to call upon a variety of connections to get the attention you deserve.

Influencers, opinion leaders, or trend-setters — whatever you want to call them, when it comes to identifying press opportunities, you want to get these people in your corner. When surveying the outlets where you can get trusted information or advice, start with those sources most immediate to you and build out from there.

When you're considering the purchase of a car, who do you turn to for advice? When you're talking money and the economy, who seems to have his finger on the pulse of it? When it comes to hip trends, who's opinion do you trust? Depending in its relevance to your product, these are the sources you want to turn to first for advice as these are your personal "trusted sources."

Have you ever turned on your TV to see some talking head communicating his expert opinion on the current news of the day, only to switch to a rival channel and see the same person reciting the same position you had just heard on the competing network not five minutes before? No, you're not suffering from some sort of very short term déjà vu. This expert has just achieved insider status on this particular topic in the media biz.

In the current climate of the 24-hour news cycle, smart TV producers know that the task of providing their viewers with credible points of view is essential to the success of their respective programs. As a result, the imperative is on these producers to present trusted sources. As you build your business, you want to do all you can to frame *yourself* as one of these experts or trusted sources.

Unlike advertising, your own personal "public relations" network can thrive by relying on getting your message in credible outlets (whether they're within your peer group, trade circle, or consumer press). Also known as *earned media,* having your message accepted in news and editorial outlets carries with it implied credibility (or what the experts like to call a *third-party endorsement*).

When you think about it, it's a lot like a romantic relationship. If someone says that she's wildly intelligent, you may just think she's is a braggart. However, if this same person gets a similarly ringing endorsement from someone *else,* you may be a little more receptive to engaging her intellectual prowess.

One of the best ways to start generating this sort of reliable-source status is to establish yourself as the go-to source on a particular topic. You can do this by participating in speaking engagements, submitting articles to trade and local publications, and actively participating in your trade and local business community. The more clout you can gain in the industry, the easier it will be down the line to attract attention and placement for your product or service. (For more on using these resources to set yourself up as an industry expert, look to Chapter 13.)

"I saw it on TV — it's got to be true!" If only consumers held that sort of naiveté. As the public becomes increasingly aware of the crossover of advertising and editorial content, brands face an uphill battle when presenting their messages. Even while you may know that the weather report you're listening to is sponsored by Tired Boy Mattresses, on a conscious level, you're less skeptical of product messages mentioned in news channels as opposed to paid ads. This small opening in the fortress of cynicism is how you can work to begin your press outreach.

Marketing guru Jack Ries lays out this strategy of tearing down this cynicism simply. Begin the launch of new or improved products with a strong public relations and press outreach first to generate baseline interest and credibility. Then monopolize on this interest by moving into your advertising strategy. Reis's rationale is succinct and sound. Win the acceptance of a skeptical public. Then, after you have your consumers abuzz with interest, drive the offering home with strong advertising efforts.

In this section, we begin with those outlets closest to you, such as friends and family. Get them to endorse you on their blogs, or drop your name on their podcast or public access program (provided they won't do any damage to your brand). From there, look to local and trade press. Do you have a good contact who you know would give your product a fair shake? Pitch them for some editorial (we get into public relations outreach in Chapter 16). Finally, after your efforts have gained momentum, call in that favor for the introduction to mainstream media that could put you over the top!

Flipping through the Rolodex: Your personal network

When your creative muse hits you and you're ready to make your announcement (whether it is a big guerrilla campaign, or the launch of a new product), your number-one stop should be your address book. Write down exactly what you're doing or what you're looking to achieve, and then make an assessment of how your personal network may help you reach these goals.

Whoever said flattery gets you nowhere? One important thing to keep in mind when you start taking inventory of existing familiar contacts is that the people in your group of targeted contacts probably has already played a role in what you plan to announce. If that's the case, cite them for their involvement where appropriate so they're able to share in a bit of the glory. Yes, there's a little ego-stroking going on here, but this kind of acknowledgement will also get contributors and partners in your corner as well, and that can't hurt.

Although it can be great to share the spotlight with partners and contributors, it's best to check with them before submitting their names and contributions. Giving credit for assistance is a gracious gesture, but such expressions could backfire if the person you're giving the hat tip to does not want to be mentioned for one reason or another. Basic rule of thumb: Ask first.

After personally handpicking all of the contacts in your Rolodex who receive your announcement regarding your campaign, product, or service, it's time to rank them. Prioritize all of those in your list who should receive the message of your announcement first. Remember to place special consideration with those who you consider can sway others about the validity of your announcement. Again, this is all about putting your message directly into the hands of the people who can do the most with it, the influencers.

After compiling your ranked list, go back through it and note how each of these people will receive it. Is there a "godfather" in the industry or community, and only a personal call will suffice? Or can you write a personal e-mail or letter directly to this person?

Whatever the mode of delivery (such as a call or e-mail), make sure this strategically selected list is advised of your big news *before* your big announcement hits the newsstands. There are three big reasons for this:

✔ **They'll provide you with some early feedback on your plans.** Especially look to those at the top of your ranked list — there's a reason you assigned them such placement. Their input and sway can help you. During this time period gently solicit reactions and pointers. This will give you the information necessary to refine and troubleshoot problems with your message.

✔ **They will consider themselves privileged "insiders," when the news is public.** We all like to be let in on secrets — it makes us feel valued and in the know. Use this status to help cultivate a powerful group of ambassadors who will be helpful once your news is released.

✔ **They will take ownership of the news after it's released.** Because you showed the courtesy of letting this group in on the secret, they'll carry this on for you once this information is disseminated to the masses. Not only that, but because they've lived with this information longer, you've also created unofficial experts along the way.

Keeping tabs on your contacts

The majority of us out there are not natural born schmoozers. Introductions, conversations, and nurturing of business (and sometimes personal) relationships for many people is, well, work. What good are those conversations, conventions, and coffee caucuses if you aren't able to call upon them when the time is right? To be able to reap the fruit of your labors, it's essential that your Rolodex is up-to-date.

When you receive e-mails of people moving onward and upward, don't just send them a monogrammed paperweight noting their achievement. Make a note of where they were and where they went and what they're doing now. The lowly entry-level person that you dealt with initially could be a senior manager at his next gig, so it's good to keep tabs on everyone.

Why are we stressing what might seem like, Working in an Office 101? Because far too often, opportunities are missed through poor monitoring of industry contacts. More important, when you're looking to extend PR to your guerrilla marketing arsenal, your contacts have to be current so that you get the most out of your media push.

Calling friends and family

Your friends and family want what's best for you. (If not, ditch them and buy new ones.) See how your friends and family may be able to help your cause by providing you with specific feedback or assistance in spreading the word about your latest accomplishments and presenting yourself in the best light.

Make a list of all your friends and family members, and make notes about where they work, where they volunteer, which clubs or organizations they're part of, who they know, and so on. For example, is your sister a prominent professor in a related field? Is your cousin a producer at the local radio station? Is your friend a sometime contributor to the local newspaper? These are ripe resources just waiting to be plucked, so take advantage of them.

Start by calling those in your inner circle who can do the greatest good, and build from there. Letting your family and friends in on your guerrilla campaign prior to going live with it allows them the opportunity to take ownership and assist you in your work.

Especially if the news you're about to release is particularly big, make sure that those you tap will respect the content and timing of your efforts. Although your dad may chat up your efforts because he's just so darn proud of you, if your competitors catch wind of what you plan on doing before you do it, they may end up beating you to the punch. To avoid this fate, make it very clear what you're asking of everyone and the timeline for your plans. That way, you can enjoy both a successful campaign and all the press you worked so hard to achieve.

Don't ask for too much too often. If you have a friend or kin with major pull, save that ace in your pocket and wait to call her until you need something that only she can deliver.

Boosting your exposure with business contacts

Say your company makes felt propeller hats for novelty shops and theme parks. It's a niche business, but one that keeps you very busy. Without even thinking, consider all the many clients, partners, and vendors you have. Plastics companies for the propellers, felt factories for the fabric and thread, the many amusement parks you sell to all over the world. . . . Think about who you spend your days talking on the phone with to ensure that your work is the best that it can be.

These people are more than just purchase orders and invoices — they're potential outlets that can spread the word for you.

Whether you're dealing in novelty bric-a-brac or artificial hearts, the people you work with have a vested interest in the success of your company. Vendors benefit from your continued if not increased sales from press exposures. Clients benefit from sharing with their consumers that they feature your industry-standard product. Make sure you business contacts are in the loop about your guerrilla marketing campaign.

When calling up business contacts, be a little sensitive to who works with whom. The person who sells materials to your company may also sell to a competitor of yours. We're not suggesting that you ask them to sign a confidentiality agreement, but be sensitive to who you can trust to keep a secret and who will best distribute your message.

Reaching Out to the Trades

After identifying contacts that can help refine your message and act as ambassadors for you, it's now time to look at building a media list for your announcement.

If your business sells directly to other businesses, you need to find media outlets that reach those businesses. These media outlets are called *trade media* — they're the media outlets that exist within a trade or industry. These outlets vary from vocation to vocation, but they're typically either magazines or Web sites that are read and known throughout the industry.

If you've worked in a particular industry for some time you're probably already familiar with these publications, and have the back issues littering your coffee table. If not, you may need a little guidance.

This direction comes to you courtesy of the North American Industry Classification Systems (NAICS). NAICS is a classification system jointly created by the U.S., Canada, and Mexico, which lists thousands of Standard Industrial Classifications (SIC). You may have heard it referred to as SIC codes, which is a good way to match your business to the industry where your customers reside. In addition to directing you to trades specifically related to you, it may also generate leads in new or budding industries that may be of use to you as well.

You've defined the outlets to receive your industry announcement, and identified the trade outlets that may be ideal for your company. Now it's time to see how you'll present your marketing concepts and in what form they'll appear.

Regardless of your business, you'll likely be able to find a trade organization and publication related to it. Depending on the size of your industry, this publication may be a quarterly newsletter or a glossy monthly publication. Whatever it is, get your hands on it, read it, and study it. Take the time to consider the articles and how they're presented. If it looks like your brand or announcement could easily be next month's feature, do some further investigation as to how you can make that happen.

For most publications, the search for finagling editorial opportunities can start on the Internet. Larger publications (such as glossy monthly magazines) have information on their *editorial calendar* (a year-long plot for intended features and stories to be promoted throughout the year), *content overview* (may be something as simple as a mission statement), *reader makeup* (basic demographics: sex, age, household income, and so on), and *circulation* (the number of people who read the publication). You can find most of these items in the About Us, Advertising, and/or Press Kit sections of their Web sites.

See if the publication's Web site says whether it's open to accepting editorial submissions. You want to find out if they'll accept press releases (see Chapter 16) about your activities, which might materialize in the form of editorial coverage for your brand. If so, add the publication to your media list.

When you begin compiling your list of trade publications associated with your service or brand, keep one thing in mind: Many times, publications need you as much as you may need them. Magazines and newsletters are always eager for fresh content — after all, without it, they don't exist. So don't feel like you're begging for attention — you're simply offering them ideas for content that'll benefit you as well as them.

If the publication does not offer the opportunity to submit editorial pitches in the form of press releases (or off the record conversations), you may want to come at it from a slightly different angle. Although most publications strive to keep their editorial content separate from their ad sales to preserve their editorial integrity, in some instances, you may be able to purchase an *advertorial*. An *advertorial* allows you to present your product in the publication as ad space that looks like editorial content. (You've probably seen similar things in magazines before — you can spot it by the word Advertisement at the top of every page of the advertorial.) An advertorial doesn't bear quite the same weight of actual editorial content, but it's sometimes a great way to get the word out about your product in more controlled form.

Depending on the caliber of the story and the size of the industry, giving a reporter the *scoop* (an exclusive first crack on your major news) could also go a long way toward getting a big bang and premium coverage.

Don't be so hungry as to present your announcement to any ol' outlet. Really consider who is going to read the publication and how your presence will be perceived. You may want as much press as possible, but make sure that your inclusion in the publication is in step with the image you want to present to both the industry and consumers.

Looking at Mainstream Media Options

The trades (see the preceding section) are great when you sell directly to other business, but if any of your customers are in the general public, how do you make them aware of — and get them excited about — your efforts? Through the mainstream media.

Approach the mainstream or consumer media only if your product or service goes direct to the consumer. If you sell bolts that can only be used on gargantuan construction cranes, the mainstream media won't be worth your time or money. Instead, your efforts and resources should be spent on wooing and exciting contractors who use your product.

Of course, there are always exceptions to the rule. You may have a product that's generally sold directly to other businesses — maybe you manufacture industrial kitchen appliances, for example — but you want to make the general public aware of your product (after all, the people who run the businesses you sell to are part of the general public, too). You can create a campaign where you show the fantastic desserts a baker can make with your oven. You finish your pitch by asking, "What kind of over does *your* baker use?" This approach is known as a *pull-through strategy*. When it works, it has the power of making seemingly pedestrian products or industries household names. (For more on the pull-through strategy, check out the sidebar "But what kind of semiconductor do you have?" in this chapter).

But what kind of semiconductor do you have?

The words *semiconductor* and *microprocessor* elicit images of studious nerds tinkering with their soldering guns. The microprocessor company Intel broke through this stigma by making computer chips cool and taking its case directly to the consumer. In a textbook example of the pull-through strategy, Intel made its product appealing by showing all the dynamic things consumers could do with their processors, and then followed up by asking exactly what kind of chip they had "inside." Intel made its chips so irresistible that they had consumers going directly into the computer retailers, and commenting, "Yeah, it looks good, but what kind of processor does it have?"

Local versus national

The good guerrilla knows to hit her target audience where they live, work, and play. The same holds true when targeting your mainstream media outlets' viewer or readership. Where are the consumers who will see this most likely to reside? Are you a diner renowned for the best banana pancakes in town or a budding rock band about to explode on the national scene? Your final decision on what media to court depends a great deal on whom your customer or prospects are and where they reside.

Think about all the places where you, your friends, and your co-workers get your news and information. Here are just a few of the more common ones with various levels of reach:

- ✔ Locally:

  - Town newsletters

  - Community bulletin boards & calendars

  - Bulletins from houses of worship

  - Municipal radio stations

  - Local newspapers

  - E-mail chains

- ✔ Nationally:

  - Newspapers from "big cities" that cover state and national news

  - Syndicated radio programs

  - Video sharing sites and blogs

  - Network and cable television

  - Magazines

If your customers are locally based, you may need to look no further than your next-door neighbor. Not only are your consumers close by, but you may even know them by name. Given this familiarity and close-knit ties to the community, you may not only have a greater awareness of the outlets but know people who work at those outlets as well.

If you're a consumer-based enterprise with national customers, your task will be slightly more complicated. To get the most out of your efforts, you'll want to examine media outlets that are national in scope and that would have an interest in accepting your news. Make a list of national outlets you may want to hit, prioritizing those that you feel would be the most receptive. As always, think targeted — if your budget allows, try to focus efforts in metropolitan areas where the greatest number of your customers are based.

If you're particularly industrious, you can find most of the answers to your questions about available options for various national media outlets online. However, if you have some extra money to spend there are other options. Commercially available media research firms such as Cision (www.cision. com) and BurrellesLuce (www.burrellesluce.com) are available with online subscription portals dedicated to assisting organizations and agencies to help define their media targets. However, as is the way in the world of business, it'll cost you.

Old-school print

Since the path forged by Johann Gutenberg and his printing press, the printed word has been the preferred method for the distribution of information. Print is where it all began. While newspapers or magazines, may not have the immediacy or reach of radio or TV, print is still an exceptional tool for consumers who are seeking more involvement with the stories they read beyond the immediate imagery.

If your product or service can't be reduced to a sound bite or begs for additional explanation, you'll want to strongly consider print. Doing so is important for two reasons in particular:

- ✔ Print publications can help to explain more complex concepts, ultimately making your product more appealing to consumers.
- ✔ This type of media has more space set aside for content.

Television

Psychologists love to hypothesize that Americans have severe attention deficit disorder due to the quick flashing of images in our lives — it's all about pictures. We watch TV and use snapshots and their associations to make instant connections to the story being told.

An assignment editor considering your message must be able to visualize the story in the form of these pictures. The story must show action and be compelling. The power of TV relies on the moving image — if the shot is static the story isn't properly communicated. This lack of communication will ultimately result in "your" airtime reallocated to an amazing dog that walks on its hind legs like a human.

When issuing a news release (see Chapter 16), think of how you can provide a visual dimension to the story. Doing so will help win over the assignment editor by helping him to tell the story. Perhaps add a sketch of what the event or installation will look like. You may even want to include bios on celebrities or talent who are expected to attend.

Radio

Like television, radio relies on immediacy. But unlike TV, it isn't burdened by the need for pictures, video, and illustrations. However, it does rely on the spoken word, dialogue, newsmakers, and the sound bite. Be prepared to offer radio news directors a spokesperson who can eloquently deliver sound bites that support your product or service. (For more on how to approach and pitch this media in a nontraditional way, check out Chapter 8.)

Chapter 16

Becoming a One-Person Public Relations Outfit

. . . .

. . . .

*Y*ou are a do-it-yourselfer. Fix the hardware in your malfunctioning computer? Cakewalk. Build a wall in your home? No problem. Yet, when it comes to the realm of public relations, you stop dead in your tracks.

We encourage you to take this fearless sensibility that you embody, rally your team around you company's message, and proudly declare, *"Sí, se puede!"* ("Yes, we can!")

The truth is, you already have many of the skills necessary to compile, distribute, and represent your press stories to the media. The ability to summarize your efforts in a concise, insightful way; the adroitness to identify and contact outlets to pass along your message (see Chapter 15); and the capability to articulately communicate your message (or find someone who can do it for you) to the powers that be — these skills are ones that you likely have. If you're thinking, "But I *don't* have these skills," this chapter shows you how to become self-reliant when it comes to dealing with the press.

In this chapter, we unlock the press prodigy that you are — just waiting to be unleashed upon trade, local, and national news outlets! You begin by getting inside the minds of the people who will publish or promote your work by crafting stories that are easy for your outlets to get onboard with. After you've defined your stories, we show you how to craft your very own press release, your personal invitation of sorts to the media to cover your story.

After the "invitation" has been sent, we look into making the most of this release — from crafting talking points that will get picked up, to making the most of the interest that you receive. Then after you've fielded countless interview requests, we get analytical and evaluate the successes and shortcomings of your public relations outreach, so you can evolve your efforts for the better in the future.

Embracing Your Inner Journalist

When Patrick was about 10, he swiped an old hammer-style typewriter from his dad; donned a fedora (with press tag appropriately slipped in the band), trench coat, and tie; and set about penning a series of dissertations on Navy jets that were way ahead of their time.

Unfortunately, these exposés never made it to the outlets they were intended for, but the experience was formative in producing an early foundation for creating good stories that the media would (someday) latch onto. It is this sense of a burgeoning reporter that you should harness when you start thinking about approaching the press.

The act of communicating your company's messaging is far less daunting than you might think. It's all about creating a compelling narrative. In the morning, on lunch, or whenever your boss isn't looking, you read online articles to pick up the news of the day. If you're like us, if the story isn't told in an intriguing way, your flighty tendencies kick in and you're off to read about the latest celebrity to get arrested.

To ensure that your efforts stand out against the backdrop of stale news and trashy media, you want to conceptualize and communicate your message in a way that has a *hook,* something that attracts the readers' attention and gets them to finish the article.

The disciplines of advertising and public relations are, at their core, journalism. In fact, many advertising and PR professionals are former journalists. They've taken the tools used in news reporting and put them to work in support of businesses, organizations, products, and services. In crossing over to the "dark side," as some journalistic purists may say, they've used the same form and structure they used in their news outlets.

Writing a Press Release

The press is a busy lot, constantly on the move. As a result, when you're producing materials for the press, you want to provide them with the tools to make writing and/or covering your story as easy as possible. To do this, the PR and press have come up with a protocol for communicating stories: the press release. A *press release* is a written submission to media outlets announcing something that the outlets may find particularly newsworthy.

Generally speaking, the press pool is a no-nonsense crowd. They can smell a fluff piece a mile away. The most successful press releases resemble stories in news and editorial pages of consumer and trade media. If your release is full of platitudes and little hard content, most editors will consider it fluff and bury it in the most undesirable section of the circular or delete it altogether.

To avoid your news ending up in the abyss of obscurity or flatly ignored, follow the basics of the news story to craft a release that's compelling, timely, and informative. The news story — or on the other side, the press release — must contain a few basic essentials:

- ✔ **Who** is producing this potentially pressworthy item?
- ✔ **What** are they doing?
- ✔ **When** are they doing it?
- ✔ **Where** are they doing it?
- ✔ **How** is this item being executed? What is particularly noteworthy about this effort?
- ✔ **Why** is this being done? To break a record? To raise awareness? To benefit a particular charity?

In this section, we walk you through the structure of a press release and tell you how to deliver it to the press.

Structure and form

In order for your press release to be read (or at least to have a greater *chance* of being read), you need to make sure the release follows the standard structure and form. The structure is there for a reason — it tells the press what they need to know quickly and efficiently.

Save your irreverence and tradition-bucking for your guerrilla campaign — when it comes to writing a press release, sure, you want it to stand out, but not because it was written with red crayon on construction paper and delivered by carrier pigeon. Follow the already established protocol — it'll pay off.

To help illustrate how to craft a press release, we'll use an example scenario of Secret Garden, a flower shop specializing in roses. To celebrate the shop's tenth anniversary, which happens to fall near Mother's Day, the shop is producing the world's largest rose sculpture crafted exclusively using roses.

In the following sections, we spell out each section of a press release, and give you examples of what Secret Garden might say in each of these sections. (You can use this example to create a press release that works for your business and your guerrilla campaign.)

Maybe it's just that we're a little unconventional, but drafting press releases can be fun. For practice, try to draft a few of your own either for past initiatives or for ones that you have coming up. Doing so, and looking at them objectively, will help you to get a handle on what you want to say and which press outlets will pick it up.

Do it backwards. Take print, broadcast, or electronic news stories you find particularly effective, and draft the press release you think might have been created to get that piece produced.

Headline

Imagine yourself going out to your doorstep, cup of coffee in hand, and picking up the morning paper. A story about your business and your campaign is on the front page. What would the headline be?

A good press release resembles a basic news story. You need to start the release with a snappy headline and an explanatory sub-headline that further supports the newsworthiness of the headline. Here's an example:

Secret Garden to Produce the World's Largest Rose

World-Renowned Rose Growers to Produce Rose Sculpture for Mother's Day

Although the heading goes at the top of the press release, you may find it helpful to write it last — after you've got the content down.

Dateline

Media outlets will want to know the where's and when's of your release. Right after the headline, put the dateline, which includes the city and state (in all capital letters), as well as the month, day, and year, followed by an em dash (as shown below):

KALAMAZOO, MI, May 11, 2010 —

If you don't know em dashes from M&M's, you can just type two hyphens, like this: --.

Lead

You've enticed them with your headline and you've told them where and when your big effort is taking place. Now what are your opening shots going to be?

The *lead* is the opportunity to tell the readers exactly who is doing what. Here's an example:

> Secret Garden, award-winning growers of long-stemmed roses, has announced that it will produce the world's largest rose sculpture using 300,000 roses.

Explanation of what prompted the news

This is your opportunity to share with the media the *why* of your efforts. Why is what you're doing significant? What forces, relating to the company or otherwise, prompted this action to take place? Here's an example:

> To thank its valued customers for ten years of patronage, and all the mothers in the community it serves, Secret Garden will produce a large-scale thing of beauty for all to enjoy.

Supporting quote from a third-party

A third party, especially one that's well known or would otherwise seem objective or weighty, getting behind a story and showing encouragement for a news item can give it weight. Additionally, a supporting quote provides media outlets with an additional point of view from which to approach the announcement. Here's an example:

> "We're thrilled that Secret Garden has decided to produce this sculpture," said Harry Donnell, mayor of Kalamazoo. "This is an impressive tribute to our community and the mothers who add so much beauty to our lives. We're very excited to see the finished product!"

Additional information about the product or service

This is your opportunity to do a little touting of your company and the services you provide.

Don't get too self-congratulatory here. You don't want to alienate the editors and keep your piece from getting produced.

> Secret Garden's roses have received international awards in Switzerland, France, and Spain, and have been featured in glitzy Hollywood awards shows, but Secret Garden has long considered Kalamazoo home. Given its commitment to the community, it only seemed natural to extend a big thank-you to the people who have made the city a wonderful place to live.

Quote from a company official

Here you want to bring in the words of a company official, which allows you to speak directly to the community you're trying to reach. Here's an example:

> "Since putting down roots in Kalamazoo ten years ago, we've been humbled by the loyalty of our customers," said Susan Smith, owner of Secret Garden. "When it came time to celebrate a decade here, we knew we wanted to do it in a big, big way, with 300,000 of our signature roses."

Additional information about the product or service line

If the lead is your opening shots, then this section is the place for your parting shots. What last messages do you want to impart to the person who will end up reading this? For example:

> Secret Garden is proud to offer world-class flowers to the Greater Kalamazoo area and beyond. Its floral arrangements provide beauty to the lives of the clients it serves.

Boilerplate

To conclude your press release you want to provide a *boilerplate,* a stock prepared summary of your company and its offerings. After reading this quick paragraph, the press should have a clear picture of what your company is and what you do.

Don't have a boilerplate? You can easily compile one by answering a few quick questions about your company. Compile the answers in an articulate paragraph and, in a snap, you've got yourself a first-class boilerplate.

- ✔ What does your company do?
- ✔ For whom does your company do its work?
- ✔ What does this work result in?
- ✔ How does your company do this?
- ✔ Why is your company different?
- ✔ Where can people find out more information about your company?

For the Secret Garden flower shop, the boilerplate would be the following:

> **Secret Garden** is a world-class floral design group located in the heart of downtown Kalamazoo, Michigan [What does your company do?]. Known internationally for its quality products and designs, Secret Garden in the one-stop shop for custom floral designs, from local weddings to Hollywood premieres [For whom does your company do its work?]. Given its breadth of experience, the Garden is able to provide an endless array

of flawlessly executed designs [What does this work result in?]. Such execution is achieved through strict attention to detail and unparalleled customer care [How does your company do this?]. No job is too small or too large, as Secret Garden seeks to provide a unique experiences for every client [Why is your company different?]. For more information please visit us online at www.webaddress.com or call 800-555-1212 [Where can people find out more information about your company?].

Obviously, you wouldn't include the questions in brackets — we just put those in so you could see where and how each question was answered.

Paste your boilerplate at the conclusion of your announcement and your release is ready to be distributed. (To see the finished product, check out Figure 16-1.)

Down to the wire

The great Chinese general Sun Tzu once said, "Know thyself, know thy media. A hundred announcements, a hundred victories!" Okay, so maybe we took some liberties with the quote, but the essence is there.

Know the media that will be most receptive to your message, and you position yourself to land that coverage. Although you can do your best to know your outlets, inevitably you're bound to miss some. Good news: There are resources to help.

BusinessWire (www.buinesswire.com), MarketWire (www.marketwire.com), and PR Newswire (www.prnewswire.com), among others, are commercially available wire services which can substantially increase the number of people who see your news release. These wire services, are linked to thousands of print, electronic, and online news editorial outlets. They can ensure that your message gets to global, national, regional, trade, and consumer press.

These services work by taking your release and sending out to desired outlets. The rates for using these networks vary based on the word count and breadth of distribution. You can achieve targeted distribution to trade, regional, national, and/or global distributions (or as they're known in the biz, *circuits*). Generally speaking (but dependent on the circuit or service you use), rates for national distribution begin at $650 per release and grow from there.

The exceptional bonus of using such portals is the trickle down effect. Assuming that you've produced a truly exceptional campaign that is worthy of press notice, all it takes is a couple of select outlets to pick up your story in order to achieve a landslide of publicity. In the digital age, and with the viral nature of news items, that could be all you need to get the most out of your effort. Sure, using the wires may be a little more expensive, but it can certainly increase the exposure of your message exponentially.

Secret Garden
43 Roses Row
Kalamazoo, MI
800-555-1212

PRESS RELEASE

FOR IMMEDIATE RELEASE

MEDIA CONTACT: Daniel Jones, 800-555-1212 x34

'Secret Garden' to Produce the World's Largest Rose

World-Renowned Rose Growers to Produce Rose Sculpture for Mother's Day

KALAMAZOO, MI, May 11, 2010 – Secret Garden, award-winning growers of long-stemmed roses, has announced that it will produce the world's largest rose sculpture using 300,000 roses. To thank its valued customers for ten years of patronage, and all the mothers in the community it serves, Secret Garden will produce a large-scale thing of beauty for all to enjoy.

"We're thrilled that Secret Garden has decided to produce this sculpture," said Harry Donnell, mayor of Kalamazoo. "This is a impressive tribute to our community and the mothers who add so much to beauty to our lives. We're very excited to see the finished product!"

Secret Garden's roses have been received international awards in Switzerland, France, and Spain, and have been featured in glitzy Hollywood awards shows, but Secret Garden has long considered Kalamazoo home. Given its commitment to the community, it only seemed natural to extend a big thank-you to the people who have made the city a wonderful place to live.

"Since putting down roots in Kalamazoo ten years ago, we've been humbled by the loyalty of our customers," said Susan Smith, owner of Secret Garden. "When it came time to celebrate a decade here, we knew we wanted to do it in a big, big way with 300,000 of our signature roses."

Secret Garden is proud to offer world-class flowers to the Greater Kalamazoo area and beyond. Its floral arrangements provide beauty to the lives of the clients it serves.

Secret Garden is a world-class floral design group located in the heart of downtown Kalamazoo, Michigan. Known internationally for its quality products and designs, Secret Garden in the one-stop shop for custom floral designs, from local weddings to Hollywood premieres. Given its breadth of experience, the Garden is able to provide an endless array of flawlessly executed designs. Such execution is achieved through strict attention to detail and unparalleled customer care. No job is too small or too large, as Secret Garden seeks to provide a unique experience for every client. For more information please visit us online at www.webaddress.com or call 800-555-1212.

Figure 16-1:
This just in. To get your message to your press in a way that will get your story out, draft a press release like this one.

Context and delivery

In Chapter 15, we show you how to compile a list of desired outlets for your news. When you have your list ready, it's time to take the leap and distribute your press release. Unless the media outlet and its editors have specific preferences, get your contacts lined up and ready to send out.

Press releases are sent almost exclusively via e-mail. Many news and editorial outlets will not accept news releases as attachments, so to be safe, copy and paste your news release into the body of the e-mail message itself.

Type all the e-mail addresses of the news outlets and other influencers in the blind carbon copy (BCC) field of the outgoing e-mail. In the TO field, put your own e-mail address.

We can't stress how important it is to BCC these contacts. Although most of the contacts placed on your outgoing list can easily be found through a quick online search, people can get testy when you broadcast their contact information to hundreds of people. Plus, it's just plain tacky.

Take the time to proofread your entire announcement, and have others in your office who are sticklers for detail proofread it as well. Some media outlets will publish sections of the release in their entirety. Taking a second glance at your release will prevent your own typo from getting published.

Calling upon one of the primary axioms of guerrilla marketing, timing is everything. To get the greatest amount of coverage, familiarize yourself with the deadlines of the editors and reporters you're trying to contact. If it's a TV producer, don't call 30 minutes before air time. Likewise, if it's a radio reporter, don't call five minutes before the newscast. Not only will your piece not get aired due to its late arrival, but you're likely to annoy the very gatekeepers who you want to distribute your message for you. Ideally, you'll want to send your release out ten days prior to an event.

Avoid sending out your press release on a Monday or a Friday.

Steee-rike!: The Big Pitch

It's not just what you say, it's how you say it. After you send out your initial press release, you need to follow up with the media outlets. Follow-up is crucial to potentially pushing your release through — taking it from some excellent writing into real, live coverage.

The most effective way to support your press release is to reach out to the news media by phone. Reporters get numerous press releases every day. So when you get an editor on the phone, don't bark, "Did you get our news release?" Instead, try a little more tact and frame your announcement as something useful to them.

Here are few quick points that may help make the media outlets a little more inclined to cover your story:

- ✔ **Instead of calling to inquire about the status of your press release, play up the beneficial aspects of your story.** In other words, avoid being petty — instead of asking if they got the thing, amp up the fact that your story is right up the alley for their listener/viewer/readership. You have them on the phone — work to get the most out of it.

- ✔ **Be respectful, and remember that these people don't work for you.** Although journalists are always looking for stories, they're people, and if their experience with you is negative, you aren't likely to land coverage.

- ✔ **Think of this follow-up as the first step toward building personal working relationships with these press outlets.** You'll probably be calling them again very soon!

For most guerrilla marketing campaigns, you're likely to know what you're planning on doing at least two weeks out. If your goal is to get press, use this time to lay the groundwork with your outlets. In particular, if you're launching something incredible that you're relatively confident will garner major press coverage, create a list of pie-in-the-sky outlets. If it were an ideal world, and you could land any media outlet, which would it be? Start at the top of the list and offer exclusive, all-access coverage to your top pick. They may pass, and that's okay — just move on to the next one on the list.

Be smart about when you go around offering "exclusives." If your big event is your friend Harold dressed up as a tube of toothpaste, not only will the media pass, but you may just be laughed at, which could hamper your ability to successfully pitch ideas to them in the future.

In tree following sections, we help you put your best foot forward when your story is picked up by the press. We begin by showing you how to shape your talking points and get what you want to say ready for broadcast. From there, we give you a quick pep talk and set you up to be the next big thing!

Talking points

After sending out your press release, you need to get ready to be interviewed. (Hey, if you don't think positively about the success of your initiative, who will?) Start by compiling a list of talking points that will help you best communicate your message and support your press release.

Put yourself in the position of an editor. If it were your job to select stories and someone was pitching to you, what would you find interesting? Frame your pitch with that editor in mind.

Here are a few places to start:

- ✔ **Draft a concise sentence that summarizes the entire event.** Take time to make this the best sound bite it can possibly be, because this one sentence is most likely what will run.

- ✔ **Identify the most dramatic, visual aspect of your campaign.**

- ✔ **Make a list of any impressive numbers you can tout about your campaign.** For example, "We've collected 25,000 clowns from across the country to perform at the event."

- ✔ **Know the basics.** Have the who, what, where, when, and Web site information readily at hand so that when you're asked about it you can deliver it with ease.

Prepare press-friendly hard copies of all your major talking points and bring them with you to any interview, so that you can distribute them to your media outlets to complement your press release.

Givin' 'em a taste

You've pitched the media and now, as expected, the media wants to interview you. It's time to put your best foot forward.

Review your talking points and make sure that you're 100 percent comfortable saying them. Practice saying them to your family and friends. Like any major presentation, there's no such thing as being too prepared. Give yourself the tools to make each interview as effective as possible. Snag yourself a playful co-worker or friend and play host and interviewee.

Strive to make your presentation as confident and conversational as possible. Use the talking points as an aid, they are not written in stone. Feel free to riff off of what you've compiled as long as you're still on message. People will be engaged by someone they feel they could have a conversation with. The worst thing you can do is sound as if you're reading a script.

If your interview will be on TV and this is the first time you've done anything like this, do everything you can to make yourself comfortable. You may even want to break out the video camera and tape yourself in a mock interview to critique what you were confident with and what you weren't. You want to introduce yourself to the audience as an expert (see Chapter 15). The best way to do that is to present yourself expertly.

The Big Hits: Measuring the Media's Response

When we execute a press initiative, we monitor the results like hawks. How was our event perceived in the press? Who lauded it, who loathed it, or heck, who covered it at all. After your news release has been distributed, start tracking the print, electronic, and online coverage.

In addition to providing a memorable token of the successes of your activities, keeping track of all the coverage you get provides an objective recap of what you did, what worked, and what didn't. From these public records, you can gain further endorsements for your product. You can even share them with future consumers, letting them know what kind of company you are!

If you're an obsessive tracker as we are, you won't be able to find *everything*. In that case, you may want to hire a media tracking service or a clipping service, both of which can cast wider nets for print, electronic, trade, and online mentions. They can automate the process with sophisticated reporting devices.

Chapter 17

Hiring Publicists and Public Relations Peeps

∙∙

In This Chapter

▶ Deciding if you need help with public relations

▶ Finding and vetting the agencies

▶ Managing your expectations and results

∙∙

"*L*isten, love the idea, babe. Have your people call my people." How many times have you had this conversation, only to walk away and wonder exactly which people should call each other?

What's that? You've never had that conversation? Well, get ready for it. If you're going to launch a major guerrilla marketing campaign targeting press, there's a very good chance you're going to need "people."

But who are these elusive "people" we're referring to? They're publicists and public relations personnel. A *publicist* is a person who drums up publicity and coordinates its execution. Similarly, *public relations* (PR), in the broader sense involves maintaining a steady flow of information between client and intended recipients.

This chapter investigates exactly what these press people can do to take your event or campaign from something that 50 people experience, to something that lands on the front page of the paper the next morning and is featured on both the 5 o'clock *and* 11 o'clock news! Before theses people can take the reins to generate a publicity powerhouse, you need to decide a few things. First, can they do anything for you that you can't do for yourself? Next, how do you find these people? Then, who do you hire? And last, what type of services can you expect for your money?

As we discuss in this chapter, not everyone needs to hire these people. But when you hit the big time (and you will), you'll want to know exactly who to reach out to get the most out of your initiative. That way when it's requested that "people" call "people," you can smile, peer over your sunglasses, and reply, "You got it, babe."

Recognizing What Publicists and Public Relations Teams Can Do for You

You take pride in owning or running a business — and if you don't, you should! After all, you set budgets, hire staff, maintain inventory, and chart your company's strengths and weaknesses. It is a Herculean task and you manage it with grace — or, at the very least, a good sense of humor. One of the key requisites of a good manager is knowing what he *doesn't* know.

For many business owners, the world of publicity and press is just one of those things they don't know. If you're launching a major guerrilla marketing campaign, it may be time to bring in those who do know it well — publicists and PR teams. Especially if you're executing a guerrilla campaign where your goal is to raise awareness, such as in a stunt (see Chapter 7), you need to pull out all the stops to get the press to cover your event.

In some instances (see Chapter 16), you may have the tools, ingenuity, and contacts to connect with your desired outlets. But if you're doing a huge push for press, you want to bring in people who know how to get the press to cover an event, the same way you know how to make quality flibbity-jibits (or whatever you produce).

Here are a few of the common client requests of publicists and PR agencies:

- ✔ **Public relations counsel:** You may just want to ask an expert whether it's a good idea if you launch 5,000 branded balloons to see where they go. The agency may then provide you feedback such as, "No, because the rubber in the balloons for past initiatives of this nature have caused the rare double-chinned pelican to suffocate." PR nightmare. So following this advice, you scrap the concept. Catastrophe averted.

- ✔ **Press mentions:** Business is good, but it sure would be nice to get a little more ink. To do this, it may be a good idea to pull in a PR crew to help you identify outlets and opportunities to gain a little more visibility.

- ✔ **Feature articles:** Ah, positive editorial content — a business owner's dream come true. What most people don't realize is that these stories don't materialize out of thin air. More likely than not, there was a publicity person behind the scenes pitching the story to her press contacts that made this dream a reality.

- ✔ **Press releases:** You have the power to craft your own press releases (see Chapter 16), but maybe you don't want to. The power of the press release should never be underestimated. This is your opportunity to give the press a taste of what you hope to do. Yes, you can do it yourself — but you may find that you want to call upon an expert to expertly craft a release for you, or at least help fine-tune the one you've created on your own.

- ✔ **Event planning:** This is the avenue where guerrilla marketing agencies and public relations intersect and complement each other. If you're planning an event, PR can work with you to hone your initiative so that you're not just creating something that is experiential, but something that the press will be able to latch onto as well. This kind of feedback is incredibly helpful when strategizing how to get the most coverage for stunts and events.

- ✔ **Consumer PR:** Crucial to the success of any business is maintaining a constant flow of information with your target audience. If your brand is one that consumers directly purchase, you'll want to make sure all your efforts (guerrilla and traditional) are relentlessly relayed to your public in order to get their full value.

- ✔ **Trade PR:** Similar to consumer PR, if the end user of your product or service lies within a specific industry or industries, you'll want to make sure that the communication loop with this group is continuous. (For more on identifying trade opportunities, turn to Chapter 15.)

Deciding on the image you want to relay is half the battle. After you've clearly articulated your goals, you can call upon outside PR resources for help communicating that vision to your desired consumers.

Ideally, your organization would be able to maintain an in-house public relations effort to oversee the flow of information, and then complement these resources with an outside PR agency or firm as needed for events and specialized PR needs.

We like to think that a message is only as good as the number of times that it is seen. Guerrilla marketing provides unique opportunities to coax consumers to press the Buy button because of their continuous exposure to product messaging. PR creates another opportunity to expose consumers to your message.

Knowing When It's Time to Hire Help

Deciding when it's time to hire a PR firm or publicist is all about deciding what you want.

Start by looking at the list of services they offer (see the preceding section). Be as specific as possible. Don't just say, "I want to get more press." Instead, say, "I want to get a human-interest feature in *The Chicago Tribune,* quarterly ink in *Knitting Today,* and as much local press as possible from our charity-driven Knit-a-Thon." Setting precise publicity goals enables you to see what you can do, and what you can't do.

Here are a few questions to ask yourself:

- Do I have the press contacts necessary to make my press goals a reality?
- Is there a certain aspect of the market that I'm currently not reaching? Maybe you're big in the trades, but you've got zilch in the consumer department.
- Do I have the in-house resources to achieve desired press within established timetables?

Sometimes, with PR, the "when" can be as important as the "what." The timing of press pushes perpetuate a particular image for the brand. As you create your list of goals, set a timeline to achieve these goals. Setting and achieving publicity goals perpetuates the image that yours is an organization that's growing, has forward momentum, and is a worthwhile investment.

One of the more obvious times you may consider calling in PR assistance is when things aren't going so well and you need to do some damage control. There's an old expression in agency circles that many clients don't approach agencies when everything is working well, but when client organizations are suffering from hemorrhaging to some degree. If you find yourself in this situation and you have to ask if you need agency help, the answer is likely to be yes.

Get your PR people in on the ground floor of your operations. If you decide that you're going to call upon external resources to push your marketing initiatives, bring them in early. Far too often, companies craft what they think is the greatest concept ever, and then they wait until the last minute to bring in some help. You'll be more likely to meet your goals for your brand if PR people get in on the ground floor.

Eenie-Meenie-Miney-Mo: Deciding Which People to Hire

After you set your goals, you need to find someone who can help you reach those goals. Consider the following:

- ✔ **How much money do you have to spend?**

- ✔ **Do you need the agency for a few months or just for a one-off event?**

- ✔ **Do you need a large agency with a wide array of resources or an independent specialist?**

- ✔ **Are you looking for someone who can coordinate on-air opportunities?** (If so, you may need a media relations specialist.)

- ✔ **Do you need to get great editorial content about your business?** Do you want to get great stories about your works in front of the general public and specific agencies?

- ✔ **Do you need people who "get" your industry and already have established connections with all related trade media outlets?**

- ✔ **What kind of personalized attention are you expecting?** Will this agency be working side by side with you or in the periphery? How important is it to you that you like the people you'll work with?

The answers to these questions will help you shape your search, but your priorities may be different than those listed here. If so, go ahead and list any questions we may not have included.

Rank the issues in terms of importance — that'll help you get to the root of who you're looking for faster. For example, you may interview an agency and find your contact there to be incredibly arrogant, but you know he's able to consistently get placement in national publications. Can you stomach the ego to get that kind of exposure?

There are thousands of PR firms out there and that doesn't even include independent contractors. With all these choices, how do you begin the selection process? By clarifying your press goals and defining the specialization of your PR, you've done the bulk of the selection work. Now it's time to find agencies that fill the bill.

Following your extensive needs analysis, you're likely to find that the duties, specialty, and size of the desired agency are evident to you. You need to make some calls and set up interviews.

Finding agencies in relatively close geographic proximity to you and/or your desired press targets is a good idea. Location shouldn't be a deal-breaker, but it makes the process easier for all parties if you're able to occasionally meet face to face.

Talk to respected peers, and ask them about PR firms they've worked with. Meet with the people they recommend. Although their criteria may differ from yours, your peers may be able to provide helpful information about who they worked with and why.

In some industries, there's a go-to agency or two — agencies who understand the industry and your specific needs. Read your trade publications and see if companies you respect list an "agency of record." If so, take note and call them in.

As you hold your interviews be sure to ask about the agency's experience in your industry and in related fields. Furthermore, pick their brains as to their understanding of industry trends. *Remember:* They have to understand what you're selling before they can go pitch it to the media.

We can't stress enough how valuable agency Web sites are as a tool to get a sense of the people you'll be working with. Scour each site. What sense do you get of the mission of the company, employees, and their attitudes toward clients? An agency's site can be useful when you're evaluating their services, and it can help you better understand how they might serve you as your agency.

If you're having trouble choosing between two agencies, you may want to ask them to present their best creative ideas based on their knowledge of your business. Be respectful, though: Agencies are reluctant to provide free creative ideas on speculation. Reassure the firms that their work will be respected and considered proprietary to that agency regardless of who is selected.

Another way of seeing how your potential agency may respond to your business, is to send out a request for proposal (RFP; see Chapter 5). In it, you spell out what your needs and budget are and ask agencies to submit their expertise and ideas based upon your request.

Be extremely wary of those who say they can guarantee press. Publicity is a tricky beast. The world is a constantly changing place and although your event may be the most important thing to *you,* on the day of execution political turmoil or celebrity meltdown may woo the unpredictable press corps away from your efforts. In trying to get press, there are no guarantees — just opportunities . . . and a little bit of luck.

When you're done interviewing agencies, keep all your notes. You'll probably have a great experience with the agency you select. But if that isn't the case, you'll want to have the contact and background on your second choice close at hand.

Part VI
You Scratch My Back . . .

In this part . . .

*N*o man or woman is an island. You need to keep a mental tally of the people who may be able to help you out in the long run. Whether you're looking to make some industry connections, team up with like-minded organizations to expand your reach, or donate to charity, partnering up is a good idea.

As you conduct business, you make contacts — vendors, clients, and general admirers. In this part, we explore how you can maximize these relationships to craft mutually beneficial partnerships. Whether your exchanges are for intellectual properties, products, or goodwill, other people and businesses can be a great resource to help your own business grow.

Chapter 18

Meeting of the Minds

. . . .

In This Chapter

▶ Getting the most out of industry innovations

▶ Making connections by attending conferences

▶ Joining and creating networking groups

. . . .

The Yalta Conference, the Manhattan Project, the International Society of Poodle Groomers. What do all these assemblies have in common? They're all meetings of the minds. One of these *may not* have changed the course of world history, but gathering professionals in specific fields to share ideas has been proven to be essential to the success of concepts, businesses, and, yes, even countries.

In this chapter, we talk about the importance of sharing industry ideas. We fill you in on immediate tools at your disposal, such as subscribing to newsletters and reading the trades. Then we take the ideas on the road by attending trade shows and conferences and showing you ways to get the most out of your attendance. Finally, we look to regional groups to promote the free flow of ideas among noncompetitive businesses.

Fostering a Free Flow of Trade Ideas

What's the big idea? Regardless of what business you're in, you know that the key to your success — maybe even your survival — is being on the forefront of industry trends. The free flow of trade ideas is essential to innovation within professions because it keeps everyone evolving, competitive, and, most important, employed.

Within most industries, resources are already in place to help keep you in the know. Most of them are free or inexpensive, and your participation in them helps you to carve out your nook and position yourself within the trade.

Some people are hesitant to join or participate in the "idea trade." Their thinking goes something like this: "Are you nuts?! I'm not going to share the secrets of my success! That'll cost me customers." We completely understand and share the reservation. This point of view isn't an irrational one.

What you want to do is share ideas in a manner that doesn't give away your "secret recipe for success," but instead discusses and addresses issues that may be affecting the industry as a whole and how your business and other businesses like yours may join together for the sake of the trade. By sharing these broader trends and ideas, you're all able to reap the benefits, without harming or compromising each other's reputation and revenue flow.

Most trades have numerous facets that may not be directly competitive and can help inform your product. Say you're in the poodle grooming industry, and you sell fur-clipping shears. At the International Society of Poodle Groomers Annual Summit and in the ISPG newsletters, you constantly hear groomers complaining that their shears keep overheating, causing the pooches to yelp in pain. This information is profoundly helpful and something you can take away from the experience to make your product better. Using this feedback, you develop the Canine Cooling Clippers, which allow poodles the perfect pain-free pompadour. You've learned from a fellow contributor to the industry about a problem, and you've create a solution that solved that problem while innovating the business — the results of which you'll see in increased sales.

Subscribing to Newsletters

One of the simplest ways to stay plugged into the industry is through newsletters. Usually, simply by placing your name on a free mailing list, you can immediately tap into the latest your industry had to offer. Newsletters are a quick, easy way to see exactly what your competitors are up to and to keep your finger on the pulse of a changing trade.

Maybe you don't want your mailbox filled up with a lot of newsletters from various organizations. See if you can opt for the online or e-mail version of the newsletter instead.

After perusing the free newsletters, you may want to see what's out there in more substantial trade publications. Although it's nice to get something for nothing, if you're in a trade with a more substantial periodical — one that has meatier, more dedicated coverage of your industry — you may want to spring for it. These publications typically offer national and sometimes international updates on the state of the industry and trade-specific events that you may not be able to hear about otherwise.

If you're cruising for ways to help promote your business (and you should be!), you may need to look no further than trade publications. You may be able to place classified ads that specifically target your industry. These ads can put your product in front of people in related fields who are looking for precisely the service that you offer.

Maybe you work in a small industry where there are only a handful of people who do what you do. If so, take it upon yourself to create a simple monthly e-newsletter about your business — this is a great way to present yourself as an expert. Budget a little time each month to report on the latest trends, innovations, or just plain exciting things that may be happening in your industry. After typing up your monthly manifesto, send it off to vendors, clients, and other trade professionals (blind-carbon-copying your mailing list, of course). Who knows where it might grow? You may pick up a few more clients, land a book deal, or end up with a new source of revenue!

Although everyone loves mail, we live in a digital age, so why not turn your newsletter into a blog? Blogs allow instant publishing of your ideas complete with pictures, video, links to relevant information, and simple distribution to your target audience. The best part? They're free to produce. As if that weren't enough, you can easily work with programs such as Google AdSense (`http://adsense.google.com`) to use ad space on your blog, providing you with some extra income. Who knows? You may just become the next blogger to ink a book deal!

Attending Conferences, Trade Shows, and Seminars

Conferences, trade shows, and seminars can be key to keeping yourself up to date on what's in vogue in your industry. A trip to Vegas every now and again ain't so bad, either!

A *conference* is a gathering of individuals to discuss a particular industry, or more specifically, a field within one. This is an overarching term for trade meetings. A *trade show* is a set of exhibitors displaying the latest offerings and innovations being offered in that industry. A *seminar* is a structured presentation (or series of presentations) involving a panel of experts followed by discussion and individual sessions on the topic(s) at hand. These three offerings can happen individually or simultaneously depending on the scope of the event.

Regardless of whether you can spring for a big trip, be sure to add your name to the mailing lists of convention and conference organizers who produce trade shows in your industry. Doing so will help you stay aware of what's happening when — which will, in turn, help you make informed decisions about what trade events are important and plan your quarter, or even your year, accordingly.

Determining your level of participation

Most conferences have various levels of participation. The first and most common level is full participation, which includes entry to all the seminars, the trade show floor, dinners, and cocktail parties. The other end of the spectrum is seminar or trade-show-only passes. Most conventions post projected offerings at each show many months in advance. Utilize this information to help you decide which shows you should attend and your level of participation.

Whether you're flying in to hear a presentation given by your favorite industry hotshot or you're there for an entire week of trade-related festivities, make the most of the opportunity. You can meet the people you've been working with, selling to, buying from, or hope to work with in the future. Here are a few quick tips to reap the benefits long after you've returned to the grind:

- ✔ **Always carry a stack of business cards.** Those beautifully printed cards aren't just to impress your friends and family — you have them to give your contact information legs. Be sure to have plenty on hand — the card swap is likely to happen more often than you realize.

- ✔ **Follow up with the people you meet as soon as possible.** If someone says to you, "I'd like to hear more about what you're working on," send her the information she's asked for as quickly as possible. If you can do it on-site, great. If not, be sure to follow up as soon as you're back in the office.

- ✔ **Know when to say goodnight.** It's important to see and be seen at these events — making yourself visible and accessible is crucial to your success — but know when to call it a night. Being around is great — being a fixture can be seen as needy.

Taking advantage of sponsorship opportunities

Most conventions have a variety of existing opportunities already available, but they're always seeking new sponsorship opportunities to provide added value for their attendees, and pick up some sponsorship fees along the way. Especially if you're an industry-based product as opposed to one that targets consumers, this may be the perfect avenue for you.

To help you grab that prime industry position, here are some pointers for negotiating with show management.

- ✔ **Have a clear understanding of what you want to sponsor and when.**

- ✔ **Ask if there are any other companies sponsoring the event as well.** If so, who are they and what are they doing? You don't want to be competing for the spotlight or, worse, get upstaged!

- ✔ **What opportunities are you entitled to with the sponsorship?** Does it include presence in marketing materials, opportunities to drop items in goody bags, the chance to make a speech at a dinner or present an award? Don't be afraid to seek additional on-site opportunities.

Conference organizers will usually have existing sponsorship packages. That said, sometimes things can be added, removed, or changed — as long as they don't mess up the flow of the event and show — so don't be afraid to pipe up with specific package requests.

After you've decided that you want to participate in some sort of sponsorship capacity, the conversation inevitably turns to what will be expected of you in exchange for your presence. There are several types of ways to go about "paying" for this exposure:

- ✔ **Cash:** Most commonly, a predetermined amount of cash is requested and paid in exchange for any combination of exposure opportunities for the product or brand. This usually includes a mix of on-site signage, presence in marketing materials, and exposure at the event.

- ✔ **In kind:** Instead of, or in addition to, paying a reduced amount of cash, you donate goods or services, usually in exchange for on-site signage and acknowledgments. These typically include equipment used for the event, or food and beverage being poured and served.

- ✔ **Media:** This is usually reserved for companies that produce some form of media, naturally. In this instance, no money is exchanged, but the cash equivalent is provided in media coverage for the event using the business's media resources. By doing so, the media group typically receives tagging on all the remaining materials promoting the event as well as opportunity on-site to either distribute its publications or solicit potential subscribers.

Say you want to sponsor something but the pricing levels are initially just too high. Be upfront. Tell the show management what your budget is and see what they can do for you. Sometimes by simply asking, you may be able to take advantage of an opportunity that you wouldn't have known existed otherwise.

You don't have the extra bucks? Or simply don't feel like spending the few you have? Look into speaking on a panel or contributing an article to the show's journal or trade publication as a way to gain exposure for you and your brand.

If you can't afford to sponsor anything and you can't get on a panel, what should you do? Take to the show like a guerrilla. Drop your company's branded pens at the registration table or at booths before conference attendees get there. Place branded notepads at phone booths around the convention hall. Put guerrilla tactics in practice and drop these items at hotels and restaurants that convention-goers might frequent. You run the risk of ticking off show management, but if your efforts are discrete and don't disrupt the show, you may come away the winner.

Giving a presentations at the show

One of the most effective ways to introduce or reaffirm prominence in your selected field is to present at a show or conference. Whether it's speaking on a panel, moderating a seminar, or presenting the keynote address of the trade show or conference, this is a big opportunity for increased industry exposure. You need to do all you can to best position your company as an industry leader.

Take the time to work on whatever materials you plan to present. Don't try to wing it — this is your reputation in the industry we're talking about. Write out what you're going to say, and conduct dress rehearsals in front of your friends and, if they're of good humor, co-workers. Use the feedback you get from them to shape your presentation.

Often total laymen — people who have no idea about your business — make the best practice audience. If they can get it (or most of it anyway), then the industry folk will as well.

When you're on-site, do what you can to make yourself feel comfortable and confident. If you'll be showing any sort of presentation — whether it's a PowerPoint deck or video — don't be afraid to request a run-through prior to the event. Run through your presentation with all materials you'll be using — the outfit you will be wearing, the monitor you'll be viewing, the computer running your presentation, and that obligatory lavaliere mic pinned to your lapel. If there are snags, work them through again — that way you won't be anxious when it comes back around.

At the conclusion of the show, get your presentation materials back from the audiovisual crew. Your outstanding showing will certainly require a repeat performance in the very near future.

We don't want to stress you out on the preparation aspect, but this could be an opportunity to generate business for your company. Preparing will enable you to make a successful presentation that will resonate within the industry.

Partnering Up with Other Businesses in Your Region

Even if you're a smaller company, never settle on the construct that your ideas or the font from which you pluck them is small! Smaller companies or regional branches are often able to draw on the agility of their resources. One of the areas in which this is most true is in the camaraderie of intellectual regional partnerships.

Trade organizations, even national ones, have regional sects or groups that meet every month or so. Sometimes independent groups — not affiliated with any national organization — also work to drum up ideas and solutions. Whichever the case, these groups come together to share ideas, hear speakers, hold events for local causes, and gain a presence and notoriety in the larger industry community.

These regional co-ops are exciting propositions because most meet with the pure goal of seeing how they can improve their skills and services for the benefit of the industry. Plus, these meetings are regional touchstones for understanding other businesses' focuses or areas of expertise. With this information, you can form partnerships with people who may put you in a position to better serve your customers — and enable you *both* to make some money in the process. This helps to galvanize the perception (and the reality) that you're a true leader in your field.

Joining a group

Depending on the industry you're in, one or several various groups may be available for you to join in order stay on top of the latest happenings in your business. Do your research and see which outlets will best fit you. Is it the regional chapter of your national trade organization? The local chamber of commerce or other civic business group? Which group or groups best serve your company by giving you the latest info on industry or business ideas and opening you up to new business?

Most groups have membership fees. Know that going in, but explore what you can leverage to get the most out of that fee. Some of the most common perks include

- Opportunities to speak as an expert before the group
- A decal you can put on your storefront letting customers know of your affiliation with a reputable and perhaps recognizable organization
- A logo or acknowledgment you can add to your Web site
- Inclusion on the organization's Web site as well, with perhaps even a link to your own site
- Free newsletters and discounts at participating members' establishments
- Reduced rates for special events, such as seminars, conferences, and trade shows

Creating a group

No matter what business you're in, staying ahead of the curve is important. As already existing innovations develop, and new ones emerge, you need to be able to share thoughts and insights with peers and colleagues to promote continued growth. If there currently isn't an organization or trade group for your particular business to spur on this sort of development, maybe it's time to form one.

We know you're busy. You're running a business, you've got a family or fish to look after, and your social life makes *Gossip Girls* look like *Mr. Rogers' Neighborhood*. We're not saying drop what you're doing and focus all your energy on starting a nonprofit (or even a for-profit) group or conference — at least not yet.

Start small and think locally. Are there colleagues, peers, or vendors who might benefit by gathering for a monthly meeting with an open discussion, followed by cocktails or some other social activity? Test the waters. Throw it against the wall and see if there's any interest among those in your immediate industry circle, and build it from there. An industry haunt could be a next stop — they may be open to hosting your meetings in exchange for your food and beverage purchases.

An alternative may be to link up with an existing group that shares similar hurdles and obstacles. Maybe grab a couple of colleagues, bribe them with food, and see if a parallel organization may be something you (and your coerced team) can get something out of.

Networking groups

Not a week goes by that we don't hear someone, upon discovering a mutual acquaintance, declare, "Well, what a small world!" Especially within industries, the degrees of separation are steadily shrinking. In an effort to help expand the circle, many people have created networking groups. These are groups where people in related fields, but not necessarily the same industry, are given the opportunity to meet and mingle in a usually more relaxed social setting.

Networking groups are helpful in seeing what's going on in other areas of business that you may not otherwise be exposed to due to your steadfast immersion and commitment to what you do. Entering into dialogues with these other "worlds" can help give you a point of view different from the ones you or your industry may hold. This could then result in an innovation in *your* industry or a new consumer base. At the very least, it could result in a titillating evening of conversation.

Chapter 19

Cross-Promotional Partnerships

. . . .

In This Chapter

▶ Discovering partnership opportunities

▶ Knowing what to consider before entering into a relationship

▶ Getting the most out of teaming up

. . . .

To help keep yourself entertained and supported, you probably have quite the eclectic mix of comrades. You've got your goofy friend who provides you with a laugh. The supportive friend who's always there to listen to your woes. The fiercely loyal (although occasionally misguided) friend who has your back in case any altercation ever occurs. Each of these people plays a vital role in your life, but what you may not realize is that your friends likely value you just as much.

To your goofy friend, you provide an attentive audience member. To the supportive friend, your quirks allow practical training for her budding psychiatric studies. To the fiercely loyal friend, you facilitate the much needed opportunity to occasionally lay the smack down. This is the reason your relationships are successful — or, at the very least, entertaining. Each person is able to contribute and benefit from the other person's unique gifts.

When executed properly, you can use your astute understanding of diverse and mutually beneficial relationships to benefit your business. In this chapter, we look to help you identify opportunities to partner up with like-minded businesses. By doing so, you may be able to save on resources and make a much greater impact than you thought possible. We also point out the possible pitfalls and help you maximize your resources and your partner's resources to get the most out of the union. We think you'll agree that partnering up will have you saying, "It's good to have friends."

Identifying and Leveraging Mutually Beneficial Noncompeting Brands

Marketing initiatives can be expensive. Throughout this book, we investigate more nontraditional methods you can use to raise awareness of your brand, at little or no cost to your company. (For a look at a few of the more inexpensive tools, check out Chapters 6 and 13.) In some instances, businesses exploring marketing options simply don't have the resources for typical guerrilla tactics. Or they may discover that these methods just aren't a good match for their brand.

If you find yourself in this pickle, it may be time to identify and secure a mutually beneficial, cross-promotional partnership. Sounds fancy, doesn't it? Well, it's not really. In the end, whether you have the resources or not, partnering up with a like-minded brand can help your budget stretch much farther.

Mutually beneficial, cross-promotional partnerships are unions between non-competitive (perhaps even complimentary) brands or services in which they work together for the benefit of both parties involved, usually at little or no cost to either one. It's actually one of the simplest, smartest, cheapest tools you should think about when laying out your marketing goals and objectives. Plus, if you drop the term *mutually beneficial, cross-promotional partnerships* at a dinner party, everyone will think you're quite the smarty, and that's always a bonus.

These partnerships are fruitful networking at its most essential. By combining resources, mutually beneficial relationships create opportunities for people and businesses to help each other out, without it costing them too much time or money.

For example, say you're a jeweler, and you specialize in engagement rings and wedding bands. Your store is naturally aflutter with nervous suitors contemplating the "big buy" and their next steps. The information you have about your customers — they're getting married — provides you with an opportunity to seek out a potential partner. Why not partner with a stationery store to supply your customers with a preprinted *Guy's Guide to Getting Hitched,* which could be distributed in your store and suggest that the happy couple next look to the stationery store for the wedding invitations. This arrangement is mutually beneficial, because you're producing something as an added value to your jittery customer at no cost to you, and the stationery store gets some referrals by planting the idea right when the beaux is in the planning stages.

The idea here is to take advantage of or create opportunities where both you and your ally can benefit by serving consumers without cutting in on anyone's turf.

In the following sections, we discuss some of the more popular ways non-competing and/or complementary brands can work together for the good of a common cause —increased exposure (in the form of consumer and trade press) and business!

You've got a wagon, I've got a horse

We're fans of old western movies. That grit, that resolve . . . a place where partnerships were forged out of necessity, people wore chaps, and the spirit of coming together allowed frontiersmen to not only survive, but thrive. For most people, chaps have gone the way of legwarmers. However, partnering up with others to fill a need is still alive and well. The only difference: The resources available aren't always as apparent. In the following sections, we cover a few of the more common offerings used to fill the need.

In this section, we show you a few successful partnerships that have proven beneficial to business owners in the past. These partnerships have succeeded because both parties were able to benefit from the partnership using minimal resources. We hope you'll take these ideas to get started and generate your own ways to partner up!

On-site presence in exchange for prizing or promotion

One way to get increased exposure is to supply an existing event with prizing or some other promotion that can be viewed as an added value or supplemental contribution to the event. You may be able to get on-site at the event that you otherwise would have had to pay for, as well as mentions in the event's existing marketing efforts.

Maybe you're the proud proprietor of a travel agency, and for every fifth person you send to Orlando, the tourism board gives you the sixth trip for free. To consumers in the Northeast and Midwest during teeth-chattering winters, a trip to sunny Florida is quite the perk! You may want to consider offering up this trip as a prize for an existing event (a craft show, community festival, street fair, charity event) in exchange for an on-site presence and placement in their signage and marketing materials.

By supplying this trip, you're able to increase your exposure, meet and establish a rapport with potential clients, and help make someone very, very tan — all of which bodes very well for your brand.

Items for gift bags

Who doesn't love goody bags?! The answer: No one. Grown men and women tear into goody bags like kids on Christmas morning to see what they got. It doesn't matter if the bags are filled with a magazine, stale breath mints, and last year's limited-edition camouflage-colored watch, getting something for nothing is just plain fun.

What many people may not realize is that those goody bags cost money, so event organizers are constantly on the prowl (and in some instances scrambling) for sponsors to help fill the kitty. (We get into this a bit more in Chapter 20.)

Look to your resources and see what you may have to contribute. A bunch of extra-large T-shirts left over from the company paintball outing, branded pens, or anything with your company name and logo will be great to drop in. The event coordinators get more swag, and your messaging gets into your consumers' hands.

Content on a Web site

Do you ever sit in front of the computer clicking through articles, blogs, pictures, and video only to discover that four hours have gone by, and you have nothing to show for your time? Suddenly, the voice of your mother pops into your head, pointedly questioning, "Do you plan on doing *anything* with your day?" Well, take heart: The reason your time flew by isn't that you're an antisocial recluse — it's that there is just so much content out there to view.

Content is material posted or published for consumption by readers or viewers. Some of the more popular forms of content are articles, pictures, games, or video.

Even though the Internet is rife with content, a lot of it isn't all that great. As a consequence, Web publishers are hustling to fill the insatiable consumer demand by tracking down and securing quality content to keep users (and advertisers) happy.

If you've got exceptional content, you may be able to leverage that content for increased exposure. By sharing archived stories, photos, and videos with a complementary site or source, you can easily be referenced and perhaps even include a link to your own site should the consumer be interested in learning more about you or your group. From there, you may even consider co-producing content that might be shared on YouTube or other video-sharing sites.

Your guerrilla tactics should always be educational and entertaining. Can you produce an entertaining video that shares simple procedures, tips from the pros, demos, or anything else that helps to set you up as the independently minded, industry leader you are? Sure you can — now hop to it!

Venue or space

You may need to look no further than your own storefront. If you have a centrally located business, you may want to consider opening your doors to host a local event or gathering. In exchange for your hospitality, it is not out of line to ask for exposure on their materials and existing marketing efforts.

While playing host may require a little more planning and involvement on your part, having a built in apparatus to drive traffic to your store and get publicity at the same time is an invaluable opportunity that should not be passed up.

Entering into a Partnership: Questions to Ask

Entering into a new romantic relationship there are lots of questions. Do I like this person? Does this person complement me well? Can I trust this person with my secrets? Will this person care that I still sleep with a stuffed monkey?

With the obvious exception of the last question, you should ask these same questions before entering into a partnership. In your day-to-day transactions you take great care when it comes to how you want your brand to appear. Consumers draw conclusions based on their brand associations, so you want to be cautions as to whom you choose to hitch your wagon to.

Here are some pointers to consider before teaming up.

- ✔ **Does this company complement my own?** One of the major stumbling blocks when it comes to partnerships is teaming up with a company that doesn't "match" your brand. For example, a luxury clothing store teaming up with the local waste disposal outfit probably doesn't make a whole lot of sense. Successful partnerships are ones that will maintain — or preferably increase — your exposure and make a positive perception of the brand.

- ✔ **What are the benefits of teaming up with this brand?** This is a nice way of asking that charming question, "What's in it for me?" Before you exert energy and resources, it's totally fair to ask what you're going to get out of the deal. What does your partner have at its disposal? Availability of a choice venue, involvement in existing marketing efforts, on-site signage, media mentions, and access to highly valuable e-mail lists or on-site acquisition of contact or other personal information are just a few of the possible benefits.

After you've nailed down options and how each of you can maximize these resources, it's time to get down to the nitty-gritty — billing in marketing materials, ownership of any acquisition generated through the course marketing efforts for your mailing lists, and whatever other benefits you want to capitalize on. This part may get a bit touchy — but it's far better to go through these few moments of unpleasantness and be clear than it is to discover later that you need a magnifying glass to see your logo on the marketing materials after they've have been printed.

✔ **Who is responsible for the costs that may be incurred during the course of this partnership?** Although one of the pluses of entering into a partnership is that you're able to minimize costs, things may pop up along the way. Regardless of your arrangement, it's a good idea to make sure that everyone involved is clear on who's responsible for picking up the check if costs arise.

✔ **When does the partnership end and what happens when it does?** Finally, to make sure that everyone is working from the same playbook, make sure that the start date and end date (if applicable) are outlined and agreed upon by both parties. Along the way, your partnership may result in the creation of printed materials, signage, and other property. Either in the beginning or as the partnership continues, you'll want to discuss who gets what at the conclusion, to avoid any misunderstandings down the line.

After hammering out all the parameters, draft a simple written agreement so that the basic elements of the arrangement are spelled out on paper. This agreement should cover all the elements in the preceding checklist. Putting down in black-and-white things like the length and details of the arrangement enables each party to fully understand who's responsible for bringing what to the table. People are human and they forget or remember things differently. This agreement is not a statement of mistrust — it's an opportunity for all parties to clearly articulate their goals and responsibilities.

In that same vein, if proprietary information will be used or revealed during the partnership, you may also want to consider engaging your partner in a non-disclosure agreement (NDA), a document used to protect both partners from the other partner using proprietary information. You work very hard to make and keep your business competitive — too hard, in fact, to have proprietary information floating around for the sake of some signage. An NDA brings with it a certain amount of trust that will likely build trust with your partner and finally give them the opportunity to declare, "I could tell you, but then I'd have to kill you," in response to internal discussions.

Seizing the Opportunities

In the process of your partnership, additional opportunities may become available to you to help increase your reach. Keeping yourself aware of what your partners are doing and looking for further chances for increased exposures are part of your guerrilla duties. Here are a few other situations where your partnership may pay off in ways you didn't expect.

Print and radio

Throughout the course of your partnership, you may find you have occasion for mainstream media exposure by way of your cohort. See how you can leverage your relationship to get included in your partner's print and radio advertising. For example, if there's an *on-site remote* (where a radio or TV personality broadcasts live from the venue) at your collaborator's event, you may want to see if the interviewee may be able to give you a quick shout-out.

If your associate is taking out an ad of some sort, can you get a mention for promotional consideration? If your partner is paying for an ad buy, they may not be entirely receptive to sharing the spotlight, so what can you provide them in exchange, to help sweeten the deal? For example, you might place their ad on your Web site, offering a gift if they mention the ad in your store, or you might offer to help with the distribution/dissemination of the ad itself.

Online and e-mail

If you're partnering up with someone, you may want to explore what online assets you both have and how you each can benefit. Maybe you have banner ads on your site that could refer consumers to their page, or vice versa? Many sites have link pages highlighting clients and local trade organizations — maybe you and your partner can include each other on your link lists.

One of the most valuable gems your partner may have is access to e-mail lists. You don't want to take that list and spam your associate's client list, but the list can be exceptionally useful to promote major events or, when used prudently, to raise awareness for your brand.

People hate junk mail. Many people get understandably disgruntled when their information is shared or sold to another company without their permission. Keep this in mind when discussing the sharing of contact information acquired through your own independent marketing efforts.

Sweepstakes and contests

You may not have the funds to send one lucky couple to Bora Bora, but combining the resources of you and your partner, you may be able to create an exciting prize package.

If you decide to go this route, you'll want to make clear exactly what each person is prepared to offer and pay for. Awarding a trip makes for a great customer incentive and opens up the potential for press. However, a contest unfulfilled can have the exact opposite effect. Good planning between you and your partner will help you avoid these negative ends. (For more on creating prize packages turn to Chapter 13.)

Chapter 20

Giving Back: Adding a Cause-Related Tie-In

*T*his just in: Money buys happiness — *if* you spend it on someone else. That's right, according to a 2008 study by the University of British Columbia and the Harvard Business School, researchers found that people who spend their money on others or in the form of charitable contributions, instead of using it to buy something fancy for themselves, experience "significantly greater happiness." What does this mean for you?

For starters, it means you should probably cancel the commission of that pricey, life-size oil portrait of yourself — or, at the very least, give it to someone else. When it comes to guerrilla marketing, it means that by directing your resources charitably, not only can you help a deserving organization and benefit your brand, but you may also end up happier!

In this chapter, we look to make your day a little sunnier by exploring the benefits of cause-related tie-ins. We begin by discussing exactly what's involved in this sort of campaign and how it can be helpful to your brand. Next, we fill you in on sharing a portion of your company's proceeds with charities or other deserving organizations as a tool to generate interest. Finally, while still maintaining altruistic sensibilities, we look to additional benefits and partnership opportunities that you can claim by embracing your company's philanthropic image.

Considering Cause-Related Tie-Ins

We make a living by what we get, but we make a life by what we give.

—Winston Churchill

That Winston Churchill fellow was a pretty clever chap — and his words can easily be used when applied toward using a cause-related tie-in to promote your brand. A *cause-related tie-in* is a charitable component that you can use to increase visibility and brand equity. Essentially, this means that by helping charitable organizations, you can get the attention of your consumers in a positive, warm-and-fuzzy kind of way. (For more on warming consumer's hearts, check out the "Let it shine" sidebar in this chapter.)

Cause-related tie-ins have been known by other monikers or jargony titles. Similar terms such as *cause-related marketing* or simply *cause marketing* have also been used been used to define the act of incorporating a compassionate component into companies' marketing plans.

Guerrilla thinking requires you to be ahead of the curve when it comes to resourcefulness and innovation. This means being as ingenious as possible to create opportunities to help others while, in a humble way, helping yourself. When done with sincerity, cause-related tie-ins can go far in helping to fulfill a cultural need while creating positive associations with your brand.

Cause-related tie-ins work because they're mutually beneficial partnerships in their most unselfish form. Much like cross-promotional partnerships (see Chapter 19), cause-related campaigns provide both the business and the charity with a host of opportunities, while the majority of available resources (be they financial, services, or manpower) go toward the greater good.

Although just getting that nice glow of helping others may be enough for companies to participate in a cause-related campaign, participating in such an endeavor offers many advantages for both the charity and the business. Here are a few of the more common benefits the two parties can enjoy:

- ✔ **Increased awareness:** Much like any other partnership, by joining forces each organization is able to raise awareness by capitalizing on each other's assets. The business may gain access to the charity's mailing lists or mentions in its newsletter and on its Web site. Meanwhile, charitable organizations are able to take advantage of the larger marketing efforts that companies can provide — marketing that may not otherwise be feasible for a nonprofit.

- ✔ **Positive associations, consumer loyalty, and goodwill:** When a business partners with a charity, the business creates a positive connection in people's minds between the company and charitable acts. Plus, the charity benefits by receiving an indirect (or direct) endorsement from the selected company.

✔ **Increased revenue:** After participating in a cause-related tie-in, businesses typically find an increase in revenue that could be directly associated with the raised awareness and consumer loyalty. The charity prospers by receiving direct contributions from the business itself or a bounce in donations due to increased awareness.

✔ **Motivating others:** We like to think that most people want to leave the world a little better than they found it. By participating in this kind of effort, all participants are playing an active role in promoting a culture of philanthropy and public service — not only about the employees, but among the public at large.

In the following sections, we walk you through the process of developing your own cause-related tie-in.

Selecting a charity

You want to hitch your wagon to a great charity and do some good. The first step is to pick your charity. With so many deserving organizations out there, trying to pick just one may seem slightly daunting. Fortunately, a variety of resources are readily available to help you make a smart, informed selection:

✔ **Personal experience:** Nothing will better you than something that's personal. Have you ever watched a TV show or read an article, and the story of overcoming adversity and fighting the good fight moved you in such a way that you wished you could do something? Do you have a specific life experience that caused you to want to help out in some way, but then life happened, and it got pushed to the back burner? If either of these are the case, now is your opportunity to fuel this fire in your belly, and use your business to help take an active role in making a change for good.

✔ **Family and friends:** Family and friends are exceptional resources. We never cease to be surprised by the selfless work that our friends and family do in their spare time. Maybe your brother spends a couple of nights each week teaching woodworking to underprivileged kids. Perhaps your talented friend goes to nursing homes once a week to sing for the elderly. Given the nature of good deeds, your friends and family probably don't wear their angelic efforts on their sleeves, so ask around. Who knows — you may learn something!

Has one of your loved ones suffered from a disease, like cancer or heart disease? If so, you were probably able to see first-hand the results of the situation or affliction, and this is your chance to give back to help others in the same situation you and your loved one were in.

If one of your friends or family members participates in a charity that you don't know anything about, but that may be a potential opportunity, ask if you can go with her to see her efforts yourself. Taking the time to get some personal experience with a charity will help you decide if it may be a good fit for your brand.

✔ **Industry-related charities:** Turning to your local trade associations may provide you with an assortment of industry-endorsed charities that could serve as a perfect fit for your brand.

You may need to look no further than what you do in your day-to-day activities. Is there a brand-related charity that could benefit from your resources, labor, or funding? For example, if you own a hair salon, you may consider partnering with Locks of Love (www.locksoflove.org), which donates hair to be made into wigs for people afflicted with cancer. If you're a tailor, maybe you can partner with the local homeless shelter to provide coats during the winter.

This situation is ideal because, in addition to helping an organization specific to your trade, consumers can look at your efforts and think, "That totally makes sense."

✔ **Online resources:** A variety of Web sites serve as excellent connectors between businesses and charities. Two of the more popular ones are

- Network for Good (www.networkforgood.org): Network for Good gives charities and nonprofits the opportunities to post their regional needs in the hopes that they can find a match.

- Better Business Bureau (www.give.org): Give.org is a charitable site run by the Better Business Bureau (BBB). It provides information on reputable charities.

These sites will give you a sense of what's out there and put you in touch with the people who can make it happen!

By calling up this wealth of existing assets, you'll be able to identify and select which charity (or perhaps even charities) you'd like to approach and possibly work with as you continue to grow and market your business or brand.

Figuring out what the organization needs

When you're working out a business proposition with a potential client or a business partner, you do your research first. Before you propose your concept, you figure out what you may be able to offer as part of a deal. You need to show the same industrious preparation before approaching a charity.

Take stock of what assets you have at your fingertips and how you might apply these to benefit the charity. Do you have financial support you can offer? Throngs of loyal customers? Media resources that you're willing to share? Good ol' mom used to always chirp, "If you have a gift and you don't share it, well, that's just a crime!"

Do a bit of research and see if there's something in particular the charity or cause is immediately in need of. Being able to fulfill a need makes your proposition incredibly appealing and persuasive.

Cash is always in demand, so this may be the gift you want to consider when approaching your charity. But maybe — given your unique background, experience, and position — your skill set enables you to give something that no other business can equal. If that's the case, make sure to leverage that special something — in the end, it might be worth as much as (or more than) your basic cash contribution.

Approaching the organization

After taking your plan into account, it's time to reach out to your charity and make your case. A quick online search will connect you with the central number of the organization, but we recommend starting your conversation with someone in the development, corporate relations, or fundraising departments. People in these departments are typically skilled in working with businesses like yours, and they'll be able to work with you to shape a program that both your business and the charity will find rewarding.

Chances are, most charities will be open to a mutually beneficial, cause-related marketing tie-in. But keep in mind that there may be more involved than just calling them and saying, "Hey, let's team up for increased exposure, awareness, and feelings of goodwill." Charities work just as hard to protect their image as you work to protect yours — if not more. For a charity to give its name and time to successfully foster and nurture the relationship, they'll often request a full proposal from you. They'll use this proposal to determine whether your tie-in is, in fact, worth their time and resources.

If the charity asks for a formal proposal, it's nothing personal. Charities and other nonprofits must work tirelessly to protect their good names. Many of them rely on public and private funds to operate, so they have to make sure that none of their partnerships disrupts the delicate balance they need in order to stick around.

Also keep in mind that, as the boss, you may enjoy the prerogative of being the Decider — but, often, charities don't quite share that same amount of freedom. Some have boards to answer to and preexisting marketing plans in place that may conflict with what you're proposing at the moment. So the answer may not be a "no" — it may just be a "not now."

You may be a captain of industry, leaving mortals trembling when you enter the room, but when you're approaching charities, you need to exercise humility. When it comes to smaller nonprofits and community-run organizations, many of their staff are part-time employees or volunteers who are trying to juggle many jobs with limited time and resources. It's in your best interest to be a humble team player. Presenting yourself as a cheerful collaborator, rather than a steamroller, will make a charity far more receptive to your efforts.

Deciding what to contribute

Isn't holiday shopping stressful? You search high and low to find the perfect gift for loved ones with frazzled determination — the intensity of which is slightly heightened by the memory of the malfunctioning electric sock debacle from the year before. Then, just when you think you can't search any longer, you stumble upon that perfect gift that was right in front of you the entire time.

Occasionally, the search for what to contribute to a selected charity can be just as taxing. Our advice? Look in front of you first. We feel pretty confident in saying that simply by looking at what's directly in front of you, and using just a little creativity, pretty much any marketer in nearly any business should be able to find a way to create a contribution that works.

Many business owners think they have to reach out to some national charity, but often the most effective charitable tie-ins are local ones that directly impact your community (and consumers). What immediate resources do you have to contribute to your own community?

Maybe Brian's Bakery can donate buns marked with a B to help out the marching band's bake sale. DJ Funky Fresh could spin the supa-fly hits at the annual senior center dance. Crunch Accounting can offer its services to do the taxes for members of the local houses of worship. Many times, gifts that require little more than time are the ones that reap the greatest benefit and yield the greatest response from the public.

Most people want to participate in some sort of charitable activity, but they don't know how to get started. If you have big-hearted employees or co-workers, you may want to reach out to them and see if they'd be interested in volunteering for an organization as a group. In addition to reflecting well on the company, it'll boost for workplace morale and help a great cause!

There are numerous ways to lend a hand — you're only really limited by your resources and resourcefulness. Here are some suggestions:

- ✔ **Donate a product or service.** What do you make? Donate something of value to the organization so that it can be used as a giveaway or grand prize to benefit the organization.

- ✔ **If you have a particularly altruistic workforce, organize an employee service program to benefit the selected charity.**

- ✔ **Promote a common message.** When partnering up with a charity or cause, maximize this relationship by promoting a common positive message.

Establishing the parameters

Pinning down the specifics of your contribution may be as simple taking advantage of an existing opportunity. For example, say you've decided to contribute an item to an event or take advantage of the placement in a goody bag for a charitable event or fundraiser — there isn't a whole lot of room for negotiation, because the trade is relatively obvious: They get the benefit of your product for their uses and gain access to their attendees and event.

The charity is able to give your product away to its guests and you're able to benefit from the associated exposure. As long as you have no strong objections (such as placement alongside a direct competitor), it's best to go along with whatever the charity suggests and not rock the boat.

If your offering is something unique or particularly sizable, you may have greater room to negotiate. Especially if you're donating large sums of money or other high-value resources, you may have the opportunity to kindly request things in return for your contribution. However, be sure to negotiate with a sense of modesty, tact, and respect.

Regardless of whether it's your first time or 100th time working with the charity, as with any business transaction, get your agreement in writing.

Sharing the wealth

Business is booming! You rise in the morning, and take a dip in a pool of gold coins. "Yes, life is good," you say to yourself.

One way to make it even better: Share the wealth — in the form of a *portion-of-proceeds component* (a marketing effort in which, for a set period of time, a company agrees to donate to charity a set portion of its proceeds from every purchase of its product up to a certain amount of money). The theory

Let it shine

One pharmaceutical company looking to lend a helping hand to those suffering from AIDS partnered with the National AIDS Fund to create a cause-related initiative to help awareness of an epidemic that had spread like wildfire. To do this, the drug company created an elegant Web site that encouraged consumers to use their mouse to strike a virtual match, and light up a simple white candle positioned on the center of the page. For every candle lit, the organization donated $1 to the fund to be applied toward AIDS research.

Aside from being an incredibly generous gesture and beautifully executed, it didn't take long for news of the site and the company's efforts to travel. In no time at all, traditional media, bloggers, and family LISTSERVs were quickly twinkling with the good feelings toward this brand, as well as words of encouragement for friends and family to go to their site and "take a second to light a candle" in the name of helping to find a cure.

behind a portion-of-proceeds is that, when a consumer in search of a product — say, spicy mustard — is given the choice of either a spicy mustard where 50¢ of every bottle goes to charity and one without that charitable aspect, the consumer will select the more philanthropic mustard. Some say people just prefer charitable condiments, but we assert that the motivation is that, generally speaking, consumers want to help out — especially when that help comes in the form of buying something that they would have purchased anyway.

Taking credit for your good deeds

You help old ladies across the street, cover your nose when you sneeze, and say "thank you" when someone holds the door for you. But do you get any credit for all your good works? No! Well, for once it's time to tactfully step up and accept some humble accolades for your charitable activities. Although just helping others is reward enough, we say if you can pick up some recognition for your brand along the way, that's not too shabby either.

Traditionally, businesses can work to leverage their donation and/or participation in ways that can help their business in the following ways:

- ✔ **Having an on-site presence at an event, function, or venue:** For example, maybe you're given the opportunity to set up a small table or display at the charity's event, as well as the chance to offer samples of your product and get attendee contact information from the guests.

✔ **Being mentioned in the charity's print campaigns:** Most nonprofit organizations offer their business partners exposure to their supporters via listings in pre-promotion, honorable mentions on-site, or ads in organizational journals, newsletters, or signage. The donation of the business is noted in some way, so that people are aware of your contribution.

✔ **Being given a presence on the charity's Web site:** Being mentioned on the charity's Web site is great, but you want to make sure that the charity also links to your own Web site, so that people can find you.

✔ **Getting a tax break:** Charities aren't the only ones who appreciate a good deed. Laws and benefits vary from state to state and charity to charity, but be sure to check with your local tax laws and/or your accountant to see what might be available to you and your business.

Nurturing the relationship

You go to conventions, you take lunches, and you place calls to check in. As a networker and marketer, you use your inherent people skills to get the most out of your business relationships. When working with charities and other organizations for the general good, you need to exercise this same sense of attentiveness toward your charitable partnerships.

Here are a few ways to learn about and cultivate a relationship with your comrades in compassion:

✔ **Meet with a member of the organization.** Getting some face time is important. Plus, you may find it inspirational — or, at the very least, informative — to speak to someone about the organization.

✔ **Visit the facility, if applicable.** Nothing will give you a greater sense of the work being done than seeing it first hand.

✔ **Add the charity's logo to your site or materials.** When you're partners with a charity, you can help increase their visibility by presenting their logo on your own marketing materials. This is usually extremely inexpensive, and it promotes goodwill with your charity.

✔ **If you have the time and they need your help, join one of the organization's committees or even sit on the board.**

✔ **Attend any functions, galas, or fundraisers that the charity puts on, whether your business is directly involved or not.**

Your initial intention may just be to partner with a charity for a campaign that's mutually beneficial. But who knows? After working with a charity and seeing their work first-hand, you may find yourself with a long-term charitable partner.

Aligning a Quality Product with a Charitable Cause

Last summer, Jonathan's wife brought home a box of Girl Scout cookies — Thin Mints, to be exact. Upon opening the box, it occurred to him that, every year, he somehow ended up with a green box in hand. To his best recollection, he never actually made a conscious effort to buy them, and yet, some how they had just sort of ended up there. One year a co-worker was selling them for her niece. Another year it was at a fundraising event that distributed them as giveaways. And this year, it just happened to be one more advantage of being married.

Not everyone has the resources to create a product specifically geared toward a charity, but maybe you do. Girl Scout cookies are probably one of the most obvious (and deliciously addictive) examples of the numerous products that are associated with charitable organizations or ends.

The implementation has been as broad as the concept. Clothing lines, MP3 players, jewelry, and even salad dressings have done very well by creating a product specifically geared toward a charitable end. Not every offering from these companies may be charitably based, but creating at least one high-quality product the profits of which go toward a good cause has proven effective to help increase the legitimacy of the product or brand.

Part VII
The Part of Tens

The 5th Wave   By Rich Tennant

@RICHTENNANT

Art's AUTO PARTS

GIFT BASKETS

Gasket Greetings | Valentine Tune-Up | Spark-Plug Sampler

SALE
~~1/3 OFF~~
1/2 OFF

"I don't know, Art. I think you're just ahead of your time."

In this part . . .

We love working in the field of guerrilla marketing. Our goal is that, as you're reading this book, you'll discover that not only are guerrilla marketing tactics an effective way to reach your audience, but often they're just plain fun!

This part functions as our informative valentine to the industry. We begin by showing you how to pair the methods detailed in this book with various budgets and needs. When you tell co-workers and friends that you've decided to "go guerrilla," you may be met with a little push-back or, at the very least, some judgmental quips. In this part, we help you survive the doubters by outlining exactly why we love guerrilla marketing and how its tactics can serve brands in a variety of ways. Finally, we tell you how you can go guerrilla on any budget — so you can eliminate cost as an excuse not to market your business.

Chapter 21

Ten Practically Perfect Campaigns

*T*he scene: a dark cave in a nondescript Middle Eastern locale. Business owners eager to get the perfect marketing program have sought and acquired a magical lamp with a genie who will grant them three wishes. Upon discovering the magical relic, they rub its side, summon the genie, and state their wishes: "Wish no. one: I wish for a marketing campaign the likes of which has never been seen! Wish no. two: I wish for press exposure that will reach to the farthest expanses of the globe, garnering me international consumers! Wish no. three: I wish for one of those leather massage chairs — you know, the ones that vibrate." (Hey, if you run into a genie you should get yourself something nice.)

If only it were that simple. One of the common pitfalls business owners tend to fall into is the idea that they just need to find that secret recipe or magic bullet that will make their campaign a success. But the uniqueness of your business demands more than a cookie-cutter marketing plan. It requires one that is tailor made to meet your goals and objectives while still fitting into your budget.

Every day we receive requests from a variety of businesses, large and small, that are looking to grow through the use of guerrilla marketing. They have a variety of specific needs and, from there, we try to match them with programs (most of which are outlined directly in this book) that will benefit them the most. To give you a sense of how you may apply these techniques to your business, we've decided to place you in the seat of the nontraditional marketing agency account executive (AE) and present a few common client groups to illustrate how we typically work to match them with an appropriate campaign.

To usher you into your illustrious new gig as guerrilla marketing AE, we pick ten common businesses and brands that may use guerrilla marketing in their media mix. From there, we break it down and craft a proposal for each of these businesses, taking into consideration the elements specific to each. We include things like goals and objectives they might have for their campaign, their strategy for achieving those goals, timing and locations, and which guerrilla methods they might apply to their plan and why.

Some of the campaigns outlined in this chapter are pulled from actual cases, some are created based on requests we've received in the past, and still others are ones we would do if we had it to do all over again. Our hope is that, by looking at these mini proposals, you'll find a group that closely represents your brand and be able to work within these constructs to handpick a campaign that will look as if you got your three wishes granted by a puffy-panted genie!

Dressing for Success: A Clothing Store

Client overview: It has long been Erica's dream to open a shop featuring her funky flair for retro T-shirts, skirts, and pants. Her designs are trendy, sexy, and perfect for her up-and-coming Brooklyn neighborhood, but in pursuing the dream, she knows there's a lot riding on the way that she gets her message to her target consumers.

Goals and objectives: Introduce Erica and her designs to the neighborhood. Drive store traffic and ultimately blockbuster sales!

Strategy: Work to make the storefront stand out among businesses on the block and in the neighborhood. Use personal consumer attention and unparalleled inventory to build a loyal clientele who will return time after time and bring along friends and family as well.

Target demographic: Young, hip, affluent consumers.

Timing and markets: Late summer to early fall. Store's neighborhood and vicinity.

Budget: $10,000

Concepts and components:

- ✔ **Mutually beneficial, cross-promotional partnerships:** Advertise in neighboring, noncompetitive stores (such as skate parks, independent bookstores, and coffee shops).

- ✔ **Online efforts:** Create a dynamic, visual Web site that makes the fashionista's designs as appealing and detailed as possible:

- Include background on the process for the designs and play up the one-of-a-kind feel for each of the garments on display.

- Provide testimonials from actual customers and local influencers to provide local credibility.

✔ **In-store activities and events:**

- Have special shopping events for local organizations and groups. Grant charities the opportunity to have exclusive shopping parties where a portion of the proceeds are donated to the cause.

- Make the shop available for poetry readings, acoustic performances, theatrical readings, art showings, and other activities that appeal to the store's target audience.

- Set aside a special section of the store to promote local designers and craftsman of noncompetitive goods and services.

- Include a subtle yet classy enter-to-win component where consumers have the chance to win an outfit personally selected for that person by Erica.

Breaking Your Back: A Chiropractic Office

Client overview: Greg's chiropractic practice has flourished for one reason: He's good at cracking those backs! However, he's looking to expand by bringing an additional practitioner to offer a more diverse list of offerings to his clients. As a result, he's hired three new staffers to provide his clients with more-personalized, all-inclusive offerings.

Goals and objectives: Alert current and potential patients to the new services being offered in the practice — the introduction of masseuses who can assist with medical and relaxation massage.

Strategy: Leverage impressive résumé and experience that this new staff member brings to the practice. Bundle special packages that introduce current patients to the new services at a slightly lower price in an effort to help spread the word.

Target demographic: Current patients of the practice and new clients seeking more diversified chiropractic and massage therapies.

Timing and markets: Three-month period, concurrent with the arrival of the new staff member. Patients who live or work within a 30-block radius of the practice.

Budget: $5,000

Concepts and components:

- ✔ **In-office signage and materials touting the new service being offered and the credentials of the new therapist:**
  - Provide small, informative takeaways such as brochures of complete services.
  - Include a limited number of small premiums, such as a branded stress ball touting the establishment as the one-stop shop for total-body wellness.
- ✔ **Online efforts:** Update current Web site with information on the services
- ✔ **Community events:** Bring new staffer to local health fairs and community gatherings to help introduce them to your team and the area at large.

Surfing for Sales: A Web Site with an E-Store

Client overview: William, the owner of Cast & Catch Fly-Fishing Store, abandoned his actual storefront when he realized he could do just as much business and cut his overhead drastically by selling his "Hot Betty" fishing lures and supplies online. Never one to go with the flow, William is eager to keep his online business going.

Goals and objectives: Raise awareness and drive site traffic and sales.

Strategy: Leverage customer base and growing interest in fly fishing to generate sales. Because other companies offer similar products and services, find a way to stand out from the competition.

Target demographic: Fly fisherman in lake regions.

Timing and markets: Summer. National, focusing on those markets where fly fishing is most popular

Budget: $25,000

Concepts and components:

- ✔ **Online efforts:**
  - Search engine optimization (SEO) making Cast & Catch the first name that pops up when consumers search for fly-fishing supplies.

- Banner ads on brand-related yet noncompetitive outdoor Web sites.

- Online infiltration targeting fishermen's online forums.

✔ **Distribute materials with URL and strong call to action offering consumers a discount or coupon with purchase.**

✔ **Partner with other noncompetitive brands to create a regional fly-fishing event.**

✔ **Produce a unique presence (such as a build-your-lure workstation) at trade shows and industry events.**

✔ **Actively court editorial press about the "Hot Betty" in consumer publications geared toward the sport to increase brand credibility and awareness.**

Laying Down Tracks: A Record Label

Client overview: Funky Tuna was recently signed to the upstart label, In Your Ear Artists. The quartet's model looks and gravely, angsty sound is guaranteed to have the ladies swooning and the guys nodding their heads approvingly. The challenge becomes shifting the group from hometown favorites to national stars.

Goals and objectives: Increase awareness of the band. Drive site traffic. Increase concert attendance and, ultimately, sales of a new album.

Strategy: Unite existing fan base to help spread the word nationally. Leverage the band's preexisting fan base to act as regional ambassadors.

Target demographic: Alternative music lovers, focusing first on females and extending to males secondarily.

Timing and markets: Coincide with album release in five select markets with strong fan base: Austin, Boston, Chicago, Los Angeles, and New York.

Budget: $10,000

Concepts and components:

✔ **Online efforts:**

- Utilize social networking sites such as MySpace (www.myspace.com) to present "raw, behind-the-scenes" concert footage.

- Release teasers of the new album, giving fans a hint of what's to come.

- Targeted distribution outside select concerts of bands with similar sounds and fan base. If budget permits, offer CD samplers of singles off the new release.

- Wild posting in top five markets.

- Wrapped vehicle — even if it's Funky Tuna's own touring van or truck.

- Event:
  - Throw an album release party at a brand-related but unexpected venue like an abandoned tuna cannery.
  - Make best efforts to secure a sponsor (liquor, clothing, charitable, and so on).

Marketing for the Greater Good: A Nonprofit Group

Client overview: Youth Mentors has grown leaps and bounds over the years by pairing at-risk youth with professionals who are leaders in areas of interest to their younger counterparts. Though they have done great work over the years, there is no shortage of kids who need their attention.

Goals and objectives: Raise awareness of the charity and the organization that supports it. Design and create an annual event that acts as a launch pad for current and future fundraising efforts.

Strategy: Leverage inherent interest in the cause and its participants. Create a unique event that stands out from other competing events at the same time, in the same market.

Target demographic: Those familiar with the charity as well as new contributors and mentors who can empathize with the cause and pitch in time and resources.

Timing and markets: Spring. Seeking to target those in the local community.

Budget: $75,000

Concepts and components:

- Produce a fundraising event presenting unparalleled entertainment:
  - Leverage altruistic sensibilities to get world-class talent to donate their time to present existing songs, dances, or other entertainment.

- • Allow patrons the opportunity to interact with any talent participating.

- • Attempt to integrate the nonprofit's most emotional success stories into the evening's festivities to put a personal face on the work being done.

✔ **Online efforts:**

- • Design informative, detailed Web site that is personal without being overly sentimental.

- • Include videos highlighting the work achieved through contributions.

- • Make it as easy as possible for attendees to get more information, participate, or donate.

✔ **Secure a notable figure to act as a spokesperson for marketing and advertising campaigns.** From a press standpoint, the more positively recognizable your spokesperson, the greater your opportunities that may become available to you. You may be surprised by the inexpensiveness of hiring a spokesperson, especially if you approach someone who has a direct connection to the nonprofit's goals. Allow people to win lunch with the face of Youth Mentors or another auctionable prize to generate revenue and promote it across your platforms (online, event, mailers, and so on).

Thinking Big for a Growing Company: A Small Business

Client overview: Simply known as IT, this information technology firm has been working to pick up steam by secretly delighting in its tag, "When it comes to information technology, we're IT." However, the steadiness of business has ebbed and flowed from quarter to quarter.

Goals and objectives: To build business and revenues by increasing networking efforts to grow the client database.

Strategy: Focus on areas of expertise and the fact that the group holds most current certifications in the area. Leverage existing contacts in the industry to help build reputation and workload.

Target demographic: Potential information technology clients and partners.

Timing and markets: Seek to build business immediately, locally, and then nationally.

Budget: $15,000

Concepts and components:

- ✔ **Online efforts:** Strong, clean Web site with principal biographies and case studies (if applicable).

- ✔ **Press:** Target trade publications (print and online) for industry nods to the quality of IT's work.

- ✔ **Industry shows and events:** Make the most of these events by arranging introductory capability meetings.

Brewing with the Best: A Coffee Bar and Cafe

Client overview: As Americans actively seek a "third home" that takes them out of the house and away from the office, Ashley's Café has created an unpretentious, roomy cafe that provides a homey alternative to the coffee leviathans that have recently dominated the marketplace.

Goals and objectives: Drive traffic to the cafe. Build a loyal customer base by presenting them with a spacious, community-based atmosphere and, of course, great fair-trade coffee products and delicious scones.

Strategy: Highlight unique offerings, value, atmosphere, and attitudes.

Target demographic: Lunchtime crowds, college students, and those looking to relax over the weekend.

Timing and markets: To coincide with opening local business district.

Budget: $5,000

Concepts and components:

- ✔ **Targeted street distribution centered around the launch of the business district opening.**

- ✔ **Online efforts:** Web site highlighting offerings of the cafe and vibrant pictures that serve to tip off visitors as to the tone of the space.

- ✔ **In-store events, incentives, and sampling:**

  - Customer reward program: Buy five cups of coffee, get the sixth one free!

  - Sampling pastry of the week every Wednesday.

Shooting for the Stars: An Independent Filmmaker

Client overview: A documentarian just wrapped on editing his new film that addresses ageism in an entertaining way as a spunky 80-year-old woman named Gertrude attempts to reenter the workforce. Set for its first screening at the local film festival, the team is sure that film could pick up a national distributor if it can generate some buzz at the premiere.

Goals and objectives: Raise awareness of the new documentary being featured at a local film festival.

Strategy: Highlight unique aspects of the film, especially the humor and human interest. Secure Gertrude, with her irrepressible wit, to be onsite for press and promotion.

Target demographic: Equal mix male and female, ages 21 to 49.

Timing and Markets: Week leading up to film festival as well as day of screening.

Budget: $2,500

Concepts and components:

- **Online efforts:** Create social-networking profiles for Gertrude featuring teasers like, "Put Gertrude to Work!"
- **Street teams and distribution efforts:**
  - Guerrilla postcard drops at hot spots around the festival and inside the theaters themselves.
  - Distribute "I'd Hire Gertrude" stickers with URL for festival attendees to wear.
  - Persuade friends, family, and fan base to wear branded gear onsite at all times during the festival.
- **Guerrilla postering in and around the festival.**
- **Press:**
  - Pitch advance screenings with Gertrude to local and national outlets.
  - Conduct overt campaigning at press gatherings for the movie. (If you can finagle a publicist, have her do the work for you.) As we say, "You don't ask, you don't get."

Living the Life: An Entertainment or Lifestyle Brand

Client Overview: *Well Heeled* is a cable program in which Katharine, a single Midwestern woman, suddenly discovers that she's heiress to a designer shoe empire and is suddenly thrown into the world of Manhattan society. A hit among women — urban and suburban alike — the network is looking for a multifaceted, nontraditional campaign to make the second season "the highest rated second-season premiere ever."

Goals and Objectives: Raise awareness of a series' second season on a popular cable network. Drive tune-in and ratings for the premiere. Garner as much press as humanly possible!

Strategy: Leverage show's existing fane base, general popularity, and familiarity. Utilize talent from the series for onsite appearances.

Target demographic: Women ages 18 to 49.

Timing and markets: Fall premiere season. Looking to target a major market such as New York City or Los Angeles, where the network sees the greatest draw.

Budget: $100,000

Concepts and components:

- **Nontraditional outdoor media** such as wild postings and bus-side advertising.
- **Put on a publicity stunt** in Times Square where die-hard female fans must swim through a pool of "champagne" and then tear into a series of branded shoe boxes to find Katharine's signature gold pumps in order to win a walk-on appearance on the show and a $10,000 cash prize.
- **Online:**
  - Create a microsite for a watch-and-win contest.
  - Buy banner ads on luxury brand sites.

Making Cents: Banking and Corporate

Client overview: A nationally recognized bank is looking to soften its image and be a little more playful by offering consumers a rewards program that provides them with immediate gifts for doing the services they do everyday.

Goals and Objectives: Raise awareness for the new rewards program. Increase loyalty and retentions amongst preexisting customers. Attract new customers to the banks and encourage them to take advantage of as many services as possible.

Strategy: Offer a strong incentive for acquisition. Target key markets where brand service is strong. Utilize exiting branch offices to assist with staffing and point of entry.

Target Demographic: Adults ages 21 to 54.

Timing and markets: Looking to launch late summer or early fall targeting New York, San Francisco, and Houston.

Budget: $100,000

Concepts and components:

- **Regional customized program-related events and national tour:** Provide consumers with an engaging, fun experience where potential customers are given the opportunity to try out the various program rewards, win premiums, and sign up for the program onsite.

- **Street teams:** Use street teams inside and outside of bank branches themselves to raise awareness and drive traffic into the bank where service experts can fully illustrate the program.

- **Local and national event sponsorship:** Select events such as three-on-three basketball tournaments, gaming events, and so on that reflect on the available rewards and can nurture positive associations between consumers and the brand.

Chapter 22

Ten Reasons We Love Guerrilla Marketing — And Why You Will, Too!

Guerrilla marketing provides businesses and marketers with many reasons to get up and cheer. The impact and reach — combined with its low cost — should be reason enough to get you to grab your pom-poms and join the guerrilla marketing pep squad! Over the years, as this genre of marketing has expanded and developed in vibrant ways, we've progressed from early practitioners to zealous fans. To let you in on why we've become such admirers, we take you behind the scenes to explore that persistent question posed by our puzzled family members and potential clients alike: "Why do you do what you do?" Here, we do you one better, as we entertain not only why we do guerrilla marketing, but why we *love* doing it — and why you will, too!

Guerrilla Is All about Reaching Your Consumers Directly

Whenever we open our mail, we read rate cards for various forms of media, with punchy tags like, "Let your ad work for you this quarter!" This quarter? Some may say it's the gluttonous pursuit of instant gratification, but we think your company is far too important — and your consumers are far too quick — for you to wait three months for your ad to work for you.

Now, don't get us wrong: Traditional media is an important (if not essential) component to figure into your marketing plan. But one of the reasons we love guerrilla marketing is because you don't have to wait for your potential customers to come to your media. Instead, you hand-deliver your message and connect to them in a targeted, immediate, and personal way.

Going guerrilla puts your message on the move, granting you the opportunity to talk to people as they walk to work, watch a movie, or make a stop at the restroom. Unlike a radio spot or a print ad, guerrilla marketing tactics don't box your message into one location. This soldier-of-fortune status enables your message to live on the street, in the mall, or on the Web. Through careful planning, you can use this trait to your advantage, deciding what sort of efforts to implement in order to target specific people at specific points in their day.

You Can Step Outside Your Daily Grind

Crackerjack psychology tells us that everyone has two sides. Maybe by day you're Betsy, actuary extraordinaire — but by night, you're Bet-say, rock goddess. Nontraditional marketing lets you shake off the shackles of more traditional techniques and open yourself — personally and professionally — to experiences that you may never have had, all the while benefiting your brand.

Whether you're commissioning a local chef to build a cake replicating your logo for your grand opening or arranging for the star of your favorite reality show to come down and pose for a picture you could use in your advertising, these experiences help to shake up the day to day, boosting workplace morale and reinvigorating consumer awareness and associations with your brand. And we think you'll agree that shaving the CEO's head for a charity stunt is *far* more fun than that 9:30 a.m. staff meeting you had planned for the day.

Guerrilla Marketing Makes You Dollars with Sense

What a difference a day makes! One day a consumer can have absolutely no idea about your product, and the next day your brand is all they can talk about. All it takes is making that connection in a meaningful way. A common misconception is that you need to have millions of dollars to be able to reach people. Not necessarily, friends.

Yet another reason we know you'll love guerrilla marketing is that you can do it on nearly any budget. Whether you have $5,000 or $500,000, you can shape a truly effective campaign. For starters, street teams can be activated for as low as a few hundred bucks, while large-scale events and media campaigns can cost in the thousands.

One of our delights is the resulting beauty when people manage to spend hundreds on campaigns that appear to have cost thousands through intelligent, targeted use of resources. Because you aren't tied to one lump sum for your efforts, you can work like a tailor and only spend money on the things that are going to make you look sharp, sidestepping the unnecessary.

You Get Your Name in the Paper

When you get your name in the paper, you're famous! (Well, until they use that paper to line the bird cage the next morning.) Maybe it appeals to our flashy sensibilities, but another reason we know you'll get a kick out of guerrilla is that it has one extremely beneficial side effect — the possibility for press!

Especially when it comes to events and stunts (see Chapters 7 and 8, respectively), guerrilla marketing is a two-way street. You can bask in the adoration and free publicity of a flawlessly executed event, and you give the press something they love: fodder for segments, articles, and big glossy photos featuring your masterwork.

The best part: It's relatively easy. All you have to do is provide the press with something brand-related that has never been done before (or an improvement on something that has). By wracking your company's collective brain, you can enjoy this huge perk for your efforts!

You Can Harness Your Inner Artist

Maybe we spent too much time watching frizzy-haired painters on PBS shape "happy trees," or maybe we just like to mix it up. Whatever the reason, guerrilla has us smiling because it's a unique opportunity to unleash our inner creative artists. Because nontraditional marketing can live anywhere, you have the playful challenge of seeing where your imagination takes you. The journey begins at the brainstorming table and it continues as you make inventive choices about what kind of campaign you'll produce, where you'll do it, and how you'll get it done.

Although we think you'll get a kick out of concocting these plans yourself, you may decide to charge an agency with the task of creating innovative, one-of-a-kind promotions, events, and communications to help promote your product, service, or brand. If so, the creativity doesn't die — it just takes a new form as you work as a collaborator with your agency to collectively produce something exciting for your brand.

Whether you employ an agency or open it up to the collective, your job as a guerrilla marketer is to be creative, to come up with ideas that are so cool they simply *must* be done. Where else can you say that other than budget and the laws of physics, you have no limitations?

You Can Track Your Way through Validation

"We like it! We *really* like it!" Everybody needs a little validation, and guerrilla marketing gives you the opportunity to track your campaign in order to certify that your energies (and money) were well spent. Pulling off a successful marketing campaign is great. Having the data to *prove* it was a success is even better.

We're fans of keeping metrics simple, and guerrilla gives you the opportunity to shape your measurements so they're easy and to the point, enabling you to effectively gauge your inevitable success. Measuring your campaigns can be as simple and easy as the following scenarios:

- ✔ **Call-in campaigns:** For campaigns where consumers are asked to call in, ask the consumer to mention a location-specific code and attach the code to your pre-promotional tools to see what's been effective.

- ✔ **Street campaigns:** In addition to calculating reach by the number of pieces distributed, add a coupon to the samples you're distributing on the street. If possible, somehow mark the coupons so that, as they're redeemed, you can determine things like where they were handed out or, even better, who handed it to them. Then you can use this information to help plan future programs.

- ✔ **Stunts and events:** At stunts or events, measuring your campaign can be as simple as having a guestbook at the entrance or positioning someone at the door with a clicker to count the number of consumers on-site.

- ✔ **Online:** If you have a Web site, add the URL to your promotional piece and see if your site traffic increases as a result of your latest promotion using online tracking such as Google Analytics. (For more on tracking sites, see Chapter 12.)

Going on a guerrilla path means being bold and exploring new avenues. However, bold and ineffective is just silly. Using simple measurement tools, you can get a sense of what's working and play to these strengths. By doing so, we think you'll find the greatest validation — the growth of your business!

Guerrilla Is Gaining a Seat at the Table

Guerrilla marketing has shaped the marketing and advertising field in such a dramatic way that it's quickly trading up its ratty T-shirt for a power suit. In recent times, guerrilla used to be done only by independent record labels looking to get attention. Then it was picked up by dot-coms that wanted to cut through the clutter of traditional advertising. These days, in some form or other, guerrilla campaigns are a must for sharp business owners and media buyers looking to make a more direct connection with their consumers.

Guerrilla is populist marketing, making the little guy just as effective as the corporate titan. Unique, direct consumer connections for all! Because guerrilla marketing techniques are achieving mainstream acceptance, upstart companies can use minimal resources to come up with big, exciting ideas and make large impacts.

Whether it's Uncle Joey's Bait Shop or a Fortune 500 company, the fact that guerrilla methods have found a place at the marketing buffet is truly a testament to the effectiveness of its methods. Your contribution to this enterprise could be the next big thing that raises nontraditional to the next level!

It Can Go Anywhere for Any Brand

Guerrilla allows its users portability — and that's always a bonus! If you've executed an extremely successful campaign, you shouldn't let the momentum crash just because the program is complete. Where else can you use it? How can you refine it to target another audience? Often, we have clients who produce a campaign that's wildly successful in one market and decide they want to send it out on tour. Maybe you don't have those kinds of resources — so challenge yourself to find new ways and places to present your creation.

On a smaller scale, the same way you use your imagination and creativity on the street, you can use it at a conference, convention, or other venue. Some of the more alternative initiatives — such as reading people's tarot cards and body painting your logo on a model over the course of a trade show — may not be completely brand-related. But if your goal is to drive traffic to your booth and get people buzzing on the trade show floor, then it doesn't really matter what you do, as long as it works!

Guerrilla Marketing Plays Wells with Others

You've set out your marketing plan for the year. You've worked with a designer to create an ad featuring a gorgeous, leggy model holding your product. It is, quite simply, the cat's pajamas. You make with the usual suspects — an ad in the trades, one in the local circular, some banner ads on related Web sites — and that's where you look to invest for the year. What happens if, midway through, you find that your efforts didn't reap the kind of results you were looking for?

Innovate. Try a street team, an event, or a stunt that works *in concert* with your stellar ad. Although print is a wonderful resource, we love the way that guerrilla efforts can pick up and work easily and seamlessly within existing campaigns or media buys. Maybe you can create a self-referential event where people can have their picture taken with the lovely lady and your product putting them "in the ad." Every time they see your ad from that point forward, it'll make a more direct connection, which could put them one step closer to being a customer.

Integrating guerrilla into other existing efforts is crucial to communicating your message. Man cannot live on bread alone, and neither should your marketing plans, so to speak. See how you can work across a few platforms and how nontraditional efforts can best help you drive your message home.

It Makes an Impression That Sticks Long after It's Left the Building

In the interest of full disclosure, we have a confession to make: We haven't bought a new T-shirt in six years. Branded T-shirts left over from an assortment of events have left our dresser drawers overflowing. We share this not to come clean about our poor fashion sense, but to illustrate that guerrilla campaigns live on (in some form or other) long after the campaign has concluded.

When a campaign is executed effectively, after it's done, the consumer is left with something that continues beyond the immediate interaction. Whatever you choose to do, you'll love the fact that it lives on like this, whether it's a T-shirt from a street team, a YouTube clip of your stunt circulating around the Internet, or someone chatting up how much she loves your brand because she won a prize package through an online scavenger hunt you conducted.

Guerrilla is all about reaching people in experiential ways. If they aren't able to walk away with something tangible, at least give them something to talk about at the beauty parlor.

Chapter 23

Ten Obstacles to Avoid When Going Guerrilla

In This Chapter
▶ Recognizing common stumbling blocks to effective guerrilla marketing
▶ Righting campaigns that go off course
▶ Acknowledging past mistakes to improve your future campaigns

*R*egret is an awful feeling. Think of all the things you would do differently if you had them to do over again. Maybe you shouldn't have quit your job to be a full-time ant farmer. Maybe you wish you would've covered your nose when you sneezed on that hot date. Or maybe you just should've listened to your own better judgment and not purchased that "up-and-coming" swampfront property.

Hindsight is 20/20, but learning from the mistakes of others (some of them things we ourselves experienced, some industry lore) is incredibly valuable — it gives you the foresight to identify and avoid obstacles when planning, tailoring, and ultimately executing guerrilla campaigns. Whether you're debuting on the guerrilla scene or you've dabbled in it in the past, there are a few common stumbling blocks that, when addressed in the early stages, can prove exceptionally useful in guiding you toward an effective campaign. In this chapter, we list ten of these.

Lacking Due Diligence

You haven't allowed yourself to be limited by anything in your brainstorming and decision to create a guerrilla marketing effort. You've adopted the "yes and . . ." mentality, where everything is a good idea and the stakes are constantly being raised to create the best concepts ever.

That said, after you've come up with a campaign that's superbly profound, it's time to hit the books, phones, and Internet to see if your idea can actually be done. To get the process started, you need to do your research and answer a few basic questions:

- **Has it been done before?** If your concept has been done before, there's good news: Assuming whoever did it didn't peeve the powers-that-be, you may be able to do it, too — with your own flair, of course! Your due diligence then works like a bit of reverse engineering. If someone else did it, consider the process he had to go through in order to make his campaign work, and do that yourself.

  If it *hasn't* been done before, it's time to press on to the next question.

- **Is it legal?** Can you parade a pink elephant across a bridge? This was an inquiry we actually researched based on a client request. Upon hearing the patron's desire, we quickly realized we needed to do the proper due diligence and see if it was even legal.

  First off, we called the city to see if they had any laws regarding exotic animals, as well as what kind of parade license or permit was required. From there, we called the American Society for the Prevention of Cruelty to Animals (ASPCA) and the Humane Society to see what kind of guidelines you need to follow in order to paint an elephant pink.

  Addressing potential legal issues initially will help you avoid problems down the line and facilitate the fulfillment of your brilliant plans. Can you parade a pink elephant across a bridge? Turns out yes, you can (though laws may vary depending on where you live) — you just have to do your homework.

- **Do you have the proper permits and permission to utilize the chosen venue?** When you're selecting a venue, you have to find out if you have the necessary permits or permissions to execute your campaign. If you're particularly spiky and you've opted not to ask for permission, consider how you'll handle it if the authorities attempt to thwart your activities.

If you're executing a stunt or event where you'll be at a specific location for an extended period of time and that location is essential to your success, it's in your best interest to play nice and work with the venue owner, as well as make sure you've acquired the necessary permits and permissions to pull off your concept without incident. And don't forget to make sure your manager has a signed copy in hand.

That said, some guerrilla campaigns can be done without permits or permissions. For example, if you're executing a street-team campaign, as long as you're not distributing on commercial or city property and you're sticking to public locations, you can usually distribute materials or branded premiums without any problems. Just be smart and come up with some backup locations in case you find yourself face to face with a prickly person/business owner/hater of all things nontraditional who may have major objections to your efforts.

Asking Too Much of the Consumer

Everyone wants something. The kids want an allowance, your boss wants you to do your work, your significant other wants to go someplace nice with you once in a while! Daily, consumers are overwhelmingly called upon either with the hard or soft sell by an array of brands to buy or do something. So when you're deciding how to engage your desired consumers don't ask too much of them.

We've sat in meetings where well-intentioned people have thought of having guests at their event run an obstacle course, offer up their e-mail, and agree to name their firstborn child after the brand in order to receive a $1.50 giveaway. We're exaggerating, of course, but not by much. (For more on giveaways, check out Chapter 6.)

You're a consumer, and *you're* busy — and so are the people in your target audience. Often you have, at the most, 10 to 15 seconds to make an impact on consumers. If you don't make that connection, you've likely lost them. One sure way to lose your target audience is by asking for too much of their time, energy, privacy, and money.

Although you may want to provide a unique experience, be wary of getting too multilayered with your guerrilla marketing efforts. If you can't succinctly encapsulate what the consumers will be called upon to do and how they'll be rewarded in one sentence, chances are you need to streamline your idea.

Whether you're having customers redeem a coupon in-store, enter a sweepstakes, submit an online order, or participate in an event, only ask for exactly what you need. If you're giving them a unique reward (for example, a VIP experience or a high-value premium), you can ask for a little more, such as providing contact information or agreeing to a trial usage of your product or service. Additionally, providing this type of high-value experience will likely make for a more positive reception when you call on the consumers later.

When gathering and collecting consumer e-mails, you may need to have them click a legal "opt-in" box that officially allows you to send them e-mails. Also, age may be an issue — online campaigns aimed at minors are subject to even stricter laws. Before diving in, check with your attorney.

Being Unfocused

Who do you want to reach? If your reply is, "I want to reach the world," we encourage your pursuits — thinking globally is a great goal — but most of the world's greatest companies started small and have grown by being uber-targeted. If you find yourself with a bottomless marketing budget, you may want to begin with an all-out traditional and nontraditional global assault. Odds are, though, your budget isn't limitless, so you need to make canny use of what you have in order to avoid waste.

Arguably, one of the selling points with guerrilla efforts are that they allow for targeted use of resources directed at a specific audience — so you need to make sure to use this power in a very specific, focused way.

If you don't have a lot of money on hand for marketing, make sure you're not adopting a scattershot approach and hoping for the best. Instead, think of your resources as a six-shooter and you've got a limited number of shots to reach your target. To get the most out of what you have, train your sights on a very specific mark, take a deep breath, and pull the trigger. This clear-cut approach toward reaching your goals will allow you to be both revered and feared in whatever frontier you occupy.

This kind of specificity can be a little scary. You may be concerned that, by targeting a specific audience, you're missing out on a larger, bigger picture. These fears are not at all unfounded. But by creating a genuine, quality connection with your target, much of the work will be done for you. How? Think about when you saw that great band, were touched by that evocative movie, or dined at that obscenely delicious new restaurant. These experiences reached you in a visceral way — and they likely made you giddy to share the experience with your friends and neighbors. That's the sway of targeted connections. By touching consumers in such a way, you create positive impressions in people who can best carry your message and, as a result, enable much of the work to be done for you!

Sloppily Preparing and Monitoring Your Staff

Bad or poorly trained staff is death to any campaign, guerrilla or otherwise. We're going to level with you: When you're preparing a campaign, the big-picture items — arranging press, securing signage, and dealing with vendors, among other things — can take up much of your prep time. What if, after all your preparations, you lure the press down to your beautifully produced event, only to be felled by staffers who are literally or figuratively picking their noses.

"Heads will roll!" you declare. Well, if you don't properly train your staff, you may be partially or wholly to blame for the results. People only know what you tell them. Especially if your team wasn't working directly on the campaign during the run-up, how could they know what you expect during execution if you don't let them in on the master plan?

To avoid this obstacle, hold a training session prior to the event where you give those who will be working on your event all the tools that they need to make your vision a reality. Introduce everyone, walk them through the schedule, reiterate decorum requests (such as don't smoke, swear, or talk on cellphones in front of consumers — sounds silly, but unless you say it, it has the potential of popping up *every time!*), and give them the opportunity to sample any items prior to the event so they can comment and interact with consumers intelligently.

Wouldn't it be great if your entire team were staffed with mind readers who could anticipate your thoughts? Unfortunately, mind readers are hard to come by and extremely expensive if you do find them. Instead, you need to stay in constant contact and provide those in your employ with feedback during the course of your activities. Guerrilla marketing efforts are constantly evolving as the facts on the ground change. As a result, you need to maintain a consistent flow of information with your staff. This will ensure that everyone is working to help you achieve your goals and maintain the integrity of your campaign.

Forgetting to Budget

As you sit at home watching *Dancing with the Stars,* you think to yourself, "I want to see every sequin on those washed-up celebrities' flouncy tops. I need a new high-definition TV." Immediately, you launch into your research on assorted brands and narrow it down to a handful of possibilities. From there, you look to your household income to see what kind of funds you've got to drop on this must-have item. After giving yourself a set amount, you make considerations for delivery, tax, miscellaneous expenses, and installation, and then you make your selection (and make sure your local TV store keeps those costs exactly as they promised). It's as simple as that.

Although it seems a bit elementary, people venturing into guerrilla marketing for the first time can forget one of those essential elements: budgeting. The goal is creating an outstanding campaign, but if you put yourself in the poorhouse in the process, the victory isn't as sweet. Side-step this fate by making — and sticking to — a budget.

If you're executing the effort yourself, make calls and get estimates. Campaigns can be made up of an array of pieces that are essential to the campaign's success. Guessing the costs for these elements may make this budgeting portion of the gig move a little faster, but if you underestimate these costs, you'll end up wasting what little time you spent on your budget in the first place. Plus, taking the time to really research and budget enables you to do the bulk of your legwork upfront. When you're ready to move forward, you've got a contact to reach out to and maybe even a quote just waiting to be signed off.

You took the time to create an attractive spreadsheet to make sure you come in under budget, now get some use out of it. Include a column on your budget called "Actual Cost," and fill it in as you make your purchases. Some things may come in over what you budgeted, and some may come in under. Maintaining an actual tally ensures that you stay within the parameters you set out for yourself and budget even better should you venture into a similar task sometime in the future.

If during the course of your budgeting, you find you still have a little bit of money left over, you may want to keep it around as a rainy-day fund. You can use it to account for overages or unforeseen expenses.

Neglecting to Brainstorm

Brainstorming is fun, and yet it's often the most undervalued resource at the guerrilla's disposal. In an industry that thrives on coming up with the most creative, unheard-of campaigns, ideas are the commodities that can make your brand stick in the minds of consumers.

To position yourself to get the most out of your brainstorming sessions, set up a comfortable environment and adopt a no-holds-barred mentality. Make sure all participants are comfortable and in the right frame of mind. Lay out samples of your product, and provide any important information related to the product or brand such as key art, taglines, and so on to get your team thinking in terms that will unlock a host of great ideas.

As the ideas start rolling, don't be a Negative Nancy. That's right, leave those negative, judgmental tendencies at the door. Aside from dissuading people from wanting to throw anything out there, you may end up quashing the beginnings of a great idea before it was able to fully blossom.

Dismissing Distribution-Piece Details

One of the prime selling points for street teams and distribution campaigns is that they literally put your brand into the hands of your target consumers. This is more than a sound bite, however. Cleverly crafted distribution pieces can allow your message to live on and be shared for days, months, and (depending on the value) years after the initial contact.

Although we celebrate the shelf life of distribution campaigns, there are a few common missteps when it comes to the distribution pieces themselves that can dampen the impact of your materials. Here are few mistakes to avoid:

- **Making it too big:** Unless you're a Sherpa, you probably don't have a lot of extra room for additional things to carry around. Neither do your consumers, so keep it small.

- **Designing something that doesn't relate to your brand:** You can come up with the coolest thing ever, but if it doesn't cause consumers to think of your brand when they see it, it isn't quite right.

- **Spending too much money on distribution materials or premiums:** The goal with distribution campaigns is to get the greatest hand-to-hand reach with your message. Although producing engraved candy dishes may make for gorgeous conversation starters, the $50-per-item cost is likely to limit the number of premiums you can have produced.

- **Not taking the time to make the piece appealing.** *Remember:* It's the thought that counts. You don't have to spend hundreds of dollars on your distribution pieces. But you do need to make sure they're entertaining and educational so that they stick around for a while.

- **Not double-checking the essentials:** Especially if you're pre-promoting an event, make sure that the premium you're distributing has the correct Web address, time, date, location, and so on. Giving it a second glance will ensure you're giving away something that will serve you well.

- **Leaving off a call to action:** Are consumers going to log in for a sweepstakes? Bring the distribution piece into a store? Give them a reason to keep it around. Plus, this gives you with a way to track the effectiveness of your campaign.

- **Not properly accounting for how many you need to produce:** Produce too little, and you miss reaching potential customers. Produce too much, and you waste funds that could have been allocated somewhere else.

Quick formula: For high-value premiums distributed in high-traffic areas, assume around 200 pieces per person distributing per hour. For printed pieces under the same conditions assume 100 to 150 pieces per person distributing per hour. (To help you further with this tally, look to Chapter 6.)

Not Taking the Weather into Account

You can make choices to plan and control your effort down to the most minute detail, but if you don't plan for weather — and many people don't — you could end up all wet. You can avoid having unfavorable weather dampen your event.

For street teams distributing outdoors, the answer is to seek shelter from the storm. Provide your staffers with clear ponchos and scope out locations with awnings that your teams can seek refuge under if they need it. If the weather is particularly awful, you may want to reschedule your efforts for a day when your target audience may be a little drier and more inclined to receive your message.

For outdoor events and stunts, look into rain dates to reschedule your event if the weather is disagreeable. Some venues may be open to this while others may not — or will charge you through the nose. If you can't snag a rain-out date, make sure you have appropriate tenting that can be popped up in the event that Mother Nature forces your hand. In short, always have a plan for stormy weather. (For more on dealing with the elements, turn to Chapter 7.)

Forgetting to Document Your Efforts

What if, while you were growing up, your parents made a conscious choice not to document part of your life. "Eh, we got Junior at 4 — do we really care what he does when he's 5?" Think how sad that would be. No finger-painted masterpieces, no artisan macaroni necklaces, no pictures of you atop a pony at the county fair. And if your parents didn't document *any* part of your life, charting your growth as a person, remembering your past successes, and learning from your failures would be that much harder. The same goes for recording a guerrilla marketing effort.

Documenting your guerrilla campaign is usually very simple — and yet many guerrilla marketers dismiss it as unessential or unnecessary. This mistake is one you need to avoid. When you create an exceptional guerrilla marketing campaign, you're not going to want to keep it to yourself. You're going to want to share it, relish your successes, and — who knows? — maybe even create and entire ad or marketing campaign around it.

You may think to yourself, "But I don't need to document it — I'll *never* forget!" You could have a memory like an elephant's, but over time the mental pictures of what you did are probably going to get a little hazy. To keep it forever young in your mind, write it out. In as specific terms as possible write out everything that was essential to your campaign:

✔ The campaign's goals

✔ The steps you took toward reaching those goals

✔ How you executed the campaign

✔ Surprising discoveries you made

✔ The number of samples distributed

✔ Weather

✔ Foot traffic

✔ Conclusions you made about the campaign

✔ Any other details that will serve to give you the most complete picture of your event

Take color photos of everything! Imagine your campaign as a newborn baby. You need to get pictures of everything, charting its growth — your event's first signage, the first attendees to your event, any VIPs who came by to wish you well. Seemingly insignificant details can prove useful for program critique, and if something magical happens at your event, you're going to want tons of pictures to be able to share with the press.

Video-sharing Web sites like YouTube (www.youtube.com) are all the rage and are constantly growing and evolving to become more specialized, all the while giving people the opportunity to share their message with a broader audience. To make the most of this opportunity, be sure to get video of any speeches or events that took place. You can post them online just as they are, or you can edit them to produce flashy sizzle reels that you can share at future client meetings.

Getting press coverage doesn't happen everyday, so when it does make sure you collect all of it to help document your efforts. Make sure you keep copies of news clippings, calendar listings, online posts, and any other coverage to further gauge the success and reach of your campaign. If you need help with this, you may want to hire a clippings service to do this for you (see Chapter 16).

Finally, at the conclusion of your campaign, don't discard all your distribution materials. You probably have made history with your guerrilla marketing effort, so like the devout historian you are, save the artifacts of your campaign so that you can refer to and learn from them in the future.

Losing Your Kudos

The protectionist in us strongly encourages you to be alert when you enter the guerrilla jungle. In this environment, ideas are essential to survival, so don't let some other guerrilla swing in and steal credit for your idea. Especially if you've created new media (see Chapter 9), seizing a new opportunity and making it your own will not only make you the envy of your friends and neighbors, it can often prove to be quite lucrative.

To avoid missing out on the rewards that come as a result of your creative prowess, tell the world that this is your invention! (See Chapter 9 for more on how to do this.)

Index

• *N* •

Notes

Notes

Notes

Notes

Notes